TRACKING TREASURE

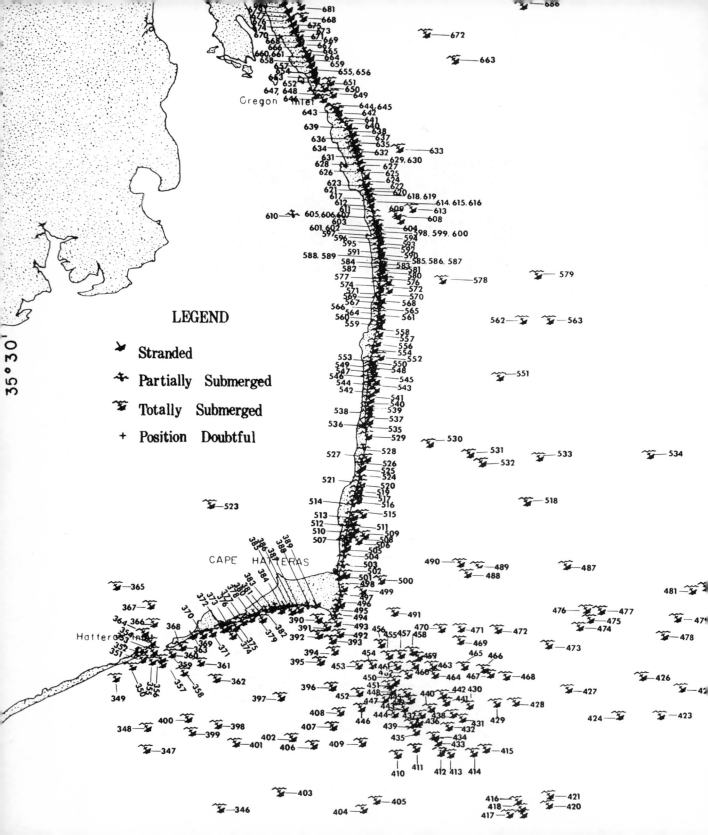

Romance & Fortune Beneath the Sea and How to Find It!

TRACKING TREASURE

573

575

by Philip Z. Trupp

522

486

485
483
484

N

ACROPOLIS BOOKS LTD.

WASHINGTON, D.C.

DEDICATION

This book is dedicated to the memory of Phillip Lee Krause, a young explorer who lost his life October 1985, in Australia in the pursuit of his dreams; and to my mother, Mary Z. Trupp, for her wisdom and great courage.

ACROPOLIS BOOKS, LTD.
Alphons J. Hackl, Publisher
Colortone Building, 2400 17th St., N.W.
Washington, D.C. 20009

Printed in the United States of America by
COLORTONE PRESS
Creative Graphics, Inc.
Washington, D.C. 20009

Attention: Schools and Corporations
ACROPOLIS books are available at quantity discounts with bulk purchase for educational, business, or sales promotional use. For information, please write to: SPECIAL SALES DEPARTMENT, ACROPOLIS BOOKS LTD., 2400 17th ST., N.W., WASHINGTON, D.C. 20009

Are there Acropolis Books you want but cannot find in your local stores?
You can get any Acropolis book title in print. Simply send title and retail price, plus $1.00 per copy to cover mailing and handling costs for each book desired. District of Columbia residents add applicable sales tax. Enclose check or money order only, no cash please, to:
ACROPOLIS BOOKS LTD.,
2400 17th St., N.W.,
WASHINGTON, D.C. 20009.

Library of Congress Cataloging-in-Publication Data
Trupp, Philip Z. (Philip Zbar)
    Tracking treasure.

    Includes index.
    1. Treasure-trove. I. Title.
G525.T78 1986   622'.19   86-3481
ISBN 0-87491-812-X
ISBN 0-87491-805-7 (pbk.)

Cover Photo by Ned DeLoach

CONTENTS

FOREWORD

If you ever see the bottom of the ocean paved with gold, you will never forget it. Very few people alive today can verify this statement. Luckily, I am one of them.

On July 20, 1985, after 16 years of searching and great personal sacrifice, our team at Treasure Salvors, Inc. discovered the mother lode of the Spanish treasure ship *Nuestra Señora de Atocha.* For nearly four centuries, she had been waiting for us on the sea bottom 40 miles from Key West, Florida. At this writing, she has yielded millions in gold, silver, and precious gems. We made history.

The *Atocha* and her sister ship, *Santa Margarita,* went to the bottom in a hurricane in 1622 with a lot more than a cargo of riches. They took with them the secrets of the New World and colonial Spain. The search for these secrets will not end as long as the spirit of adventure stays with us.

Tracking Treasure, by Philip Z. Trupp, is a part of the spirit. It tells of men and women who are driven by their dreams and desires to unlock the riches and mysteries of the sea. In these pages, written by a man who knows first-hand the value of this adventure, you will find your own place. It is your personal passport. I hope you will join us on the voyage of discovery. Welcome aboard. There is room enough for all.

Mel Fisher

This elegant silver service once belonged to the infamous pirate-turned-governor of Jamaica, Captain Henry Morgan. The silver, and much of Morgan's ill-gotten loot, plunged violently into the sea in 1692, when an off-shore earthquake sank Jamaica's city of Port Royal, near modern Kingston. Morgan's fortune wasn't the only loss. Port Royal, "the wickedest city on Earth," was a haven for adventurers and pirates. When the earthquake struck, most of Jamaica's wealth was concentrated in the city. Modern explorers, working with the Jamaican government, are piecing together Port Royal's remains.
Photo by Roy O'Brien, courtesy Jamaica Tourist Board.

INTRODUCTION

This book is an adventure. It takes the reader deep into the fantasy world of sunken treasure—and it goes one step beyond, into reality.

In these pages you will join the men and women who have dedicated their lives and their fortunes to make discoveries most of us only dream about. Meet Mel Fisher, "The Greatest Treasure Hunter of Them All," who, in July 1985, after 16 years of searching and tragic sacrifice, found his dream galleon, the *Nuestra Señora de Atocha,* and a $400 million treasure trove of gold, silver, precious gems, and priceless artifacts. You will also meet Kip Wagner, the retired home builder who discovered silver on the beach and launched the greatest treasure boom of modern times. And you will go to sea with Arthur C. Clarke, the man who wrote *2001: A Space Odyssey,* as he searches for Mogul silver at the Great Basses Reef in Sri Lanka—and nearly loses his life in the bargain.

You're invited to tour the battlefields where the "treasure wars" rage between trained archaeologists and the growing army of paraprofessional, home-grown treasure hunters. The issue: Who really owns all that treasure? Is it finders-keepers or shared public patrimony? Get to know the field generals and learn why Washington may legislate treasure hunting out of existence.

If you make it through unscathed, you're invited to get wet—to start your own expedition. Like Captain Nemo in Jules Verne's *20,000 Leagues Under the Sea,* this book lets you explore the bottom of the ocean in real-life detail, to trace the footprints of civilization 30,000 years through the fog of time as it advanced across the world's seas and oceans. Along the way you'll learn of the lost wealth of empires still waiting to be recovered—from the earliest sailing ships to the ghostly remains of the *Titanic.*

Intrigued? If so, this book will allow you to sketch your own treasure hunter profile and show you what it takes to make dreams into reality. If you're an armchair adventurer, but still want in on the action, there are tips on how to invest in treasure digs. Salty explorers and Wall Street brokers tell how to get the most out of your investment dollar and how to avoid getting "soaked" by seagoing scams. In coming face-to-face with these high rollers of romance your odds in the treasure game will be greatly enhanced.

Part Three of *Tracking Treasure* takes you out of your armchair and into the mysterious world of tropical treasure. You will explore the gin-clear waters of the Caribbean Sea, where sunken galleons and whole cities are hidden beneath the waves. True to its spirit of adventure, this book does more than speculate; it takes you there, places you directly on that spot on the map marked "X."

For those more attuned to the water's edge, there is an extensive list of the most exciting "money beaches" in North America. There is gold and silver—and a lot more—awaiting the reader along both coasts.

Finally, you are invited to join in five real-life modern treasure hunts at Key West, Aruba, Bonaire, Curacao, and Cayman Brac. The prizes are sensational and all the clues you need to participate and claim a prize are in Part Four, waiting for an adventurous spirit.

Good luck—and good hunting!

Philip Z. Trupp

ACKNOWLEDGMENTS

This book is a synthesis of my own experiences over the past ten years and the talents of many other people.

I wish to thank Daniel A. Koski-Karrell, one of the busiest archaeologists in America, for his unselfish support. He provided worlds of advice, tested me at tricky turns, supplied libraries of source materials, and cheered me on at times when it seemed I was hopelessly outnumbered. Dan proved that archaeologists, like writers, need the instincts of a club fighter.

Special thanks to Pamela Warner who kept me in constant touch with the diving community. Her tireless stream of news, views, and opinion added much to the book's perspective—all this without ever losing her sense of humor.

Those who forced me to soul search through some very difficult human and political issues were Charles M. McKinney III, who has made deep personal sacrifices to keep the world of undersea exploration in the public domain, and his wife, Ilene, whose patience is a wonder in itself.

I am also indebted to Bob Fleming, whose research has added color and reality to many books aside from my own; R. Duncan Mathewson III, who freely shared his experiences as the embattled archaeologist of the famous *Atocha* dig; Ellsworth Boyd, dean of sport diving writers and master shipwreck sleuth; Robert Cembrola, director of the Maritime Museum at Fall River, Massachusetts, who made pirate "Black Sam" Bellamy come to life; Warren Riess, of the Mariner's Museum, Newport News, Virginia, whose down-to-earth advice added muscle to the work; Dan Lenihan, U.S. Park Service archaeologist, who has worked in the public interest, fashioned whole underwater parks, and can debate with the best of them on the course of future history; Burt D. Webber, Jr., whose discovery of the Spanish galleon *Concepción* brightened this text and gave the world a bit of much-needed magic; Peter Throckmorton, the conceptual godfather of underwater archaeology and a philosopher who will leave a lasting impression on the future; Mel Fisher, who persevered with superhuman strength to find his own dreams and shared them with the rest of us; Don Kincaid, explorer/photographer, who taught me the art of "aerial archaeology"; Bill Wible, a naval engineer in the mystical world of undersea warfare who always found time to explain things to an occasionally puzzled writer; Bleth McHaley, public relations superwoman, who had a warm human touch when the going got tough; and Edwin "Ted" Dethlefsen, the poet/archaeologist who impressed upon me that history is first and last in the public domain.

Among the many scholars who influenced this work, I am most grateful to Robert F. Marx, John S. Potter, Jr., Carl Clausen, Dr. Eugene Lyon, and the late "Kip" Wagner. They have made a tremendous contribution to history beneath the sea.

Among the divers who have rendered more than the usual assistance are Bob Landers, my first real underwater mentor; Richard Bailey, creator of the American Underwater Band; Jim Hamill, whose insight and humor were extra added attractions to his love of exploration on land and in the sea; Daphne Harden, who remade my life when she insisted, "You'll still be able to surface, even with all those lead weights." Thanks, too, to Elliot Finkel, director of NOAA's manned undersea program, who made it possible to spend three days beneath the ocean in Hydro-Lab, and who spurred me on to all manner of seagoing adventure. His inspirational toughness is between the lines of this book.

I am also grateful to Jerome Burke, of Underhill Associates, who filled me in on the dollars and cents of treasure as a business; Harwood Nichols, vice president for investments, Mercantile Safe Deposit & Trust, who helped make the bottom line more than an illusion; and John Amrhein, historian and author, who revealed the pitfalls with elegant clarity.

Those who helped to make *Tracking Treasure* pure fun were Joyce and Scott Wiggins, of the Divi Hotels, and Debra Slater, the sharpest PR woman in the Caribbean or any other sea. Thanks, too, goes to Andy Newman, who added yet another flash of gold to the treasure trove at Key West, and Lee Dodez, of the East Martello Museum in Key West, whose sense of adventure added another mystery "X" to the *Tracking Treasure* map.

Neil and Kathleen Hughes are also a part of this book. Neil's remarkable experiences in Central American archaeology opened a new world to me, and Kathleen's knowledge of the writer's craft helped make the gears mesh when I thought they might never move again. To Barbara Hendra, a bright light of Manhattan, thanks for casting me off; and to Peggy Whedon, of Public Affairs Satellite, thanks for the bright pennants for my little ship of exploration. Chris and John Kidner provided steady navigation.

Lou and Flora Krause gave blessed moral support throughout and the ladies of the American Newswomen's Club smiled through the stormiest of seas.

At Acropolis Books, I wish to thank publisher Alphons J. Hackl for being a lot more than a publisher. His editorial insight, logic, prodding, and fine-tuning were invaluable. I am convinced that if he ever went to sea full time, he might rival Mel Fisher. Another star was Lisa Shenkle, a true believer from the beginning; she and Rob Chickering kept the spirit alive in all kinds of weather. I would sail anywhere with them and feel safe. Other voyagers were Val Avedon, who added her own knowledge of the sea and who knows quite well how it is to swim upstream and make it. Muriel and John Hackl have always been hearty seapersons under sail on the Chesapeake or on land making books. Dan Wallace was out there keeping the writer off the rocks. Fran Liebowitz read the barometer, while Robert Hickey, Chris Borges and Pamela Moore made it possible to view the illustrations to best advantage.

To my talented and tough-minded editors, Steve Blount and Lisa Walker of Communications Design, I offer a treasure chest of admiration and respect. They know how to make books that carry the reader to far horizons.

Warm thanks to Mike and Sharon Smith, my close friends, who have somehow weathered many, many projects with me. Not once have they faltered; their friendship is more valuable than gold.

To my family, who have literally followed me into shark-infested waters, and are inordinately patient with a writer who not only roams far and wide but also spends most of the night banging on an old-fashioned typewriter, I can only offer love and whatever royalties come my way. Sandy, Becky, and John, this is a small gift that can never repay your greater ones to me.

And to my friend and crony of many years, musical artist and historical scholar Robert M. "Bob" Bruno, my heart-felt thanks for backing me against the wall one hot summer night not so long ago and growling, "Write that book—and not another word until you do!"

To one and all in this fantastic crew, thanks and well done.

Philip Z. Trupp
Washington, D.C.

Spain's New World trade routes left a trail of lost treasure and blood across the bottoms of the world's seas and oceans. The fleets departed Spain in the spring and sailed down the coast of Africa, then west with the trade winds. Two months later, they arrived in the Caribbean and separated to pick up cargo from the colonies. The so-called "New Spain Fleet" coasted around Mexico's Yucatan and headed north to Veracruz, where the riches of the New World mixed with the wealth of the Orient, shipped in from the Spanish-held Philippines aboard the Manila Galleons. The Manila Galleons unloaded their Far Eastern treasures at Acapulco, and from there the wares were transported over-land by slaves to Veracruz. From there the fleet sailed with the currents of the Gulf of Mexico, north to Texas, then down Florida's west coast to Spain's most powerful outpost: Havana, Cuba.

Another fleet, the *Galleones de Tierra Firme,* called first at Cartagena, Colombia, then sailed on to Portobello, Panama, to pick up treasure from Central America. Eventually, the New Spain Fleet and the *Galleones de Tierra Firme* met in Havana for the trip together back to Spain. The timetable for one of these round-trips was seven to nine months.

The voyage home was incredibly perilous. The ships sailed north from Havana to the tip of Florida, where they navigated up the Straits of Florida on the powerful north-flowing Gulf Stream. The reefs of the Florida Keys lay to the west and the treacherous Bahama Banks bordered the ships to the east. If all went well, they made it to Cape Hatteras, then turned east into the deep open Atlantic. But many times the voyage did not go well. Sudden storms drove the ships onto the Florida reefs or the shoals of the Bahamas. If the reefs didn't snare the heavily laden slow-moving galleons, pirates often did. It is estimated that at least 10 percent of all New World and Far Eastern treasure was lost at sea, but the true figure is probably much higher.

PART ONE

Treasure: The Meaning of It All

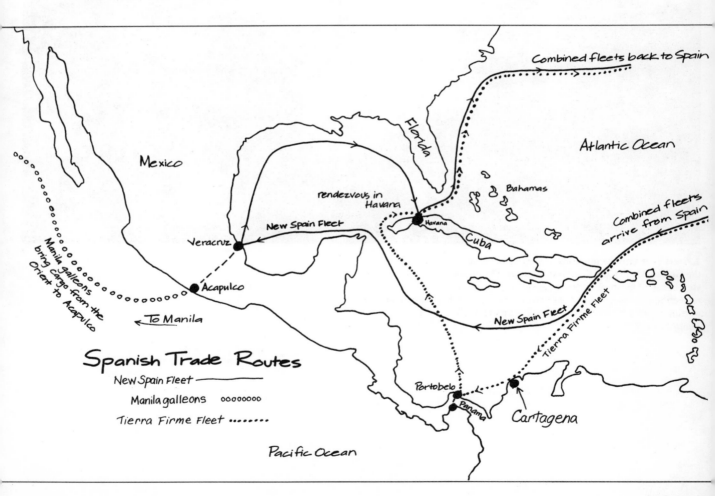

Combined fleets back to Spain

Atlantic Ocean

Florida

Bahamas

rendezvous in Havana

Mexico

Havana

Cuba

Combined fleets arrive from Spain

New Spain Fleet

Veracruz

Manila galleons bring cargo from the Orient to Acapulco

Acapulco

To Manila

New Spain Fleet

Tierra Firme Fleet

Spanish Trade Routes

New Spain Fleet ——————

Manila galleons   oooooooo

Tierra Firme Fleet ·········

Portobelo

Panama

Cartagena

Pacific Ocean

Divers peer into the pitch-black interior of an unknown ship, lost in the Gulf of Mexico off Key West, Florida. The ocean bottom is a vast storehouse of mysterious "time capsules," lost ships and men reflecting a cross-section of the culture from which they came, now waiting silently for modern explorers to unlock their secrets.
Photo by Carl Purcell.

CHAPTER ONE

The Lure of Treasure

Could you be a successful treasure hunter? It's a question worth asking. The rewards, in dollars and especially in personal satisfaction, have lured more than one "commonplace" citizen away from the workaday world to look for the remains of history. Some search on weekends, others during week-long vacations. And some search their entire lives. What they find ranges from spare change and lost jewelry to mega-fortunes and traces of lost civilizations.

The risk? For the weekender, practically nothing—a bit of equipment, some time spent looking over maps. But treasure hunting is what you make of it. Those who choose to seek bigger rewards must take bigger risks: they risk their savings, their families, even their own lives.

Sir Edmund Hillary, nearing the summit of Mount Everest in 1953, turned to his Sherpa guide, Sidar Tenzing Norkey, and asked if he thought their chosen route would take them safely upwards.

"What do you think of it?" Hillary asked.

"I don't like it at all," Tenzing replied.

"Shall we go on?"

Tenzing looked around and shrugged. "As you wish," he said.

Hillary later said that in ordinary mountaineering the risks associated with that particular route would not have been justifiable. "But this is Everest," he said, "and on Everest you sometimes have to take long odds, because the goal is worth it."

The search for treasure incorporates the same logic. It is so special, so compelling, that one is willing to accept certain risks. Like Captain Nemo in Jules Verne's *20,000 Leagues Under The Sea,* the treasure hunter has to preserve a kind of child-like (as opposed to *childish*) belief in the importance of something which the everyday common-sense world believes is too far removed to be of any consequence, not to mention risky. Because of this acceptance of the Nemo Syndrome the successful treasure hunter never entirely "grows up." The spirit of Captain Nemo removes him from the mundane world. His instincts cry out for something unique, something remarkable and lasting. The search for treasure, he knows, will give it to him in a big way.

Every explorer must confront this issue of personal motivation: *Why am I doing this? Am I truly built for an undertaking that is exciting, unique, liberating, and important, and at the same time incredibly demanding?*

So far, no one has devised a quick and easy test that supplies all the answers. Motivation varies with the individual. Over the past ten years, however, I have noticed certain common characteristics among treasure hunters of all types:

1. They are risk-takers.
2. They believe that what they are doing is important.
3. In action, they are tenacious, persistent, tough-minded.
4. They are good planners, meticulous about details.
5. They trust their gut reactions and instincts. They're willing to endure the harshest skepticism.
6. For the most part, treasure hunters are individualists with a unique twist: they realize they can't do it alone—barring sheer luck—and they work well with groups.
7. A fair dose of healthy ego is involved, but no vanity. They enjoy being patted on the back but almost always place the results of their search, the finds, at center stage.
8. There is a powerful element of goal-orientation, almost obsessive at times, but always constructive in nature.
9. Finally, there is the essential romantic element; a "poetic" disposition that lures the explorer onward in search of secrets unknown to others.

This last characteristic, the desire to unlock secrets, is central to the Nemo Syndrome. Inevitably, it leads to action.

An energetic Philadelphia woman, Pamela Warner, provides an excellent example of how this works. To the outside world, she is a successful real estate executive. But her inner circle of friends know her as an accomplished underwater explorer who systematically searches the depths of Lake George, New York, a cold water storehouse of Revolutionary War relics and early American Indian watercraft.

"Most people only see the beautiful mirror-calm surface of the lake," she says. "But I know its secrets."

Each new discovery pleases her, makes her feel special, energizes her to probe further and bring back to life the long-lost artifacts concealed on the lake bottom. It is pure joy, Warner says. "To be the first—to see with your own eyes something that has been hidden from the world for hundreds of years."

Her experience applies not only to SCUBA divers, but to non-divers as well. To succeed at the painstaking job of finding treasure you may never don SCUBA gear or even get wet—but the thrill of discovery has to be there.

Different Strokes

Dan Stack, a Washington, D.C.-based entrepreneur who once helped finance a number of underwater digs, has classified treasure hunters into four neat categories:

1. The single largest category are the "armchair adventurers" who vicariously follow the exploits of treasure hunters as reported in the newspapers and on television. They entertain wonderful wispy dreams of their own, such as stumbling across pirate gold while vacationing at the seashore, and they are cheered and thrilled when real-life treasure hunters strike it rich.

2. Archaeologists, historians, scientists—a very small but important group which generally cares nothing for profit and is concerned mostly with gaining new knowledge. This is essentially a category of purists.

3. Active adventurers. These are the men and women who spend their own time and money in the pursuit of treasure. Rarely are they systematic or scientific. Mostly, they chase the wind. It is the hunt, the raw adventure, that appeals to them. If they find anything, it is usually through pure luck.

4. Professional treasure hunters and shipwreck salvors, such as Mel Fisher, who recently found a Spanish treasure trove worth $400 million. While these rare individuals enjoy glamorous public images, beneath the glitter they are businessmen with more headaches than most. They keep the Nemo Syndrome alive for the general public. They're the ones who, at times, appear to have cornered the attention of the media. Often they are at the center of some controversy. They become larger-than-life folk heroes; legends spring up about them. The purists, horrified by what they perceive to be unscientific salvage methods, imagine them to be a nest of villains bent on destroying history. The active adventurers and the "armchair" sailors adore them for the swashbuckling images they create. Meanwhile, the professional treasure hunters, often impervious to both criticism and adoration, hustle hard every day to maintain their expensive and highly ambitious operations.

The four categories of treasure hunters were outlined by Dan Stack in 1960. There is one group he failed to mention, and still another which in the intervening years has become a revolutionary new power in the underwater world—the paraprofessional explorer.

The first of these groups has a justifiably grotesque reputation; these are the "looters." On land, the looter is a cat burglar, the thief who steals religious artifacts from American Indian burial grounds. The looter chips pieces out of public statues and buildings and, if he could get away with it, would tear down the pyramids of Egypt and sell them as trinkets. In the ocean, the looter will destroy by any means possible any shipwreck or other cultural deposit that might hold negotiable precious metals or historic artifacts. In Florida looters have been particularly destructive. Along the east coast of that treasure-rich state a number of truly breath-taking galleons have been blasted to pieces by dynamite for little more than a handful of antique coins. Looters never stay around long enough to get at the mother lode, and the coins and other objects they come up with are sold at any price the market will bear. No matter how much is paid for these items by naive and unsuspecting persons, the rest of us pay even more. The looter has knowingly destroyed forever a piece of history that can't be replaced. The cultural manuscript, which is the ship itself, has been torn and scattered and will never be read.

I don't blame Dan Stack for ignoring the looter, for he is very properly outlawed in every civilized country in the world. In the Middle East, looters may have their hands chopped off if they're caught. We don't do that here in the United States; we hand them a monetary penalty for defacing public property and send them on their way. I mention them because it is important to know that a looter is *not* a treasure hunter. He is a thief and a pirate who robs us and future generations of a rich cultural inheritance.

That cultural inheritance is the pithy, redolent residue of our past, preserved in artifacts. Some, like the cakes of Chinese beeswax that wash ashore on the northern Pacific Coast, aren't worth a lot of money. Others, like the gleaming gold coins that creep up onto the beaches of Florida after violent storms, are worth a fortune. But the monetary value of the artifacts is not the issue, particularly not for the paraprofessional explorer. These are the private citizens who, driven by curiosity and a desire to contribute their time and talents, pursue the recovery of lost history.

The most important thing is the spirit of the search. The essential chemistry is a sense of wonder and persistent curiosity. If you feel these emotions, I can promise you (almost) that with a little patience and self-application your own fantasies will become reality—and all of us will be the richer for it.

Search For a Sunken City

The lure of treasure began for me in December 1975 on the Caribbean island of St. Maarten, in the Netherlands Antilles. I had gone there to explore the wreck of the British man-o-war, H.M.S. *Proselyte,* which went to the bottom in 1801 when she struck a submerged reef known as Small Bank. Whatever gold and silver the vessel may have carried had long since been salvaged. As a journalist I was more concerned with documenting the wreck site as a dash of color in a larger story I was writing about the Antillian island chain.

"She been down a long time," my island diving guide remarked as we prepared to make our first dive. "Still plenty to see if you look for it." Apparently the British attempted to salvage the cargo soon after she wrecked, and later the Dutch cleaned up what the British had overlooked.

First sight of the drowned vessel came at 15 feet below the surface, where the seabed forms a small underwater cliff. There were two large anchors encrusted with living coral and a scattering of less recognizable wreckage—a jumble of ballast stones, twisted iron fittings, and bronze spikes that once secured the hull planking. My guide motioned with a sweeping gesture, signifying that such bits and pieces were strewn everywhere.

We knelt on the bottom and gently fanned the fine white sand, removing a little of the overburden that had covered fragments of *Proselyte* for nearly two centuries. Within minutes we uncovered broken porcelain, still white with fine blue edging, and bearing a hint of the royal seal. It was an eerie feeling. Here was a small piece of an object from the past—a simple porcelain shard—and yet it set my imagination spinning. Someone had eaten from this plate, probably an officer. I wondered who he might have been, wondered if he survived the sinking. This small shard was like a magic icon which, when touched, allowed me to visualize the life of the ship and its crew.

The guide motioned for us to swim along the reef to a place where the bottom suddenly dropped away to 50 feet. We floated gently downward and, as the deeper bottom came into focus, I saw more ballast stones and larger pieces of wreckage decorated by red and pink coral. There were barrel hoops standing upright in the white sand. A school of silvery mulletts swam elegantly through them. Again, we fanned the sand, uncovering broken black grog bottles. The guide picked up one of these and pretended to take a long belt of the grog, the generic name for anything alcoholic served aboard ship. He then cupped his hands and pointed to the bottom, indicating that the hull of the ship, or what remained of it, lay buried below the sand. For an instant I could imagine it, the blackened skeleton of an ancient vessel waiting in silence for the day when perhaps other men would come to uncover it and bring it back to the world of the sun and sky. It was captivating, and the hour or so we spent underwater raced by very quickly.

On board our little dive boat I sat silently, still wondering about the *Proselyte,* as my guide revved up the engine and headed back to our base of operation in Phillipsburg.

"They be lots more down there," he shouted over the noise of the motor. "These islands be surrounded by ships from all over. Some, they carried treasure. I have been told of this, but I never found any treasure."

What kinds of treasure?

"All kinds," he replied. "Coins. Gold bars. Silver. Lot of galleons sunk around here. More than anybody knows. These waters got more gold in them than all the banks in the world."

That evening we sat and talked at the beach bar. It was a clear night and the stars reflected with a burning intensity on the calm, black Caribbean. I could not take my eyes off the sea or dismiss, even for a moment, the shadowy ghost of the *Proselyte* hidden beneath the surface.

"You be going on to St. Eustatius?" the guide asked. St. Eustatius (or "Stacia," as she is known in these parts) is another tiny spit of an island in the Windward chain. Formerly a thriving Dutch mercantile center and military garrison, it is now a little-known destination among the countless volcanic island peaks in the area. "If you be going there," he continued, "they be something you should know for sure."

He told me that soon after the American Revolution the Dutch at Stacia had been the very first to recognize and formally salute the new American Navy when the fleet sailed by the island. There had been a diplomatic exchange aboard the vessels anchored at Gallows Bay, topped off by congratulatory cannon volleys from Fort Oranje.

"The Brits, they heard of this and became very angry," he explained. "So they sailed into Stacia. She be a big trading place then, but the Brits put an end to it."

He told a tale of British seamen storming ashore in 1781 to sack the old city of Oranjestad. Then, standing offshore in Gallows Bay, their frigates bombarded the city with cannon fire, totally destroying the sea wall that protected the low-lying island. The sea rushed in, drowning Oranjestad.

"A whole city be there underwater—what be left of it," he said.

"A city?"

"Yes, truly. Maybe you will get to see it."

My imagination kicked into high gear. I had read tales of sunken cities, such as Port Royal, which in 1692 sank into the harbor at Kingston, Jamaica, when an offshore earthquake shook the island. Port Royal was infamous in an era of infamy, the hub of every pirate operation in the Caribbean. In one catastrophic moment, "the wickedest city in the world" trembled and plunged into the sea, burying a vast bank of pirate treasure beneath the waves. I had long dreamed of exploring Port Royal, and years later I would make a concerted effort to do so. But for the moment, I was captivated by the sunken city of Oranjestad only a few miles away on Stacia. I did not fix on gold or silver or great riches; instead, it was the ghost of the sunken city itself that captured me, the lure of actually seeing a drowned civilization that appealed so intensely to the Nemo Syndrome, which was slowly overtaking me.

I did not sail to Stacia that year. Other expeditions took precedence. But the image of Oranjestad lingered, darkly glowing with mystery.

Finally, in the summer of 1979, I landed at Saint Eustatius' dusty Franklin Delano Roosevelt Airport. Ours was the only plane in sight. If I did not know better I would have guessed that Stacia, simmering silently in the tropic sun, was deserted. The tiny island-hopping aircraft which had brought me here seemed like something out of another time. I took all of this as being symbolic of the lost civilization I had waited so long to see.

The city I found directly off the beach of the Old Gin House hotel was an undersea ruin. To me, however, it might have been Atlantis. A patch-work of low tumbled-down stone walls outlined the pattern of the life that had been here two centuries before.

Old Oranjestad, or what remained of it, was close to the surf and, over the years, had been worn down to the curbstones. But slowly, as I grew accustomed to the patterns, the ruin took on shape and form. Low walls covered by coral and colorful sponges revealed the rectangular shapes of houses. Sand had clogged every passageway, and here and there a vacant window opened onto the empty sea. The dark sand on the bottom was littered with shards, bits of clay pipes, and encrusted pieces of blackened glass. Along one wall which stood at right angles to the beach I saw the remains of a cannon mount. A few feet farther on was the breech of the cannon itself, poking mournfully out of the sand like a sad, rusting statue.

The chaos of Oranjestad was not Atlantis, surely not the unearthly spectre of imagination and dreams. But to me, it was better. I was fortu-nate to explore the remains of a city built by man and destroyed by man. I knew that beneath this ruin lay the wealth of a forgotten world. I was in no way equipped to dig through the remains and recover that wealth. I knew that others had tried, some successfully, others not so successfully, and that the sea does not give up her bounty without a fight. No ship dies an easy death on the high seas, and this sunken relic of a city had been no less violently destroyed. Among its broken walls and along the path of scattered cobblestones that had once been the avenues of Oranjestad, a current of tragedy swept over me. The broken ceramics littering the bottom had once been useful human tools; the bits of clay pipes helped while away the hours of real men long ago; the cannon buried askew in the sand, now a gathering place for tiny blue fishes, once pointed defiantly seaward.

Farther away from the beach, in about 60 feet of water, the clean sand bottom sloped away into cobalt blue depths. The water was perfectly transparent and sunlit. Countless bottles and broken ceramics, which caught the rays of the sun and showed a distinctive blue edging, were scattered randomly. Fanning the sand with my hand, I came upon bits of iron and wood and handfuls of pottery shards. Out of this fragmented mine of objects that had once been whole and useful came a surprise—a tiny silver spoon. I held it in my palm and wondered if it had adorned a condiment tray. Maybe it belonged to a child. The spoon was slightly bent and tarnished by a dark oxide coating, which dissolved in an ink-like cloud when I rubbed it. So this was the old city of Oranjestad two centuries after the British invasion. Piece by piece it had worked away from the shore and into deep water. I knew that many tons of artifacts were hidden below the sand, and the endless tides and currents would continue to pull these remains of a former life into the deep cobalt depths. In another century much of it will be hidden away forever in the sunlessness of the abyss.

When my dive guide touched my shoulder I nearly jumped out of the water. I had gone so deeply into my imagination that I had forgotten he was there. It was time to go, he indicated, motioning with a thumb toward the surface. When we reached shore I had a sense of having lived in a time capsule. Two centuries earlier merchant ships called on this port. Gold and silver were exchanged for the vast resources of the Indies. Men built and lost their fortunes here. Now it was hidden mutely beneath the sands and the turbulent sea.

"You are so quiet," my guide said. "What is on your mind?"

"Treasure," I replied. "Treasure and the meaning of it all."

Mel Fisher, the "greatest treasure hunter of them all," spends a sultry afternoon showing long golden chains to visitors outside his treasure museum in Key West, Florida. The chains and other treasures were recovered by Fisher from the *Nuestra Señora de Atocha,* a galleon lost in 1622 near Florida's Marquesas Keys. After nearly two decades of constant searching, Fisher discovered the Atocha's mother lode in July, 1985. Part of the recovered cargo, sometimes called the "primary cultural deposit," consisted of 47 tons of solid silver bars, stacked like cordwood on the ocean bottom. The total treasure trove, including the silver, is valued at $400 million.
Photo by Don Kincaid.

CHAPTER TWO

Mel Fisher: Lucky Like a Fox

As the Las Vegas blackjack dealer slipped another hand out of the shoe that night in January, 1985, a large, deeply-tanned, yet oddly inconspicuous man appeared out of the murky innards of the casino and stood quietly behind us. Melvin A. Fisher, the world's most famous treasure hunter, grinned, showing his 24-karat fillings, and toyed with the $12,000 Spanish gold coin suspended on an ancient gold necklace which circled his sunburned neck. The golden display characteristically did not elevate the persona of the man beyond the ordinary. Only Mel Fisher can remain inconspicuous in a wreath of glitter. The man who had gained world recognition in his quest for a rich Spanish treasure galleon, *Nuestra Señora de Atocha,* appeared to be just another gambler in a town awash with gamblers.

The dealer dealt the cards and Fisher observed us quietly as the hands were played out on the green felt table. We won a few and lost a few. Fisher was unimpressed with our mixed fortunes.

"Heck, you can't make any money playing cards," he whispered in my ear. "You're wasting time, wasting money."

Now there are innumerable "experts" in Las Vegas who gladly hand out free advice on gambling, and generally you can count on getting your money's worth. But when the world's greatest treasure hunter, the ultimate odds player, tells you to fold, the wisest thing to do is to heed his words. Yet neither I nor my table mate, Charlie McKinney, were prepared to play it smart. We considered ourselves pretty canny players and had come to Vegas armed with the famous blackjack treatise *Aus Boss.*

"Really, fellas, you're just giving it away. Tonight's the night for slots. That's where the action is," Fisher said.

"Sure, Mel," I replied. "Later."

Fisher watched us for a few minutes more, and, seeing that he was getting nowhere with us, slipped back into the cavernous dark hollows of the Las Vegas club.

We had what we believed to be good cause to question Fisher's advice. We were slightly ahead, luck was with us (sort of) but Fisher's luck had been running cold—not just on this particular night, but for the past decade. His long quest for the *Atocha* and her sister treasure ship, the *Santa Margarita,* had peaked in 1975. That was the year a massive display of his treasure finds were exhibited in Explorer's Hall at the National Geographic Society headquarters in Washington, D.C. In the glare of the *Atocha's* bronze cannons, returned to Queen Sophia of Spain, and an article in the Society's magazine, *National Geographic,* Mel reported that the gold, silver, and artifacts recovered by his adventure company, Treasure Salvors, Inc., of Key West, Florida, were worth more than $60 million. On this night, all of that seemed like a far-away dream. The treasure business had fallen on hard times, and now Fisher's stockholders wanted to know what he had done for them lately. Fisher had tried to reassure them that the mother lode, worth perhaps as much as $400 million, would soon be discovered. "Today's the day!" he told them, without much tangible feedback. We knew he had faithful, powerful, wealthy, and believing allies who would not let him down. But no amount of faith could satisfy his long time supporters. He came to Vegas to look for new believers, new investors.

We forgot about Fisher and continued at the blackjack table. Then, over the din of the casino, we heard the unmistakable, cheerful sound of dollar chips clattering into the metal bin of a one-armed bandit. Charlie gave me a look. Could it be . . . ?

Fisher reappeared, still the inconspicuous everyman figure with blurred edges. "Hey, what did I tell you," he said. "The slots are running. You guys should be in on it."

We followed him through the crowd to a bank of gaudy slots. He seemed to be sniffing the smokey air, sensing something we couldn't understand. He stopped in front of one of the slots and introduced us to his new chum, a native desert rat type wearing a tattered baseball cap with an oily brim. Also standing at the machine were two long-time Fisher associates,

R. Duncan Mathewson III, Treasure Salvors' pioneering marine archaeologist, and Pat Clyne, a diver, ship captain, and underwater video expert. They were beaming.

"She still running?" Fisher asked the desert rat.

"Could be better," he replied.

Fisher offered to buy into this particular slot. He would finance an all-out assault and all of us would split the winnings. It sounded good to us. We pooled our money to buy more chips, about $100 in all, and the treasure hunt resumed.

Fisher dropped some chips into the slot without results. Then a very strange thing happened. He turned away from the machine so that his back was to it. He reached around with his right arm so that it passed under his left and took hold of the slot's long, silver handle, his back still to the machine. "You do it like this," he explained. "You drop the chips and I'll play a few." In this awkward posture, with the rest of us feeding the slot, Fisher played on. After a half-dozen pulls, $50 clattered noisily into the bin. A few more pulls and another $50 spewed forth. Fisher smiled, goldenly. "Now you fellas do it like I did." We took turns with Fisher feeding the machine; another score, $70. We were ready to call it quits, but Fisher said we were hot. He said we had to pour our winnings back into the game. Good businessmen know that to win big, the profits need to be reinvested, he said.

Fisher cheered. He coached us on proper one-armed bandit pulling. "Don't stop," he urged. We were dropping chips into the slot as fast as humanly possible. The music of money pouring into the bin continued. Within an hour, the brazen glow of the slot machine sputtered and died, like a juke box unplugged in the middle of a fast tune. As we gleefully stacked nearly $1,000 worth of winnings into bright red trays, we noticed a dark-suited Vegas pit boss a few yards away, glaring at us with arms folded across his massive chest. Fisher smiled at him innocently.

"Nice casino you got here," Fisher said.

The pit boss remained sober.

Later on, Charlie, Duncan, and Pat sat in a bar discussing Fisher's uncanny luck. "You need it in the treasure business," Duncan admitted.

I agreed. But somehow this crazy experience in the casino seemed to be more than luck. It had to be. Fisher was too consistent. He had scoped the casino for the "right" machine and "right" player. He trusted his instincts. Playing the slots is a risk—a very large risk at a dollar a roll— but somehow Fisher had intangibly shifted the odds in our favor. I don't know how he did it, but there was something cool and calculating in his method. He wasn't shooting in the dark. In the casino, as in the search for sunken treasure, Fisher did not trust luck alone. That would be an act of simple-minded faith, and that's not what treasure hunting is about. Fisher is often politely called a dreamer by his detractors, of whom there are legions. He is in fact a plotter, a resource gatherer who knows precisely what he's looking for, where he might find it, and what will be required to take delivery.

Six months after his remarkable display at Vegas, his biggest gamble paid off—Treasure Salvors found the mother lode of the *Atocha*: gold, silver, precious gems, and priceless artifacts worth more than $400 million. Fisher never doubted that he would find it beneath the sand and mud bottom of the Gulf of Mexico near the Marquesas Atoll, some 40 miles from Key West. When, on July 20, 1985, his jubilant divers reported over the marine radio that they were recovering intact treasure chests crammed with riches, Fisher maintained his obscure, stoic composure. On hearing the news he smiled very faintly, nonchalantly lifted an eyebrow and drawled in a voice that seemed to say *I told you so.* "Treasure chests, huh? Well you don't say. . . ." It was the response of a hard-line winner.

On the Ground Floor

I interviewed Fisher for the first time in 1978, aboard his floating office and museum, a life-sized replica of a Spanish treasure galleon named *Golden Doubloon,* moored at the gasoline docks in Key West. Atop a counter in the ship's gift shop stood a remarkable display—a small round receptacle in the middle of which sat a bright Spanish gold coin. When I tried to pick up the coin, however, my fingers closed on empty air. The coin wasn't there; it was an optical illusion, Fisher's idea of a clever practical joke. The coin was actually below the counter surrounded by trick mirrors and several layers of protective glass. To me the illusion was a symbol of the difficulties of chasing after treasure, and it is the perfect metaphor of Fisher's struggles over the years to hold onto the precious objects he's recovered from the sea. Even now, almost a decade after the first interview, that metaphor remains accurate. The *Atocha's* mother lode is slowly coming up from the sea bed but in the end it may prove as hard to hold onto as the trick coin in Fisher's gift shop. For most of the 16 years he'd been looking for his galleon, Fisher has had to fight the state of Florida and the federal government for title to the wreck.

Fisher received me in the cramped, sweltering sterncastle office of the treasure museum. The gold coin around his sunburned neck was the first thing that caught my attention. He stood to shake hands, towering over me, and flashed that engaging gold-spiked grin.

"Welcome aboard," he said over the whir of an over-worked air conditioner. "Excuse the mess, but we're getting ready to put our treasure on the road, like the King Tut exhibit."

I had already toured the shipboard museum. Frankly, the exhibits seemed rather dark and musty. Comparing them to the King Tut treasures did not compute in my mind, but Fisher assured me that the really flashy items were being packaged for shipment and when properly displayed would compare favorably to the Tut show or any other exhibit I'd ever seen.

Fisher toyed with a couple of silver *reales* and a gold object I could not identify on his cluttered desk top.

"We're going to open at the Queens Museum in New York," he continued. "Wait till you see it. You won't believe your eyes."

Like most serious treasure hunters, Fisher struck me as a man of great ego and extraordinary drive. His single-mindedness stood out as clearly as the gold coin around his neck. He was the kind of man, all too rare these days, who lives out his fantasies so that they spill over and touch the rest of us in dramatic, extravagant terms. His answers to my questions seemed larger than life, yet he was anything but verbose. He was sizing me up, chain-smoking and filling the room with a gray fog. The ashtray was piled high with butts. He spoke softly, almost laconically, his answers short and to the point, doing nothing to lead me on to the next question. I now understood why he had the reputation of being a difficult interview.

After a while, Fisher's wife, Deo, entered the room. The moment she stepped through the door, the whole place brightened. Deo was truly striking, a tall, slender woman who might easily have made herself a career as a fashion model. She had a warm, disarming smile and fabulous red hair. Her bright, energetic manner contrasted sharply with her husband's somewhat sombre presence.

Deo answered most of my questions and the more we spoke the more I liked her. Fisher, meanwhile, leaned back in his king-sized swivel chair, taking in every detail, fingering the silver *reales.*

"We've been through a lot," Deo said. "More than most people could stand."

At the head of the list were the deaths of the Fisher's oldest son, Dirk, their daughter-in-law Angel, and diver Rick Gage. On the night of July 20, 1975, they were trapped in their bunks and drowned when one of the Treasure Salvor dive boats, *Northwind,* capsized and went to the bottom while anchored over the *Atocha* site. Ironically, ten years to the day after the tragedy Fisher's youngest son, Kane, discovered the mother lode.

"Sure, we thought of quitting," Deo said. "We wondered why this had happened. Was it a curse? Were we being punished? But we knew that if we didn't go on, Dirk's death would have gone for nothing."

Fisher leaned forward, reached into a trouser pocket, and removed a long gold chain, dropping it on the desk top. It was one of the "money chains" recovered years earlier during the endless search for the *Atocha.* The chain was made up of delicately fashioned links, which were snapped off and spent like money. It was dazzling.

"What does this say to you?" Fisher asked, moving the chain over the desk toward me.

Treasure had been placed before me many times, but this was something special. I didn't wish to appeared awed, even though I was, so I mustered up my courage and replied, "It says gold. It says—blood."

It seemed a long, long time before he spoke. "That's right," he said, his booming voice deepening. "It's blood. History. A piece of something that was alive. You can't put a price on it."

It was one of the few times I've heard him speak with passion. Some people say he has a sleepy, almost introverted manner. But during that moment in our interview, I realized that, inside, he burned with a hard, clear intensity. He is the classic man of few words, but every word comes from the blood level where everything counts, where words and thoughts are at critical mass; there was no trace whatever of the hyperbole that so often pervades the atmosphere of big-time treasure hunting. It made a profound impression. In a flash, I knew that Mel Fisher was for real.

At this writing, there is talk in Hollywood of a movie about Fisher's life. It will have to be an epic drama, for the man is infinitely more impressive than his treasure trove. No one I have ever known has lived more intensely or endured so many wild swings of the pendulum of fate.

Fisher was born to the extraordinary. He grew up in Gary, Indiana, played saxophone in high school, and formed his own jazz band. He went from jazz to engineering at Purdue University, working his way through college as a music booking agent. In 1944, he was shipped to France with the Army Corps of Engineers. After the war, he worked as a carpenter in Chicago and Denver. Later, he moved to Tampa, Florida, set up a general contracting company, and spent his spare time spearfishing in the Gulf of Mexico. Locals knew him as the young man who swam out the farthest and bagged the biggest fish. To prove his fish stories to doubters, he took up underwater photography and learned to SCUBA dive. He discovered his first treasure, a very modest one, while diving off St. Petersburg. "I used to dive on the old wrecks around Tampa and St. Pete because that's where you find most of the fish," he recalled. "But when I picked up that first piece of silver, that was the end of spearfishing."

In 1950, he moved to Torrance, California to help his father build a chicken ranch. He continued his undersea explorations and, when the SCUBA craze hit California, he built a dive shop—one of the first—in the feed shed at the ranch. He then formed a SCUBA club, appropriately named "The Sharks," and taught novices to dive.

Mel met Deo (then 15-year-old Delores Horton) when her family purchased the Fisher chicken ranch. Fisher stayed on to help the new owners get started—and also to spend time with Deo. The feed shed dive shop remained open.

Deo attended a meeting of The Sharks where Fisher showed underwater footage that he had filmed in Tampa. Deo was spell-bound by the colorful, incandescent undersea world. Fisher taught her to dive. "It was like nothing I had ever seen or done before," she recalled.

Bubbles apparently led to love, and they were married in 1953. The newlyweds took a diver's honeymoon in Florida, filming a movie about spearfishing for the Voit Company, which markets SCUBA gear. Back in Torrance, the Fishers went into the dive business full time, opening Mel's Aqua Shop in Redondo Beach. In addition to oceanic adventure, Mel's Aqua Shop also marketed gold prospecting trips to the Sierra Nevada mountains. Naturally, the prospectors needed equipment to get at the gold, and Fisher sold them dredges he had designed.

SCUBA was growing in popularity in the States. The patented air tanks and regulators invented by Jacques Cousteau and Canadian Emile Gagnan were being imported from Europe. For a modest price, virtually anyone could become an instant underwater explorer. Treasure hunting grew in popularity, particularly in the warm, clear waters surrounding the Florida Keys. In 1951, Art McKee, who had been investigating old wrecks since the 1930s, led a treasure hunting team that included Edwin A. Link, inventor of the Link aircraft trainer. They discovered the famous H.M.S. *Looe,* a British frigate lost off Big Pine Key in 1743. Link later claimed the discovery of the *Santa Maria,* Columbus' flagship, which sank off the north coast of Haiti on Christmas Day, 1492. Across the Atlantic, in Bermuda, Edward "Teddy" Tucker began a four-year underwater search which yielded a stunning collection of treasures.

The Ultimate Survivor

Mel soon supplemented his Sierra gold trips by purchasing a 55-foot diesel-powered boat. With a select group of friends and his most able SCUBA students, he formed a marine salvage club. It was during this period that he met a diver named Fay Feild. A highly-skilled electronics expert, Feild had built a device called a flux-gate magnetometer. The Navy had used similar devices, which work like metal detectors, during World War II to find submarines, but Feild's device was far more sensitive. Light and portable, it could be towed behind a boat. Even in deep water it was capable of "seeing" all the way to bottom and honing in on metal objects buried in the seabed. Thus, in partnership with Feild, Fisher's quest for sunken treasure took on bright new dimensions.

After a test of the "mag" on the Cortez Bank, a shallow ocean area off California, Fisher and his associates headed for the Caribbean Sea. The first stop was the island of Cozumel, off Mexico's Yucatan Peninsula, in the Gulf of Mexico. At Dzibilchaltun, Fisher explored the mud-clouded water of an inland *cenote,* a Mayan sacrificial well, and recovered an intact ceramic vessel. He gave the pot to an archaeological team from Tulane University which was excavating the site. Cozumel yielded no vast treasures, so the crew returned to California to regroup.

Their next destination was the famous Silver Shoals, located north of the Dominican Republic. It was here, in 1687, that Sir William Phips, the most celebrated treasure hunter of his day, recovered a substantial cache of silver from a Spanish vessel lost in 1641. Fisher was convinced that Phips, severely limited by primitive salvage techniques, had left much treasure behind. Fisher found a group of investors, put together $25,000, and set out to explore the Shoals.

So, in 1960, the *Golden Doubloon* sailed out of the California port of San Pedro, along the west coast of Mexico, and through the Panama Canal. But half-way across the Gulf of Mexico, the vessel developed a serious leak. The pumps failed and the boat began to settle ominously by the stern. Fisher had met a marine mechanic, Demosthenes "Moe" Molinar, in Colon, Panama and they had instantly become life-long partners. Together they struggled desperately at the end of a lifeline, slapping together a plywood shield around the fantail to keep out the sea. Miraculously, it worked and the pumps were repaired. Then, without warning, the engines quit. Fisher and his crew drifted for days in the open sea before the engines could be restarted. They limped back to Panama for an overhaul.

Portobello, an ancient terminus for the treasure fleets along the Panamanian coast, gave Fisher his first genuine Spanish shipwreck. Fay Feild's magnetometer recorded positive hits on the site and Moe Molinar went over the side to investigate. Within seconds, Molinar shot to the surface, breathless, and reported seeing cannons and a big pile of ballast stones. Fisher strapped on a SCUBA tank and leaped into the water carrying the small water jet he had developed for gold prospecting in the Sierras. Planting himself firmly on the bottom, he used the jet to burrow into the jumbled wreckage. but the device wasn't powerful enough to make much of a dent. The Fisher team turned up pottery, nails, and musket shot—but no gold or silver. Years later, after much hard-won experience, Fisher reflected that he had probably left behind a fortune on this wreck.

This Caribbean foray had absorbed the $25,000 Mel had raised from investors plus an equal amount out of his own pocket. He had learned the hard way that if big-time treasure hunting was exciting it was also difficult, fraught with danger, and very expensive. There would be no more seat-of-the-pants operations.

The Fishers were prospering. The SCUBA shop was doing a brisk trade, the family owned a home and a boat, investors had come through for another Silver Shoals expedition, Fisher was writing magazine articles and selling movies to various underwriters. Despite this success, Fisher felt compelled to become a full-time treasure hunter. He had assembled a group of dedicated adventurers, many of whom were prepared to fund treasure hunts, while others were ready to go to sea on short notice with their considerable diving skills. As for Deo, she had become a superb diver and had broken the world's record for underwater endurance by a woman, staying submerged for 57 hours.

The turning point came in the winter of 1962 when a group of visitors from the East Coast came to see the Fishers. They were Clifford "Kip" Wagner and several of his partners. These men had formed a company called Real 8 which was salvaging a fleet of Spanish treasure galleons which sunk off Florida in 1715. Already their finds had been estimated to be worth more than $1 million, and they were developing new technology to recover even more treasure.

Wagner's meeting with Fisher was useful to both men, and a special kind of camraderie was born. Wagner was impressed by Fisher's leadership qualities. Not only was he something of a swashbuckler, but he possessed hard-won ocean skills and inner toughness—important attributes in this unique profession.

Wagner struck a deal. The Californians would become partners in Real 8. They would support themselves in Florida for a year and handle all of their own expenses while working the 1715 wrecks. Fisher's finds would be split 50-50 with Real 8. Any division of the spoils, of course, was subject to the group's salvage permit with the State of Florida, which claimed 25 percent of anything the divers brought up from the bottom.

Fisher and Deo considered their options. Wagner's offer was spiked with risks. But with risk comes opportunity. It would be a golden entree to the real professional treasure action in Florida, a stepping stone to bigger and better things. They would be working wrecks known to contain great treasures and gain priceless hands-on experience. What's more, Wagner was connected with a number of recognized experts and some very high-rolling investors.

The Fisher team left California with high hopes, arriving in Fort Pierce, Florida on July 4, 1963. Events moved quickly. Almost immediately, the Fisher group found its first treasure on the 1715 wrecks—a large silver wedge and a respectable collection of silver coins. Inventiveness shifted into high hear. The shallow waters of the work sites tended to be extremely murky because of wave action; the mag registered hits, but divers on the bottom could see just scant inches in front of their facemasks. Fisher called Fay Feild, who had remained in California, and the two talked the problem over. Their solution was a device they called the "mailbox." Large, elbow-shaped deflector tubes were fabricated and mounted on hinges on the stern of a workboat. When lowered over the boat's propellers, the mailbox would force the prop wash downward. The mailbox was tested in 50 feet of inky water near Fort Pierce. The propellers were turned on, beating slowly into the deflectors. Below, the divers watched as a bubble of bright, clean surface water was forced toward the bottom, providing a ten-foot circle of clear water. They quickly discovered an uncalculated benefit: the mailbox dug a six-foot crater in the bottom sediment, removing centuries of sand in minutes. It was a quantum leap in excavation techniques. In Panama, Mel's small gold dredge hadn't been able to move the vast amount of sand required to fully investigate the wreck. Now, the group was able to blast away tons of sand, quickly getting down to bedrock, where heavy objects like precious metals and cannons often settled over the years. Shortly, Feild made another contribution—a second-generation magnetometer able to tell the difference between ferrous metals, such as iron, and non-ferrous metals, such as silver and gold.

While working a site south of Fort Pierce on May 8, 1964, Moe Molinar recovered a pair of large gold disks. Two weeks later, after a mailbox "blow," the divers shot to the surface shouting that the bottom was "paved with gold." Indeed it was. In one day, they recovered 1,033 gold coins. By the end of that week, they had netted 2,700 coins in denominations of two, four, and eight *escudos.*

The following summer brought yet another bonanza when a random mailbox blow unearthed 1,128 gold coins in a single day. When the diving season ended with the coming of the north winds of winter, the combined treasure operations had recovered, in addition to the gold, thousands of silver coins and a rich collection of artifacts, including rare intact pieces of Chinese K'ang Hsi porcelain.

Kip Wagner was reveling in the group's success, which was beginning to attract national attention. An article in the January, 1965, issue of *National Geographic* recounted how Wagner had started the gold rush on Florida's east coast after he found Spanish coins while walking a deserted beach. Wagner had found more coins, and had followed the trail of treasure right out into the surf, eventually discovering the bones of the 1715 fleet. Yet, despite Wagner's well-deserved and hard-won fame, Mel Fisher was the true rising star. Among the "brotherhood of the coast" he was the man who attracted the most respect—and the most envy. Fisher was always prepared to roll for the highest stakes and take the greatest risks, and, according to observers, he was willing "to exaggerate more than anyone."

But there was a dark side to this fame. Archaeologists employed by the state of Florida, perhaps miffed by their own relative obscurity, attempted to seize the 1715 treasures. They did get some of it, and followed up with tight regulations governing the reporting of finds. They argued with more venom than common sense that the treasure hunters were destroying precious cultural resources, the public's rightful patrimony, for the mean purpose of making a profit. Huge tracts of ocean bottom were placed off-limits to the salvors, and a campaign of character assassination attempted to paint them as "pirates," "looters," and wanton destroyers. Only trained underwater archaeologists—of which there were fewer than 25 worldwide—should be permitted to excavate the wrecks, they said. The salvors shot back: they pointed out that the state was doing a lot of talking but virtually no underwater exploration. Besides, they added, excavation is very costly and the state had little money for such projects. Wouldn't everyone be best served by continuing to allow private companies to salvage the wrecks using private funds? The public would get to see the patrimony the archaeologists were so concerned about, and the salvors were free to develop the technology to find more of it.

The state's answer was to place even more ocean tracts off limits. In 1966, only ten salvage permits were granted. And though Governor Haydon Burns disapproved, Florida's young marine archaeologist, Carl Clausen, and the Secretary of State, Tom Adams, lobbied hard to outlaw *all* treasure hunting. These were the opening salvos of the treasure wars that even today are raging in State Houses up and down the East Coast and even in Congress.

Characteristically, Fisher refused to be intimidated. He expanded his operations to include the marketing of Feild's new magnetometer. While continuing to work the 1715 wrecks with Real 8, Fisher formed his own corporation, Treasure Salvors, Inc. Perhaps it was Fisher's positive momentum that killed his partnership with Real 8. Troubles with state officials also clouded the scene. Wagner charged that Fisher hadn't kept Real 8 fully informed about work on the 1715 sites. There was an underlying fear that Treasure Salvors was stealing the show to further its own ambitions. Yet there was more inevitability than malice in the Wagner-Fisher split. The heyday of Real 8 appeared to be waning, while Fisher, the young upstart of the partnership, seemed born to the spotlight. He was rapidly building a reputation as one of the best promoters since P.T. Barnum; his innate flair was in sharp contrast to Wagner's relatively quiet style. The relationship had soured. In December, 1969, Real 8 filed suit in a circuit court asking for a clarification of its contract with the Fisher group. Charges and counter-charges flew. The Internal Revenue Service appeared briefly to question Fisher's financial dealing. While no irregularities were found, it was clear that the Wagner-Fisher partnership was no longer workable. Joint salvage operations faded and, in the end, Real 8 declared bankruptcy. The treasure hunting world now focused on Fisher, the ultimate survivor.

The Quicksands

Early in 1970, the Treasure Salvors team pulled up stakes again, this time moving to Key West. Always the showman, Fisher offered a gold bar as collateral against future payment on the dock space needed for his museum/office, the *Golden Doubloon,* Fisher's custom-built replica of a 17th-century treasure galleon. It was the right public relations gesture for a man whose reputation was growing larger than life. To the world he appeared to be the high-rolling adventurer with a treasure chest groaning under the weight of a vast fortune. Beneath the image, however, he was struggling with the maddening financial realities of his cash-hungry profession. Florida's treasure laws added to his worries. All finds were consigned to Florida officials until a division of the artifacts could be made. At the division, the state and the salvors bargained, with the state taking 25 percent and giving the rest back to the salvor. The process was painfully slow, often dragging on for many months. When the state finally released the salvor's share, further distributions had to be made to Treasure Salvors' stockholders. Marketing the remaining treasure came with its own frustrations.

To generate cash, Fisher borrowed heavily from banks using coins as collateral. Typically, these loans amounted to about 60 percent of the treasure's retail value. But even with bank loans available the company was constantly short of cash, and Fisher's bottom line undulated as wildly as ocean waves.

Most of his energy now concentrated on finding the *Nuestra Señora de Atocha* and her sister ship, *Santa Margarita.* Fisher knew about these fabulous prizes, part of a treasure fleet sunk in a hurricane in 1622, even before he moved to Florida. They carried vast cargos, the yearly output of the mines and mints of the New World. The *Atocha* had sailed from Havana with over a quarter-million silver *reales,* nearly a thousand 60-pound silver ingots, plus uncounted gold bullion and gems—fabulous diamonds and emeralds from Columbia. His search for the vessels during his partnership with Real 8 extended from Matecumbe, in the middle of the Florida Keys, north to Key Largo, just south of Miami, without the slightest trace of success. Of course, he wasn't the only treasure hunter looking for these galleons. There was competition from Art McKee and a relentless protege of McKee's named Burt D. Webber, Jr., now head of Continental Explorations, Inc.

Search and Research

There are many things that go into a successful treasure hunt—capital, strong divers, hard work, persistence, determination. And faultless research. The location of the wreck must be pinpointed as accurately as possible from historical records before boats and men are dispatched to comb the vast ocean bottom. Most of what Fisher had read pointed in all the wrong directions. The salvor's Bible was a book by John Potter, Jr., *Treasure Hunter's Guide,* published in 1960. Potter's reading of the early Spanish accounts of the 1622 fleet disaster placed the wrecks near Matecumbe, in the Middle Keys. An English account seemed to place them near Key Largo. Fisher aggressively explored these areas but when the trails turned cold, he moved the operation south to Marathon, conducting aerial surveys from there to Key West.

Meanwhile, Burt Webber was searching, too, with his 136-foot vessel *Revenge.* This didn't worry Fisher. Treasure Salvors had already searched the area covered by Webber's state salvage lease without uncovering a trace of the galleons. Fisher was content to sit back silently as *Revenge,* outfitted with every piece of modern salvage equipment available, gobbled up Webber's precious working capital, crossing and recrossing a barren tract of sea bottom.

But, while Webber was coming up empty, so was Fisher. Then Mel found an edge. He contacted an old friend, Eugene Lyon, the former city manager of the city of Vero Beach, Florida. Lyon was studying for a doctorate degree in Latin American history at the University of Florida. Lyon's area of research was the Spanish exploitation of the New World. Now he was on his way to Seville, Spain to study the original Spanish government records of the era in the Archive of the Indies.

"When Mel discovered that I would be going to Spain for a year to work in the archives there, he asked me to let him know of anything I might turn up on the 1622 shipwrecks," Lyon recalled in his book, *The Search for the Atocha* (Harper & Row Publishers, 1979).

Lyon agreed, and though Fisher could not have known it with any real certainty, his agreement with the historian would place him on the inside track in the race for Florida's hottest, richest treasure trove. Characteristically, he was lucky like a fox.

Almost immediately, Lyon began finding original documents relating to the wrecks, which the Spanish had desperately sought to salvage themselves for several decades. His information indicated that the *Atocha* and the *Santa Margarita* had gone down 40 miles south and west of Key West near the Marquesas Atoll. This was both good and bad news. The good news was a relative fix on the wreck sites; the bad news was that the search would be moved to a trackless expanse of open ocean far from land. Costs would escalate and danger would increase.

Fay Feild arrived in Key West with his newest electronic gear, a very sensitive proton magnetometer, and the search was launched. It began in an area known as The Quicksands. The bottom here is covered with deep, shifting sands. Tides and currents constantly move the sand around, creating sinuous dune formations that continuously change the entire landscape. The Quicksands are also littered with modern refuse. The area has been a favored bombing range for Navy aviators since before World War II. Fisher's team got a horrific demonstration of this fact when they accidentally got in the way of a practice bombing run. Huge mushrooms of water rose not more than 100 yards behind one of the search boats as the series of bombs crashed into the sea. Miraculously, no one was killed or injured, and the shaken crews dashed out of the area unscathed. Old bomb casings, torpedoes, winches, anchors, fish traps, and tons or other modern garbage confused the magnetometer, keeping the divers working overtime checking out "hits."

Once again, persistence and faith worked to Fisher's advantage. On June 12, 1971, one of Fisher's diehard associates, Bob Holloway, was trolling the mag along the edge of The Quicksands. His sister, Marjory Hargreaves, had been assigned the tedious job of keeping an eye on the dial. Suddenly, she saw the mag needle dip and then jump to the right—a clear indication of something big and metallic below. Over the groan of the engines Hargreaves shouted, "Anomaly!" Holloway cut the throttles as crew members quickly heaved a heavy marker buoy into the water to mark the spot. Within minutes, the boat tugged at its anchor alongside the buoy as Holloway, in SCUBA gear, slipped into the water.

Fourteen feet below, Holloway swam over the featureless white sand around the buoy. From the air, these waters appear to be clear as thin air; on the bottom, however, currents and wave action stir the sand, blocking the surface light, and the water is a milky, dark-green color. In the gloom Holloway saw something half-buried in the sand. Using his hands like a fan, he swept away some of the sediment. The object was an iron ring about three feet in diameter. It was connected to a large, thick metal shaft buried deep in the sand. Holloway hardly paused; it was obvious he had found an anchor—a very, very old anchor.

News of Holloway's discovery sent Fisher's salvage boats churning out of Key West. At the anchor site, the 46-foot work boat, *Virgilona,* set three anchors in the sand. These would hold the boat in place when the mailboxes were turned on. Within minutes, centuries of sand disappeared, revealing a galleon anchor. On board the *Virgilona,* Fisher turned to Deo. "That's it," he told her. Mel was convinced they had found the *Margarita* or the *Atocha.*

Fisher dove and inspected the anchor again. When he surfaced, he was holding a small, round object—a lead musket ball.

Another diver, Rick Vaughan, came up with pieces of pottery and a blackened, round disc, which he gave to Fisher. Carefully rubbing away the black stain, Fisher saw the Cross of Jerusalem and a silver lion—the seal of the Spanish Hapsburg kings. More rubbing revealed lettering: Philippus IV. "That's right for 1622," he said.

The next day, following another mailbox blow, a new member of the Fisher crew came out from Key West to photograph the anchor. Don Kincaid adjusted his diving gear, checked his cameras, and rolled backwards into the sea. I've known Kincaid a long time, and observed him in many situations. Now a vice president of Treasure Salvors, he's the man who can pull a rabbit out of the hat, just when you need it most. And on this particular occasion he once again demonstrated his unique gift.

As he headed for the bottom through the cloud of sand kicked up by the mailboxes, visibility was no more than a few inches. When it began to clear, he saw the crater *Virgilona* had created. "I was looking at the crater wall and getting myself oriented," he told me later, over drinks at the colorful Pier House bar in Key West. "The sand was sliding down the wall pretty quickly, and I saw something shiny, just a few links of a chain; the sand was covering it. It was kind of dark and it looked like brass, and I made a stab at it. I pulled this little ball of shiny links out of the sand and headed up. I was looking at it, and at some point just below the surface, I noticed it wasn't brass—it was gold!"

The Credibility Gap

It was certainly a world-class start for what was to become the heavy weight championship of undersea treasure digs. But if the road to the top was paved with gold, it was also spiked with jealousy, greed, bureaucratic confiscations, insolvency and personal tragedy.

Fisher's troubles with the state began immediately after he applied for a salvage contract covering the anchor site. There were endless delays. When the permit was at last granted, a group of state archaeologists were assigned to duty on Fisher's work boats. Their job was to record all finds. It seemed like a reasonable procedure, but it soon became clear that these classically-trained archaeologists were sea-going detectives who made no secret of the state's distrust of Fisher and his crews. Alienation was at the core of the game. They began a mud-slinging campaign in the media to destroy Treasure Salvor's credibility. The fraternity of marine archaeologists is a tiny, air-tight community; it is also a collusive one. The nature of this fraternity revealed itself when articles began to appear in various publications alleging, among other things, that the *Atocha* dig had been "salted" with Fisher's 1715 finds to make it appear to be a producing wreck to investors. A constant barrage of such accusations began with the state's archaeological overseers and spread like a fire out of control. Fisher's hucksterish nature fueled these attacks and soon the "Fisher factor" was being pointed to as the telling sign of a massive floating con game. The erosion of credibility seriously impaired Fisher's ability to attract new investors at a time when capital was crucial to keeping the hunt alive.

On October 23, 1971, two gold bars were recovered; they bore no mint marks or other identifying symbols. They were contraband, a great amount of which was carried aboard all Spanish treasure ships. In Seville, Dr. Lyon had uncovered the *Atocha's* cargo manifest, showing that the vessel carried 901 silver ingots, more than 250,000 silver *reales,* and 161 gold pieces of varying weights. There was no telling how much contraband had been smuggled aboard the galleon, but it was assumed to be a substantial. Lyon told Fisher it was essential to find numbered bullion that could be checked against the registration numbers on the manifest. The numbers could prove conclusively that the wreck was that of the *Atocha* and put an end to the charges that the dig was a scam.

As sources of cash dried up, Fisher conducted a mildly successful sale of some of the 1715 finds. It wasn't enough, however, to keep up with his ever-mounting costs and payroll needs. At one point, a friend in Washington allegedly offered to put him in touch with "Bebe" Rebozo, a close associate of President Richard M. Nixon. For a million dollars, Nixon would get ten percent of the *Atocha*. Nothing came of this bizarre offer, but it stands as a peculiar comment on Fisher's money woes.

As the search for investors continued, Fisher's troubles were compounded by leaky boats and equipment failures at sea. The weather turned nasty and forced the divers to abandon their search. For a brief period, Fisher went around Key West humming "It's the Real Thing," the Coca-Cola Company's commercial ditty. He was hoping for a $2 million investment from Coke, but the deal never materialized.

His run of bad luck was briefly mitigated when the National Geographic Society decided that a good story was in the making. It contracted Fisher for exclusive rights to a future magazine piece and a film documentary of the *Atocha* dig. This upbeat development was offset when Fay Feild decided to call it quits. Treasure hunting, he said, was a "disease" that had ruined him financially, given him a bleeding ulcer, and wrecked his marriage. Feild eventually returned to the fold, but his temporary walkout cast a gloom over the entire operation.

The arrival at Treasure Salvors of Bleth McHaley in 1972 proved to be one of the most valuable finds the company ever made. A former writer for *Skin Diver* magazine, McHaley possessed an excellent treasury of public relations skills and was completely seaworthy. For a time she ran the supply boat from Key West to the Marquesas, and proved to be a better-than-able hand at sea. Her real gift lay in insightful trouble shooting and diplomacy. When she moved into the front office as Fisher's chief publicist, her most pressing job was to deal with the company's horrible relations with the state. When archaeologist Wilburn A. "Sonny" Cockrell was assigned to oversee the operation, a joke went around that McHaley would have an easier time facing down Godzilla.

More bad news came in 1973, when Burt Webber, now convinced that Fisher was searching in the right area, moved the *Revenge* to the Marquesas.

Webber was no small fry. His presence might lead to the ultimate coup—beating Fisher to the *Atocha.*

After more months of indifferent luck, good news! On May 25, 1973, the Fisher team uncovered a substantial cache of artifacts, including some weapons, barrel hoops, locks and keys, and a pair of scissors. A few days earlier, 380 silver coins had been recovered. They were closing in and the mood was high. Intensive digging in the area brought in 1,460 silver pieces of four and eight.

Bleth McHaley phoned *National Geographic* with the news, and a film crew was dispatched to the scene. She then radioed the divers and told them to stop work until the film crew arrived. For the moment, she said, "The Bank of Spain is closed."

But finding the "Bank of Spain" encouraged Fisher's enemies to redouble their invective. The whole trove was a fraud, they said, a position seconded by several state senators and some academic archaeologists. Soon afterwards, another Fisher foe filed a complaint against the firm with the Securities and Exchange Commission. The SEC moved in, halting Treasure Salvors' stock sales and cutting off the company's primary source of cash.

Then, on August 13, 1973, the *Golden Doubloon* sank at dockside, its bottom chewed up by teredos, small wood-eating marine worms. A number of the exhibits were ruined.

Somehow Fisher rose above these disheartening ups and downs. There was more to the "Fisher factor" than mere hucksterism. He was bigger than his detractors, unafraid of his competitors; he believed in himself, and, most of all, he believed in the *Atocha.*

The arrival of marine archaeologist R. Duncan Mathewson III, whose background included graduate work at the Universities of Edinburgh and London, and work on archaeological digs in West Africa and Jamaica, helped shore-up the credibility gap, but not much. Critics scoffed at Mathewson. An "outsider" who wasn't a member of the tight inner circle of American marine archaeologists, Mathewson lacked a Ph.D. The critics reasoned that no self-respecting archaeologist would be caught dead working with a treasure hunter anyway. They said Mathewson was bastardizing his profession by helping treasure hunters find and loot the 1622 galleons.

Though Mathewson brought solid archaeological methods to the dig—sometimes to the annoyance of the divers, who were slowed considerably by his methodology—nothing could stem the epidemic of mud slinging. It became vital that Fisher clear the air once and for all.

In August, 1973, the company was tapped out financially. It was broke, and the state's investigations and smear campaign were keeping investors away. The 1715 artifacts remained unsold. It became impossible to meet the payroll; crews began to fall away and the divers refused to go to sea. But the inner circle held fast. Bleth McHaley was relentless in her counter-attacks against Fisher's critics. For a long time, the situation appeared hopeless. Then, the other side of the "Fisher factor" began to show itself—the luck turned again to the persistent salvors.

Delaware contractor Melvin Joseph, a long-time supporter, bought a half interest in the 1715 wrecks for $315,000. Joseph, a self-made million-aire, also brought in other investors. At the same time, the SEC concluded its investigation. No charges were brought against the company, although Fisher agreed to halt the sale of unregistered securities. He hadn't realized that the agency's complex rules barred investments in his company without SEC oversight.

Next, an internationally-recognized authority on Spanish coins certi-fied the authenticity and dating of the coins of the *Atocha*. Next came an ever bigger break: three silver ingots bearing assayer's marks were found on the site. When compared to the ship's manifest, one of them matched a bar registered aboard the *Atocha*. Mel Fisher had clearly found "the Big A."

Back in Washington, *National Geographic* swung into high gear on the *Atocha* project. Now that so many dues had been paid, it seemed everyone wanted a piece of the action.

Treasure makes fast friends and fearsome enemies. Fisher's detractors leveled more blasts in the press: The *Miami Herald* ran a blistering attack reasserting some of the old charges, and *Forbes* magazine, in a piece titled "The One Billion Dollar Hobby," repeated some of the stories that Fisher had counterfeited artifacts. The SEC was soon involved in another probe, this time focusing on a subsidiary of Treasure Salvors, Inc., Armada Re-search. A Fort Lauderdale man filed a fraud action against Fisher, and Sonny Cockrell openly declared that Fisher was an enemy. *National Geographic,* on the other hand, held steady, its editors satisfied that the *Atocha* was for real.

The state continued to hold up renewal of the company's salvage permit on the *Atocha* site, but after a considerable delay, reissued the permit. Back in the water again, Duncan Mathewson and Mel's oldest son, Dirk, were working on an idea they called the "Deep Water Theory." Their notion was that what had been found in The Quicksands area was nothing more than the upper decks, the superstructure, of the ship. They felt that the ship's lower hull—with its cargo compartments bulging with treasure—lay in deeper water to the southeast. The elder Fisher reacted instinctively against the theory and, for a time, avoided it. He disliked working in deep water because of the danger it posed to divers.

Early in March, 1975, the state made its division of materials recovered to date from the *Atocha*. They had held the precious artifacts in Tallahassee, keeping them out of Fisher's hands and off the antiquities market. The state agreed to release Fisher's share of the artifacts only after the U.S. Supreme Court, ruling in a case unrelated to the *Atocha,* had placed the wreck site outside of state waters and beyond the state's jurisdiction. Ultimately, a Federal judge held that all of the *Atocha's* treasures belonged to Fisher. Florida had no right to require Fisher to obtain a state salvage contract because the wreck was in federal, not state waters.

Though state overseers continued to go to sea with the crews, all finds were kept by the company. Though Fisher tried to stay in contact with Tallahassee, a strange silence descended from the capital. Unknown to Fisher, state officials were quietly negotiating with federal authorities over what to do about the *Atocha*.

In June, Fisher showed that not even the greatest treasure hunter of them all was immune to world-weariness. He briefly weighed the notion of heading for Walker's Cay, in the Bahamas, where a lobsterman had found 67 iron cannons and a ballast pile. I had seen this wreck for myself, and it didn't look like a treasure ship. Later, Dr. Lyon found it to be an 18th-century British frigate, pretty well picked over and barren of silver and gold. Walker's Cay faded from Fisher's mind, and he picked up his pace— a grueling schedule of meetings with investors, visitors, job applicants, and curious reporters. It was rigorous, but helpful therapy. Fisher once again assumed his hard-earned public position, and the search went on.

The following month of July would bring great joy and unfathomable sorrow. On July 13, Dirk Fisher was resetting the *Northwind's* anchors in 40 feet of water southeast of The Quicksands. Here the bottom was hard, covered with deep mud; visibility was poor. But as he dove down the anchor line, he saw a jumbled heap of large, dark objects. He quickly swam over to the pile and, staring him in the face, were five of the *Atocha's* cannons! Within hours, the news had brought a convoy out of Key West. Divers, on-lookers, friends, reporters—all had come to savor this great moment. Now everyone knew that it was only a matter of time; the mother lode was getting closer. Soon the whole world would know if Mel Fisher was a prophet or a madman.

Mathewson checked the markings on the cannons against the *Atocha's* gun list, which had been found by Dr. Lyon in the Archives of the Indies in Seville. They matched. Fisher did not gloat, and, for the first time in years, his archaeologist critics faded into their ivory towers. Only one swore the cannons were fakes.

"It was really special," Fisher told me later. "We'd been looking for cannons for four years. Until we found them, I wasn't really sure they existed."

I wondered how he felt when Dirk reported the find.

"I felt a lot of things," he replied. "I figured they were worth maybe $20,000 or $30,000 apiece. But then I didn't think of them as *treasure,* you know. I just felt—happy."

The deep water theory was proving itself. Mathewson and Dirk Fisher were right all along. They were in deeper water all right, the deep water Fisher had always mistrusted. One week later, Dirk, his wife, Angel, and Rick Gage were dead. In deep water.

The sea was as calm as a lake. But the *Northwind* was overworked and in need of repairs. Don Kincaid was aboard the salvage boat that night as it lay anchored in the Marquesas. He says he was awakened by a loud voice, and that he knew instinctively that something was wrong. And then it hit him. The ship was listing heavily to starboard. Kincaid and crewman Don Jonas found their way to the engine room. A leaking valve on a toilet had partially flooded the *Northwind's* bilge. In addition, a fuel valve that regulated the balance of fuel between the boat's two forward fuel tanks was also leaking. As Jonas attempted to even out the load of water in the hull to stabilize the boat, the fuel suddenly shifted, heeling the ship over even further. "I knew this was it," Kincaid recalled. "I warned Jonas, yelled to the others. It was happening pretty fast. So fast I couldn't believe it."

Northwind turned turtle and went to the bottom. Dirk and Angel Fisher were trapped below in the stateroom. In the pre-dawn darkness, escape was impossible.

Moe Molinar and the *Virgilona* crew found Kincaid and eight other survivors clinging to a tiny life raft the next morning. When the survivors arrived in Key West, Deo Fisher hugged each of them and told them she was glad they had made it. Pressed by reporters for a comment, Mel said, "It's a powerful ocean. It takes people and ships."

"I Do It For People"

The Fisher family struggled hard to overcome its terrible loss. In routine fashion, the salvage boats continued to search the area where the cannons had been found, but Fisher seemingly could not bring himself to order raising the guns still on the bottom. In his mind, they were woven into the painful fabric of his son's death. Deo did her best to go on as corporate secretary of the company, but she, too, was in the grip of the same depressing thoughts. Discovery of the cannons had solved many practical problems. Now they were a symbol of an unbearable reality.

But events did not allow much time for reflection. In Washington, the Department of the Interior now claimed that the federal government owned the *Atocha*. With Florida removed from control by the Supreme Court's boundary decision, the federal authorities honed in like vultures. While Interior had laid claim to all shipwrecks within the U.S. territorial seas, the *Atocha* was its primary target.

Interior was not acting alone, either. Before the end of the summer, Fisher was informed by former Florida Senator Robert Williams that the state had applied for a federal antiquities permit on the *Atocha* site. The permit, he said, had already been drawn up and was ready to be signed. This would place the state in control of the wreck, with the U.S. Coast Guard to back them up. Under the circumstances, the very best Treasure Salvors could hope for would be to work as a subcontractor to the state on a month-to-month basis. Fisher was warned not to contest the action. If he did, the company would be removed from any participation in the dig. To put teeth into this ultimatum, the U.S. Justice Department dispatched attorneys to Miami with an order to the Coast Guard to police the site and keep Fisher away.

With the stroke of a pen and a few terse words, everything Fisher had worked for was being torn away. The loss of Dirk, Angel, and Rick Gage was rendered meaningless. It was outrageous. Grotesque. And it was being carried out under the cover of "the public interest." The bureaucrats were protecting a "priceless cultural resource" for future generations. Fisher, they said, was a treasure hunter, not a scientist, and he was "destroying" the *Atocha* for profit. His museum, the work of archaeologist Mathewson, even *National Geographic's* support amounted to little more than raw plunder. As sworn guardians of the public welfare, the bureaucracy had a duty to remove Fisher, "the pirate."

A meeting, held in August in Washington between the salvors, Department of the Interior officials, and Robert Williams, who represented the State of Florida, made a court battle inevitable. An Interior spokesman said flatly that the *Atocha* and all related artifacts were on the Outer Continental Shelf and therefore belonged entirely to the federal government. Treasure Salvors might be able to petition Congress for some special dispensation to compensate the company for the work it had done over the years.

Next, Senator Williams launched into a heated attack. The *Atocha,* he insisted, was an object of substantial historic value. Surely, the place where history dwells has no room for private enterprise. And Mel Fisher seemed to Williams to epitomize the free enterprise approach to historic wreck salvage.

True, he had hired Mathewson, but everyone knew a "real" archaeologist wouldn't work for anyone who sold artifacts. No archaeology was being practiced out in the Marquesas, Williams charged, only wanton destruction. Besides, he added, consider the character of Mel Fisher, his troubles with the SEC, with former partners. How could such a man be trusted? If the *Atocha* was to be preserved, Williams said, the only course was to give Florida a permit to control all salvage operations.

Fisher filed suit in the Federal District Court in Miami. And, despite the threats of state and federal officials, the salvors prevailed. On August 21, 1978, the late Judge William O. Mehrtens of the U.S. District Court for the Southern District of Florida, wrote, "The finding of a great treasure from the days of the Spanish Main is not the cherished dream of only the United States and Florida citizens; countless people from other lands have shared such thoughts. It would amaze and surprise most citizens of this country, when their dreams, at the greatest of costs, was realized that [government] agents . . . would, on the most flimsy grounds, lay claim to the treasure."

Mehrtens decided that the United States had no claim on shipwrecks on the Outer Continental Shelf. Indeed, the United States had signed an international treaty which gave it the right to exploit mineral resources on the Outer Continental Shelf of the oceans surrounding them. However, the treaty specifically excluded shipwrecks and bullion on the Outer Continental Shelf from ownership by the signatory nations. The law cited by the Department of Interior as justification for their attempted seizure of the *Atocha* was merely statutory law. But the United States Constitution stipulates that the treaty, ratified by the Senate, supercedes any statutes which conflict with it.

Stunned by the Mehrtens decision, Interior appealed, to no avail. The decision stood. If Interior wanted to assert its authority over sunken treasure, it would have to ask Congress to pass new legislation. This is exactly what they did. Since 1979, various "shipwreck bills" have been making the rounds on Capitol Hill. None have yet been signed into law.

One has to wonder if the *Atocha's* mother lode would ever have been found and brought to the attention of the world if the bureaucrats had beaten Fisher in court. Would Fisher have found it without their interference? Perhaps. His practicality, persistence, and intuitive genius enable him to do what others believe is impossible. But it was pressure from bureaucrats and academics—to improve archaeological practices and bring skilled workers from many fields into the hunt—that forced Fisher to develop the multi-disciplinary team of professionals that eventually helped find the $400 million treasure.

Today, Fisher maintains an impressive museum and conducts workshops for people who want to know how to find, document, and preserve treasure. He has invested heavily in a state-of-the-art computer installation that will maintain images and data on each artifact recovered in an electronic study collection. The entire collection will be available instantaneously to scholars anywhere in the world who have access to a microcomputer and a telephone line. Treasure Salvors now has an archaeological team that includes the former head of marine archaeology for Parks Canada and a half-dozen other scholars of equal skill. And, he's proved that credible research and responsible historical salvage can be conducted by a commercial salvage operation.

Fisher is on the speaking circuit, constantly in the public eye, and he continues to oppose laws that would keep people from realizing their dreams.

Did the *Atocha* make him a multimillionaire?

Maybe. Fisher's share of the treasure is about five percent. Over the years, the enormous cost of finding and salvaging the wreck forced him to sell most of his interest in the project to investors. And undoubtedly his legal battles have made fortunes for his attorneys. He continues to work the sites of the *Atocha* and *Santa Margarita,* and he's always looking into other treasure possibilities, not the least of which is the mythical city of Atlantis. It's as if there's a hole in the ocean and Fisher and company never tire of tossing cash into it.

Deo once told me that Mel never aspired to be a millionaire. "It's not his way of life," she said. "Other men seem more practical. Mel is more of a poet than a businessman."

Two years before the *Atocha's* mother lode was found, she made a prophecy: "The way I see it, Mel is very special. He's here for a special reason. I believe in destiny, and I believe he's destined to make history."

Now that he's made it, Fisher goes on speaking simply, disclaiming the status of "millionaire," but always thinking big.

"People come up to me and shake my hand and say, 'Keep it up.' So I do. I love it, and I do it for people."

Examples of glazed pottery recovered by archaeologists working a 7th century Byzantine shipwreck at Yassi Ada, "Flat Island," bordering the Chuka Channel in the southeastern Aegean Sea, near Bodrum, Turkey.

At *left* is a slender carrot-shaped amphora, a clay "packing crate" which often held wine, olive oil, and seeds for water-bourne transport. The pointed bottom made it easy to fill the amphora from larger casks of liquids; the point was dipped into the substance and sealed at the top. The shape was so popular that it lasted well into the 17th century. Archaeologists have sprouted seeds that had been sealed for centuries in these reddish brown amphora.

Next to it (*center*) is a 7th century "Wine Thief," used to draw liquid from closed containers. The lower portion was open and dipped into a barrel of wine; the thumb was then placed over the mouth of the Wine Thief, creating a vacuum to hold the wine in the lower tube. When the thumb was removed, the wine flowed out into a pitcher or some other smaller vessel. Today, similar wine thieves called "pipettes" are used by Turkish street vendors.

At *far right* are glazed pitchers, coated internally by resin. The decorative lines were raised in the clay.

The plate (*bottom*) is in the style of late Roman types dating to about 660 A.D. The rims are rounded and the inside design forms a continuous curve. Plates such as these were found in the cabin area of the Byzantine shipwreck.

Drawings by Kathryn Williams.

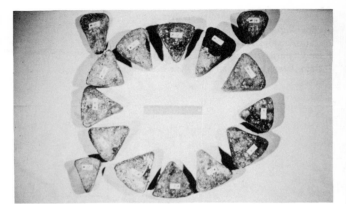

Imagine a huge pie of solid silver sliced into 15 neat wedges. This silver pie was recovered by archaeologists exploring a sunken Spanish treasure ship near Fort Pierce, Florida, under several feet of overburdening sand and silt. The Conquistadors stored the wedges in round wooden crates for shipment home from the New World. Though each wedge is worth thousands of dollars, they are only a hint of the wealth taken from the New World.
Photo by the Florida Division of Archives,
History and Records Management.

The symbols of blood, conquest, and empire, these silver coins—6 Reales—were found scattered like common shells along the seabed less than a mile from shore near Vero Beach, Florida. They were part of the glittering cargo of a Spanish treasure fleet destroyed by a hurricane in 1715. Such losses were not uncommon. No less than 10 percent of all New World riches—stolen by the Conquistadors from the Aztec, Incan, Mayan and other indigenous peoples—went to the bottom of the sea because of weather, human error, and the relentless activity of pirates. Today these lost treasures amount to billions of dollars, and each new storm casts a few more reminders onto Florida's endless beaches.
Photo by the Florida Division of Archives,
History and Records Management.

Peter Throckmorton, the self-taught conceptual godfather of underwater archaeology. In the early 1960s, Throckmorton and his friend Arthur C. Clarke, the famous author of *2001: A Space Odyssey,* pieced together the puzzle of a Mogul silver trove discovered in 30 feet of water in the Indian Ocean, off the southeast coast of Sri Lanka, at the Great Basses Reef. Dangerous surge conditions made it nearly impossible for Throckmorton to map the site in pristine detail, but toward the end of his research he discovered a solid wall of silver coins embedded in the reef. Clarke, drawn to this remarkable discovery by his own intensifying "treasure fever," nearly lost his life when huge waves and powerful currents dashed him against the razor sharp coral heads of the Great Basses.
Photo courtesy Peter Throckmorton.

CHAPTER THREE

Treasure Hunter Profiles:

Kip Wagner: At the Water's Edge
Arthur C. Clarke: Innerspace Silver

Along virtually every beach in the civilized world you can find men and women who, during the off-season, scour the empty sands for treasure left behind by the crowds of summer. I recently met one such gentleman at Rehoboth Beach, Delaware. He was ordinary looking, small and lumpy, wearing baggy Bermuda shorts, a bright Hawaiian shirt, and rubber flip-flops. Between Labor Day and Halloween he patiently strolls up and down the beach, sweeping the flat, black disc of a metal detector before him. Every few minutes a red light on a black box attached to the handle blinks on, and the black box issues a high-pitched whine, signaling the presence of some metal object hidden in the sand. He scoops up these "hits," placing them in a net bag, and continues his quiet, contemplative wandering.

"It's sort of a hobby with me," Freddy Swanson explained. "I'm retired on Social Security. My 'hits' give the wife and me a little something extra."

Freddy showed me how the metal detector discriminates between different kinds of metal. He says it bypasses bottle caps, beer cans, and other non-negotiables, but sends out a loud signal in the presence of gold or silver. "She's a jewel," he sighed. "Great on silver. I find a load of change, and believe me, it's not to be sneezed at."

Freddy occasionally gets a big strike, such as the gold Benrus pocket watch he found in near-mint condition. On the back of the watch case was an inscription: *To Billy With Love, April 1933.* Freddy's also found gold-plated Rolex watches of more recent vintage, sterling silver cigarette cases, rings and jewelry of every shape and description.

Freddy got into this activity soon after he retired a decade ago. He was idly walking the beach with his wife when he spied something bright and shiny on top of the sand near the surf line. It was a two-carat diamond in an ornate gold setting. "I thought, 'Well, isn't this the luck!' Later, I got to thinking about how many years people have been coming to Rehoboth—at least 100 years. Generations of people have been losing valuable stuff here." So Swanson went to a local sporting goods store and purchased a metal detector. "It didn't take long to figure out that this place is a gold and silver mine, just layers and layers of it, going way back to the old days."

Freddy is quick to point out that he doesn't get rich from his finds, though it could happen. He's proud of having spent two weeks in the Bahamas thanks to a couple of rich "hits." And even when the pickings are less valuable, Freddy finds another reward. "You know, it isn't all cash and carry. Just coming out here by myself, finding things, is a thrill. It keeps me young."

Ironically, the great Florida treasure bonanza that eventually led to Mel Fisher's find of the *Atocha* bounty began in much the same way. In the 1950s, a homebuilder named Clifford "Kip" Wagner happened on something "too shiny to be a seashell" on the beach near Sebastian Inlet, north of Vero Beach, on Florida's east coast.

Wagner had chanced on a Spanish piece of eight, those irregularly-shaped silver coins (sometimes called cobbs) of pirate fame. It was the size of a modern half-dollar, weighed about an ounce, and was worth eight *reales*. The polygonal coin had been deposited on the beach by a hurricane. That occurrence isn't uncommon along the state's Atlantic coast, and hundreds of collectors have found similar coins on other Florida beaches. But Wagner was no ordinary collector. A bit of a romantic whose favorite book was Robert Louis Stevenson's *Treasure Island,* Wagner wasn't the sort of man who's content to dream or leave anything to pure chance. He understood that fantasies are an outline used by determined people to build a solid reality. This single piece of silver was enough to get the process started. Somewhere just off Vero Beach was a vast hidden storehouse of treasure. It was out there waiting for him; it was no dream, it was a hard, tangible fortune, and Wagner was determined to find it.

He bought a metal detector and explored his "money beach." Soon, he'd collected nearly 40 coins, none dated later than 1715. He began to research the strange-looking coins, and soon found that a flotilla of

Spanish vessels bearing at least $14 million worth of gold and silver from Spanish colonies in the New World had been destroyed by a hurricane near Vero Beach in 1715. Wagner looked out to sea. Those ships were out there, on the nearby reefs and shoals; the question was where—and how to recover their precious cargo.

Writing in the January, 1965, issue of *National Geographic*, Wagner tells about stepping over the invisible boundary between fantasy and reality: "On that gray day following the hurricane, when I sat on the bluff a decade ago and looked out at the heaving sea, I think I made my decision without being conscious of it. From that moment began a series of circumstances that changed me from a curious beachcomber into a serious searcher after treasure."

No one ever truly stumbles onto treasure. Wagner, though he had been lucky as a beachcomber, understood that finding the remains of the famed 1715 Spanish treasure fleet would be demanding. The first step was to find out whatever he could about the fleet. He obtained a copy of an early map of Florida drawn in 1774 by Bernard Romans. It showed clearly the bulging outline of Cape Canaveral. Near the confluence of Sebastian Creek and the Indian River Romans had written: "Opposite this River, perished the Admiral, commanding the Plate Fleet 1715, the rest of the Fleet . . . between this and the Bleech Yard." Checking modern landmarks, Wagner found that the "Bleech Yard" was on the peninsula near the mouth of the St. Lucie River (about 50 miles south), a location that provided early sailors with fresh water for cleaning salt-encrusted sails. Wagner also contacted Robert I. Nesmith, an authority on Spanish colonial coins. Nesmith reported that Wagner's *reales* had been struck in the Mexico City mint and were of the type made prior to the installation of the screw-type coin press there in 1732. He informed Wagner that, in his opinion, "these are the most important finds from a Spanish Plate Fleet ever made in Florida, both historically and numismatically. . . ." Just how important, neither Nesmith nor Wagner could tell at the time.

Wagner continued searching the beach with his Army surplus metal detector. He eventually found the inland campsite where the Spanish who came to salvage the 1715 fleet had lived for three years. The first metal detector "hits" were parts of a Model T Ford and assorted metallic junk. A half-mile to the north, Wagner struck pay dirt. A few inches below the sand and scrub he found clusters of cannonballs, broken earthenware, a pair of cutlasses, and blackened rectangles of silver. A day after these discoveries, a yellow glint caught his eye. Wagner reached down and picked up a gold ring set with a 2 $1/_2$-carat diamond. Around this diamond were six others, each about the size of a match head. It was a crude, but extremely valuable, find. "A diamond cut in the shape of an uneven, truncated pyramid is not the fiery, multi-reflecting thing that all girls yearn for," Wagner said, "but the effect of this drab stone on a treasure hunter's heartbeat is identical."

Wagner badly wanted to get into the ocean to look for the wrecks. He needed no further proof that Bernard Romans was right, that the fleet was there, probably in water no deeper than 20 feet. He went to the local airport and hired a small plane, which was piloted by a SCUBA diving enthusiast. Wagner was an early advocate of airborne treasure hunting, even though he had no idea of what a treasure wreck might look like. His first flight revealed the floor of the ocean as a confusing collage of gray and black shapes. Frustrated, he asked the pilot to fly just above the wave tops while he hung out of the cabin door, dangling at the end of his safety belt, hoping to make some sense out of the confusing welter of shadows. As the little plane passed south of Palmar de Ais, Wagner signalled for a steep turn; he had sighted a long, dark area that formed a rude ellipse. Sticking out at angles from this odd shape were long, straight objects. The dark shape must be ballast stones, the rocks carried in the belly of a sailing ship to steady it, Wagner thought, and the straight objects projecting out from either side must be cannons.

The following day, Wagner and the pilot launched a skiff through the surf. It was October, a time when high tides draw the clear waters of the Gulf Stream over Florida's inner reefs. With his face mask in the water, Wagner saw something that made his heart pound:

"I had a hard time matching what I saw underwater with my imagination's image of a treasure wreck. No timbers remained—probably all having long since passed through the digestive tracts of the soft, insatiable teredos. . . . Then I swam over my first gun. It loomed larger than its original bulk. The sea had wrapped it in a limy crust embedded with shell fragments and plumed with streamers of bright green seaweed that fanned with each surge of current. Swimming along the edges of the heaped-up ballast stones, we counted the guns, 18 in all, that marked the final resting place of the ship. . . ."

If the discovery was at first thrilling, Wagner's sense of what it takes to realistically deal with a jumble of centuries-old wreckage was less than encouraging. A building contractor, he translated the find into its components; building a shopping center, he imagined, might be easy compared to resurrecting treasure from beneath tons of ballast stones and the even greater volumes of sand that eventually cover most ancient wrecks. If the ship had been down 250 years, he thought, it might take another 250 years to actually get at it.

From a surplus outlet he purchased a 40-foot Navy shore leave boat, christened her *Sampan,* and set out to find a crew. In a short time, he had recruited a team of eight, all amateurs in the business of treasure, and formed the Real 8 Company, Inc. The name was taken from the *ocho reales,* the piece of eight he had first found on the beach. Wagner and Real 8 were soon well along in recovering treasure and historical artifacts from a half-dozen Plate Fleet vessels. Thousands of silver coins had been found, and, in one day he and his companions would never forget, more than a thousand golden doubloons—eight gold *escudo* coins—came up from the bottom. By the time Mel Fisher's crew moved to Florida to work with Real 8 in 1963, the prizes totalled more than $1 million.

Compared to Fisher's later find of the *Atocha* hoard, Wagner's early fortune seems pale. Yet cash value is just one part of the reward. It's almost impossible to put a monetary value on Wagner's discoveries. The gold and silver remain impressive, but artifacts such as the intact K'ang Hsi Chinese porcelain found among the wreckage gives us a historical perspective that can't be translated into cash. Wagner also pioneered important underwater recovery techniques.

Wagner gave the outward appearance of a simple, almost introverted man. Yet inwardly he was a revolutionary with a practical Yankee genius for industry. And he found the very essence and meaning of it all.

"The excitement of the search, even the months of waiting and despair, have provided moments that could not be bought," he wrote. "Every find comes as a gift from the sea, and our best reward will always be the unforgettable thrill of discovery."

Arthur C. Clarke: Innerspace Silver

Arthur C. Clarke, author of *2001: A Space Odyssey,* is a treasure hunter—or he was back in 1961, before film maker Stanley Kubrick contacted him in Ceylon (now Sri Lanka) and asked him to work on the film that was to become an enduring box office smash.

Few people, including his fans, are aware of Clarke the avid underwater adventurer. It may surprise them to learn that it was from his exploration of Australia's Great Barrier Reef and other aquatic wonders that he drew so many of his written impressions of space travel which subsequently appeared in *Rendezvous With Rama* and the celebrated *2001*. His undersea science fiction, of which there is quite a lot, is little known. This is unfortunate, for in the pages of his relatively obscure story, *The Deep Range,* published in the 1950s, his readers will find some of the most penetrating insights on the future of the sea to be published in modern times.

But his is another story. What concerns us here is the mild-mannered, bookish figure of Clarke, the intellectual futurist and inventor of the communications satellite (which he donated to NASA), finding himself a treasure hunter. In the spring of 1961, he and his associates found what they believed to be a vast fortune in Indian Mogul silver entombed in a treacherous death trap of a reef off the southern coast of Ceylon. Recovering it was a gamble that cost him his health—and very nearly his life.

Like many divers, Clarke had dreamed of finding sunken treasure. But, unlike the hard-core treasure hunter, he was not obsessed by the idea. In fact, if it hadn't been for his young friend, Mike Wilson, it's doubtful he would have gone in search of submerged fortunes. Wilson, an ex-British merchant seaman and a daring commercial "hard-hat" diver, introduced Clarke to SCUBA in 1951, in the English Channel. That first dive was to 80 feet in rough, murky winter waters. Ten years later, Wilson discovered the Ceylon treasure by accident, then told Clarke about it.

Wilson had grown tired of the risks involved in commercial diving and, at the time he and Clarke were living in Ceylon, had decided to become an undersea film maker. Together they visited the Great Basses Reef to obtain shark footage to be spliced into *Beneath the Seas of Ceylon,* a promotional film they were producing for the Ceylon Tea Propaganda Board.

The area they were working was ten miles out to sea, about 30 feet deep, and located approximately 100 yards from the Great Basses Lighthouse. It's a dangerous place—a maneater of a reef—swept constantly by huge waves. The underwater surge is so powerful that it seems almost a miracle they accomplished any work on the bottom. The divers, in the grip of the unrelenting surge, were constantly in a state of violent, pendulum-like motion. That's bad enough in an area of clear water, but the reef was anything but clear. On one side, near the lighthouse, a limestone wall rose from the bottom. It was a killing machine, encrusted with concrete-like corals and razor-sharp barnacles. To be swept against this wall was a sure invitation to serious injury or even death. After a few forays to the site with Wilson, Clarke had had enough. He considered himself too old and living too comfortably to be risking his neck in such a menacing place. A sensible decision. Yet the powerful lure of treasure finally overruled his better judgment.

The lure was dangled before Clarke the following spring when Wilson was busy filming a fantasy he had written called *Boy Beneath the Sea.* Wilson's plot was about a little boy who constantly daydreams about life beneath the waves and wakes up to discover that his dreams have come true. The heroes were Mark Smith, 13, and Bobby Kriegel, 14, both members of the official United States diplomatic community in Ceylon. Ironically, the underwater setting was only a half-mile from the spot where Wilson and Clarke had worked on *Beneath the Seas of Ceylon.*

Clarke wasn't on the reef when the discovery came, much to his regret. One afternoon, Wilson and his two young actors arrived at Clarke's office with the battered tin trunk Wilson used to carry his underwater photo gear. Wilson locked the door and said, "Look at this." He opened the lid, and there lay two small, worn brass cannons, polished smooth by the sea.

Wilson lifted the cannons out of the trunk and showed Clarke some objects hidden beneath them. At first, Clarke thought he was looking at blackened lumps of coral about the size of coconuts. When he finally realized what the lumps were, he was too amazed to speak.

In his book, *The Treasure of the Great Reef* (Ballantine, 1964), the usually unemotional Clarke writes: "It was one of the unforgettable moments of a lifetime, for I knew then that I was staring at something few men have ever seen—genuine, honest-to-goodness treasure. These unimpressive-looking lumps were masses of coins—hundreds of them, cemented together. When I bent down to pick one up, I could hardly lift it. It was not—alas!—heavy enough for gold, but it could only be the next best thing—silver."

In addition to the big conglomerates there were hundreds of loose coins, most of them heavily corroded, but others were in good condition. They were covered with Persian letters. When Clarke and Wilson weighed the haul, it totalled 150 pounds. In addition, there were small copper bars and about 20 lead musket balls. "There's a lot more where we found this," Wilson said.

The tin chest had at one time been used to hold explosive blasting gelatin. "I could not help thinking that the chest's new contents were almost as explosive as the old; what it now held would undoubtedly change our lives, in ways that it was impossible to predict," Clarke wrote. For two years, the chest stood in a corner of his office, an object no less incredible than his most imaginative science fiction. To assure himself that it was indeed real, he would open the lid and stare at the contents. But even with his eyes shut, the reminder was there. The walls of the chest issued the peculiar metallic aroma of iodine and seaweed. Clarke called it "the scent of treasure."

He was hooked.

Clarke soon learned that discovery brings about "treasure fever," the classic symptom being that normal routines fade and the possibility of finding great wealth overwhelms the hunter. The need for secrecy is another symptom. Clarke and company were intensely fearful that the lighthouse keepers, only 100 yards from the site, would get wind of the discovery. If news got back to land, other divers might come and clean out the wreck. This paranoia, which was not unfounded, dogged them night and day to the very end.

The potential net worth of the find, according to Wilson, was mind-boggling. A little restoration work revealed that the coins were rupees, minted in 1702 in Surat, India. Extremely cautious inquiries among local numismatists proved that the coins, bearing the Muslim date 1133, were from the Year 45 in the reign of the Mogul emperor Aurangzeb, who ruled much of India between 1658 and 1707 A.D. Apparently, they didn't ask the exact market value of the rupees, as such questions were bound to draw suspicious and unwanted attention. Wilson told Clarke that one entire section of the Great Basses Reef was encrusted with silver. At least a ton of it had worked its way into the coral over the past two and a half centuries. Their dreams of vast riches soared into the stratosphere.

As salvage work began, the team cautiously researched their legal position as well. The identity of the wreck was unknown, and documents indicated the site was outside of Ceylon's territorial waters. This was very good news, for it meant that, under international law, it was finders-keepers.

The filming of *Boy Beneath the Sea* came to a halt, and Wilson decided to help finance the expedition by making a movie about the treasure hunt. Though it may seem unlikely, the team was not in the best financial condition. They really had no firm idea of how much it would cost to excavate the site and initially set the figure at $10,000. It was an absurdly low estimate but, according to Clarke, it represented ten times more than they had between them.

Fortune of another sort soon helped flesh out their crew. A crucial member of the Great Basses team was self-taught archaeologist Peter Throckmorton. The brilliant, tough, bespectacled Throckmorton had contacted Clarke from Athens, Greece, asking if he knew the locations of any ancient sunken vessels near Ceylon. Throckmorton was in luck. Of the hundreds—or perhaps thousands—of ships that came to grief on the Old Spice Route between the East Indies and Europe, this wreck was the only treasure ship that had been discovered. In 1960, Throckmorton lured to Turkey a University of Pennsylvania team that later excavated a Bronze Age merchant vessel which had gone down in deep water at Yassi Ada, an island in Aegean Sea. Work on this site proved to be an historic turning point in the development of the infant science of underwater archaeology. Land-based archaeologists weren't convinced that any useful work could be done under the sea; the whole idea seemed silly to them. A popular academic sport at the time was to scoff at the lunatic fringe which argued that underwater sites offered, in most cases, infinitely more potential for research than most land digs.

The scientific techniques pioneered at Yassi Ada changed the archaeological scene forever. Throckmorton's team proved that sunken ships, unlike the weather-worn, eroded, and pilfered land sites that are the mainstream of archaeology, represent a frozen moment in history, wonderfully preserved in the airless environment of the sea. His articles in *National Geographic*, "Thirty-three Centuries Under the Sea" (May 1960), and "Oldest Known Shipwreck Yields Bronze Age Cargo" (May 1962), stirred a great deal of jealousy among his landlocked colleagues. They now found themselves in the position of the ancient astronomers who had insisted that Earth was the center of the universe. His credentials assured, Throckmorton now joined forces with Clarke, Wilson, a friend of Wilson's, commercial diver Rodney Jonklaas.

A real treasure hunt always involves risk. Some are financial risks, others are emotional, and there is always a chance of losing life or limb. The dangerous environment of the reef placed these in sharp focus. Yet, when disaster first struck Clarke, it didn't come underwater. Rather, he was on a shopping trip to Colombo to secure equipment for the team's dive boat *Ran Muthu*. On the way out of a nautical shop, Clarke misjudged the height of a doorway and banged his head against the lintel. It didn't faze him at the time, so he climbed on his motor scooter and drove three miles home, played a few rounds of tennis, and ate a big meal. It proved to be his last for nearly three months. He wound up in the hospital. His knock on the head had left him delirious and virtually paralyzed. He had missed winding up in an iron lung by the frighteningly small margin of a few nerve fibers. His left arm, he says, will never be much good, but, thankfully, good enough to work the space bar on a typewriter. His doctors claimed he was lucky to escape with his life.

Still, treasure fever pushed the work forward as Clarke, miserable and weak, was consigned to the beach as security guard and keeper of the salvage permit the team had obtained from the Ceylonese government. He was also the group's Minister of Propaganda, keeping the details of the underwater dig vague, yet specific enough to satisfy the curious onlookers who daily poked around the shore station at Kirinda Bay.

Wilson, Jonklaas, and Throckmorton worked the site. The first two searched for silver while the latter made a systematic survey of the wreck. Throckmorton calculated the site at 60 feet in length, with two large anchors at one end. He found a variety of cannons, about ten of them, in a jumbled pile. He recovered a wooden pistol stock and collected other samples of wood, hoping they would lead to the identity of the ship. If they could identify the vessel, they could likely find a cargo manifest in an archive somewhere that would tell them exactly what the ship was carrying and how much silver was on board.

Throckmorton had little interest in the silver as treasure; he concerned himself mostly with piecing together the history of this mysterious wreck. This was by no means the clean, scientific dig run at Yassi Ada, where the vessel lay in quiet water from 70 to 100 feet deep. The Great Basses wreck lay in just 30 feet of water, in an area where surge and currents tossed divers along the bottom like cockle shells and threatened to smash them against the jagged reef. Later, Throckmorton refused to call this research archaeology, instead classifying it under the less imperious term "salvage," which is not so exacting.

On April 14, 1963, Clarke decided that, despite his weakness, he wanted to see the wreck site. Holding a line attached to a dinghy, he snorkeled slowly and cautiously above the area they now called "The Valley of the Wrecks." Both sides of the reef were littered with the remains of ships old and new, so this seemed an appropriate name. Though he was only in the water a short time, Clarke was exhausted. When Wilson surfaced and reported that most of the silver had probably been recovered already, Clarke felt a sense of relief: "This meant the end of our main worries . . . I had no intention of ever going back."

Then it happened. In mid-afternoon, Throckmorton surfaced with news that he'd found the mother lode—tons of silver, there was no telling how much. Soon massive cylinders of lime-encrusted coins were being hoisted to the deck of *Ran Muthu.* Each cylinder weighed about 30 pounds. Gray and corroded, they looked like something out of a rubbish heap. "To us," Clarke reported, "they looked beautiful."

Each mass contained 1,000 coins. Clarke was rather vague on just how many conglomerates were recovered. In a lump of coral they found an earring. "It made the wreck come suddenly to life across the centuries," he said, "linking us to an unknown crew whose hopes and dreams had foundered with her." The silver was stowed aboard, along with a bronze cannon, apparently of British origin, which had been recovered.

The divers seemed to lose interest in the silver, and spent much of their time mapping the wreck and bringing up objects of no commercial value. They found a fine copper plate, a bronze pestle, thimbles; dreams of riches were being replaced by intellectual curiosity, and this with the mother lode just 30 feet below. Sooner or later, most treasure hunters come to the simple truth that, in the sea as on dry land, there is more to the chase than money. (*See illustration, page 112.*)

On April 21, Clarke, against all caution, decided to dive on the wreck with SCUBA gear. The treasure fever had placed other values ahead of good sense. The thrill of actually being there was more important to him than survival. He descended slowly with the air tanks strapped to his back, constantly equalizing the pressure in his ears as he headed for the sea bed. Eight years earlier, while diving on Australia's Great Barrier Reef, he had gone down too quickly and ruptured an eardrum. At the Great Basses, yet another near-catastrophe struck. He was too buoyant and sinking much too slowly toward the relatively calm water on the bottom. The surge caught him, and Clarke found himself being driven violently toward the reef. The current was so strong that it nearly tore the mouthpiece of the air hose from between his clenched teeth. Alone, in the grip of the mute and insensitive sea, Clarke fought against panic, the deadliest killer in any environment. He was carrying a four-pound hammer, which was immobilizing his good arm, but for a long time, he used it to keep himself just an arm's length away from the reef's razor-studded walls; it was all that remained between him and an untimely end. This sort of struggle can only end in a loss, he knew; he dropped the hammer and swam for his life, out to sea and away from the surge. When he reached *Ran Mathu's* dinghy, hovering over the wreck site, he was too weak to climb aboard, and was towed back to the safety of the dive boat.

Clarke was badly shaken but, operating on the theory that, once thrown by a horse, one must immediately remount if one is ever to ride again, he made another attempt that day—this time using a mask and snorkel as he couldn't manage the bulky SCUBA gear. During this last sight-seeing tour, the divers brought up two more large conglomerates of silver. This was the last of it. There was no attempt to dig the rest of the treasure out of the coral, where it was imbedded. Thus, between 1961 and 1963, the total haul of silver amounted to 350 pounds.

No one made a fortune. Antique dealers informed the team that the market was awash with 1702 rupees; the coins were not the rare, costly antiques they had hoped for. The team felt it would be a shame to break up the conglomerates; the coins were much more interesting cemented to-gether, and some of the masses showed traces of the canvas sacks in which they'd been shipped.

One of the conglomerates was donated to the Smithsonian Institution in Washington, D.C. Much of the rest went to the museum in Colombo, Sri Lanka. Throckmorton's report on the wreck site, while lacking some of the detail he would have liked to obtain, still makes good reading.

The actual market value of the rupees was placed at about $1 each. Hardly a king's ransom. In the end, it was the chase and the spirit of discovery that held Clarke and his comrades enthralled.

Years later, in 1986, I interviewed Throckmorton about the Great Basses Reef dig. At the time, he was a professor of nautical archaeology at NOVA University in Florida and was working to establish a field school for graduate students in archaeology in the Caribbean.

"There were a lot of reasons why we didn't go further with that wreck," Throckmorton said. To begin with, it was virtually impossible to place a reasonable value on the silver; the team couldn't establish how much was on board. The Dutch East India Company records of the ship's manifest had been destroyed. "It would have cost us $30,000 or $40,000 to work the wreck for a few days or weeks before the monsoon set in. It was a very expensive gamble.

"We took it as far as we could. The wreck was a mess, and the working conditions were just awful. We had to crawl around on the wreck site. Aside from a few cultural items, all we could find was money. I got sick of the money. It doesn't give you much history."

Throckmorton acknowledges that there were a few moments when everyone believed they were going to be millionaires. "You know how it is, treasure brings out the worst in everybody—especially the government. Certainly, like everyone else, I'm turned on by payday. But we were more turned on to finding out something about the people associated with this wreck. In that sense, a clay pipe is more interesting than gold.

"Besides, if you want to get rich, go into commercial salvage. I have a wreck right now I'd like to get at that's full of copper ingots. That's business. History is another matter. I don't feel I have the right to own historical objects. That's a moral thing. History belongs to everybody."

Throckmorton was critical of treasure hunters and of Mel Fisher. The work being done on the *Atocha* is superficial, he says. "A clear picture doesn't emerge, and that's because they [the Fisher group] don't have a real conservator on board. To me, conservators are the unsung heroes. If you don't have good conservators, you're doing nebbish archaeology."

He was also blunt in his appraisal of classically-trained archaeologists. "They're stuffy," he said. "They have their own little world and they become creatures of it. They're pedantic; they seem to want to be bureaucrats, they don't seem to get out there and get wet and do the work."

In Europe, Throckmorton noted, archaeology is a genteel avocation, while in America, it has become a full-time vocation. "That's fine," he said, "but you must get out there and *do* it!"

What did Clarke gain from the experience?

In *The Treasure of the Great Reef* he wrote that the Great Basses wreck had provided him "a series of experiences which very few living men can share, and which are unique in this generation; nothing can take that away."

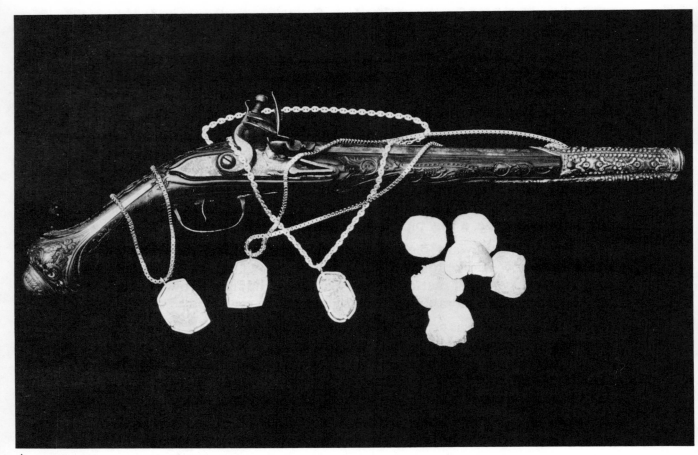

An ancient flintlock pistol, gold chains, and doubloons—
visible symbols of today's bloody "treasure wars" raging
between archaeologists and treasure hunters over access to
sunken riches. But the battle involves far more than gold,
silver, and precious gems. In the balance hangs the course
of future history and how we will write it.
Photo by Rick Frehsee.

CHAPTER FOUR

The Treasure Wars

There's a saying among treasure hunters that the romance of treasure can end abruptly the minute you find it.

There's more than a little truth in this. Arthur C. Clarke wisely observed that with perhaps the exception of a flying saucer landing in one's backyard, nothing is more disruptive of normal life than the finding of sunken treasure.

One reason is that treasure is a magnet for publicity. Treasure makes news, in the papers, on television, in books. And, because a fair percentage of treasure is old enough to be deemed historic, there are many who feel that the riches somehow belong in the public domain. This in itself excites controversy, anguish, and outright passion. Those souls who are lucky enough (or unlucky as the case may be) to discover it must be prepared for a siege by fiercely competitive and occasionally self-serving interests, all of whom want a piece of the action for their own purposes. In short, if you find the mother lode, or even a tiny fragment of it, be ready to defend your ground in a long-suffering battle of the on-going "treasure wars."

This leads to still other questions: Are paraprofessionals and professional salvors qualified to assist in the effort to retrieve drowned history, or should the digging be left strictly to academics? Should some artifacts be sold to raise the money to continue digging for more bits of history, or should each artifact—no matter if it's identical to hundreds or thousands of others already in the public domain—be preserved in a scholarly or academic institution? Are historic shipwrecks in danger of disintegrating and should an all-out effort be made to survey and salvage the thousands of historic vessels? Or should they remain safely tucked away in the ocean until lettered marine archaeologists get around to finding and excavating them?

To those who may not be familiar with the battle lines, the answers may seem obvious. They may argue that, if an individual spends his own time and money, and assumes the physical and financial risks of recovering sunken treasure, anything he might find should belong to him. In essence, that's the position of Mel Fisher, Burt Webber, and other treasure hunters. It's common sense, right? Well, not quite. On the other side of the line there's a well-entrenched school of thought that maintains an opposite point of view. This side takes the position that treasure amounts to a lot more than a flashy collection of gold or silver. It's history. And history transcends all claims to individual ownership. The very fact that it's part of our cultural heritage makes it the property of the public at large. This is the position of the orthodox archaeologists and some government bureaucrats.

These opposing camps of treasure warriors have been attacking each other for the past quarter-century. I lump them all into the generic category of treasure warrior, although I'm sure some of the archaeologists would blanch at any connection with the word treasure, since it seems to imply loot, booty, spoils. They will argue that their only concerns are science and history, that treasure and the scandalous hint of a profit motive is not part of their world. The archaeological Hippocratic oath states quite clearly that anyone who engages in the sale of artifacts for any reason is destroying history; hence the slogan, "Thou shalt not sell the goodies." They argue further that, after all, we don't allow people to dismantle national monuments brick by brick, nor do we allow private interests to plunder national parklands. Like these public properties, they argue, historic shipwrecks are finite sources, shared by all. The difference between treasure hunters and archaeologists, they say, is that treasure hunters will tear a ship apart to get at the goodies—in a sense wrecking it a second time—while an archaeologist will destroy nothing, but works carefully, piecing together the life of the ship by recovering its parts; they may happen upon real treasure, but it is treated as incidental to the search for historical knowledge.

The scholars also contend that our present laws are inadequate to protect historic artifacts in state and federal waters. We have preservationist laws to protect some dry land sites, so why not similar laws for shipwrecks?

Presently, historic shipwrecks are governed by Admiralty law, a collection of case law and judicial tradition that originated in English common law. Anyone can file an Admiralty lawsuit in federal court and thus lay claim to a wreck. The court may hear arguments from other interested parties (such as governmental agencies, others who claim the wreck, or the ship's original owner) and will ultimately decide which of them should be appointed as the salvor in custody of the wreck. Generally, the person filing the suit is named salvor. From that time on, the salvor has the protection of the court. If the government sent the Coast Guard to keep him off the wreck, he could ask the court for an injunction to get the government off his back. If a pirate moves in to plunder the site, the salvor can have him arrested and charged with larceny and contempt of court.

The archaeologists contend that Admiralty law was not written to protect cultural resources; its purpose is to regulate commercial salvage, essentially the recovery of a vessel and cargo from the peril of being lost to the ocean. But historic vessels are in no peril, they say; if anything they are securely tucked away—as they have been for centuries—beneath tons of sand or thick, protective coral. Such vessels can, and should, be left on the bottom for centuries to come. The great danger is man, specifically the treasure hunters who, archaeologists say, would steal the stars out of the sky if they could. Finally, no self-respecting archaeologist would work with a treasure hunter, and those who do should immediately turn in their sheepskins.

Of course, absolute rules don't stay absolute forever. Over the years, archaeologists have worked with treasure hunters in various roles. Some have even engaged in the sale of goodies to finance further excavations. Further, many archaeologists have adopted the work methods of treasure hunters, methods once criticized as destructive. Notable among these is the "mailbox," which uses a ship's propellers to direct clear surface water to the bottom. The mailbox improves visibility for divers and can quickly clear away tons of sand covering a wreck. The device, invented by Mel Fisher and Fay Feild, was once considered too destructive to use on a "fragile" historic wreck—a howitzer where a small-caliber rifle was needed. Today, it's an accepted part of numerous archaeological digs.

Just because archaeologists have commingled with treasure hunters in these ways, and others, is not to say they're hypocrites. For the most part, these accommodations have been sensible and productive, but in the struggle for dominance in the treasure wars, they try to maintain a spot-less image for public consumption.

Edward Dethlefsen, a professor of archaeology and anthropology at William and Mary College, recently worked on "Black Sam" Bellamy's pirate ship *Whydah,* off Wellfleet, Massachusetts on Cape Cod. Directing the underwater dig was the man who found the ship, commercial salvor Barry Clifford. Dethlefsen took more than a little heat from his professional colleagues because of this association and, in 1982, resigned his post as president of the prestigious Society for Historical Archaeology.

The resignation was motivated by what Dethlefsen perceived as "snobbism" among the Society's members and what he believed to be a campaign to blacklist archaeologists who worked with treasure hunters or other private organizations. The Society refused to accept research papers by those who had associated with treasure hunters because, he says, the organization believed that it alone was responsible for defining what belonged to the national historical heritage. "It was clear to me that [Duncan] Mathewson [Mel Fisher's archaeologist] was being marked," Dethlefsen says, "and he wasn't the only one. There is a lot of this going on. Archaeologists spread paranoia among themselves. I just couldn't operate in this atmosphere."

The issue, he says, is to balance the rights of individuals with the rights of society. "We need to define public goals that people can identify with. Let's face it: the academics don't get much press and they're jealous."

Dethlefsen says it became clear to him through the dust kicked up by his association with Barry Clifford that his academic cohorts were living in an Ivory Tower. Thus, after years in the classroom and extensive field work, Dethlefsen resigned from the 2,000-member SHA.

"I have since found," he says, humorously, "that some of my colleagues expect me, at the risk of Inquisition, to behave like a high priest whose vested purity allows only consort with temple virgins according to a strict ritual of academic cohabitation."

The treasure wars are by no means confined to academe. Millions of dollars have been spent on court battles, and nowhere has the fighting been more costly than in Florida, the treasure warrior's legal Maginot Line. The state has literally spent a fortune defending its treasure statute, known as Chapter 267. This law says that Florida owns historic shipwrecks in its territorial waters and is entitled to 25 percent of anything that might be found on them. Further, it says the state can at its pleasure, grant or withhold permits to conduct salvage of historic shipwrecks. Poachers are subject to arrest and prosecution. Unfortunately, after the state's legal bouts with Mel Fisher, Chapter 267 has been found lacking in legal merit by several federal courts. Despite the adverse court rulings, the state has continued to push its claims. There is no way the cost of these legal battles to taxpayers can ever be recouped through confiscated treasure, since the state won't sell anything it might win.

While the state has squared off in court with many of the salvors working in Florida waters, the battle with Mel Fisher has easily been the most expensive. An editorial entitled "Burying Treasure," published February 21, 1985, by the *Miami Herald,* lamented, "If Florida had spent hundreds of thousands of dollars looking for lost treasure, it might have found some of the gold-laden Spanish galleons that sank off its coast. But the state did not do that. Instead, it has spent hundreds of thousands of dollars to pay lawyers to claim for the State the gold and artifacts found by private treasure hunters. For all its effort, the State has been reversed repeatedly in court on its claims to the treasure. . . . Still, Florida pursues its dubious claim. . . ."

In 1983, the state paid out close to $400,000 in legal fees to get at the *Atocha* cargo; it also put up $1.6 million in bond money to stop Fisher from distributing some of the treasure to stockholders. The *Herald* concluded that these futile battles were "a high price for a case of improbable merit. Too high, in fact."

Another target of the state's legal campaign was the late Gerald Klein, a Miami restaurant owner and part-time spearfisherman. In 1979, while spearfishing in Biscayne Bay, a portion of which is a national park, Klein happened on the remains of an 18th-century British warship, H.M.S. *Fowey,* which sank in 1748, after running up on a reef. On board were a contingent of captured Spanish seamen and a sizable treasure trove. The impact opened the *Fowey's* hull, and for a time, the ship hung on the reef, unable to maneuver. The wind and tide finally lifted her off, and carried her five miles north to a place that is now called Legare Anchorage. The ship's captain, Sir Francis Drake, knew the *Fowey* was done for, and he ordered her stripped and scuttled. The treasure, taken from Spanish treasure ships, was put ashore. When Klein discovered the wreck, the hull was deep in the sand. He was led to the spot by the ship's cannons, which were slightly visible on the bottom.

It was clear that if any negotiable treasure was left it would take a long time to recover it, but Klein wanted to try. Word of this discovery spread and, on October 4, 1979, the National Park Service went to court, seeking an injunction, claiming the *Fowey* was on Park Service bottom lands and thus off limits to private citizens. Why the Park Service hadn't discovered the wreck before Klein did is not clear, but the court issued the injunction, preventing Klein from any further activity on the wreck. The Park Service's local archaeologists were delighted, because to them, Klein was just another pirate, a looter who would destroy the wreck in search of goodies.

What Klein might have done with the *Fowey* will never be known. His battle to claim the wreck was long and intense. He didn't expect to unearth treasure chests groaning with booty. He argued that if he hadn't found the wreck no one would have known of its existence, and at least he deserved some credit for discovering it. His wife carried on the legal fight after his death, but to no avail. When the court finally awarded custody of the wreck to the Park Service, she had its exact location printed on the placemats at the restaurant. No one, however, seemed interested.

I was sent to visit the site in 1983, by *Smithsonian* magazine. The first thing that hit me was not the intrinsic or historical value of the *Fowey* or the archaeological work being done on the site. Rather, I heard a barrage of insults against Gerald Klein. And before 24 hours were gone, I learned that I, too, was suspect. Over the years I had written about treasure hunters; that was enough, apparently, to instill fear in grown men that I would clandestinely give out the *Fowey's* location to my supposed "friends" who would sneak in under cover of darkness and loot the site. Until that moment, I had doubted that archaeologists could be so fearful and downright paranoid. Even though I was there representing the *Smithsonian,* an unimpeachable friend of conservation, the cloud remained.

Soon enough, it seemed apparent that obstacles were being put in my way to keep me off the site. First it was the weather (too rough). Then I was told I couldn't dive on the site without first being checked out by a Park Service dive master—this despite my thousands of underwater hours in all kinds of conditions, from the cold North Atlantic to a saturation mission living in the government's own underwater laboratory. I had no objection to being checked out by the dive master, but the dive master never arrived. Too bad for me, I was told sarcastically. Finally, the weather cleared and, with glowering faces on all sides, I bullied my way onto the dive boat with my gear. I was determined to see the *Fowey* and complete my assignment.

On the site, I was confronted with more frustrations. I was told that the dive master had appointments and couldn't accompany me on the dive; once again, too bad for me! It was disheartening because I have a long-standing respect for the Park Service; it's not often given the credit it deserves. I wondered how this tiny group in south Florida could so carelessly cast a cloud over the entire organization.

Finally, standing out in worsening weather at Legare Anchorage, knowing this might be my last chance, I announced that, dive master or no dive master, I was going into the water. Feeling like a defector jumping ship, I headed 30 feet below to the bottom. One of the students working on the dig came in behind me, hovering over my shoulder like a big shark. To be shadowed on dry land is unpleasant enough; underwater, it's intolerable. Fortunately I managed to lose him in the murky waters of Biscayne Bay. Before he caught up with me I had obtained the impressions I had come to get. Here are the passages as they appeared in the October, 1983, *Smithsonian* cover story:

> ". . . Floating above the site, I found myself extraordinarily touched by the scene. After 235 years on the bottom, the *Fowey* looks nothing like a ship. For more than two centuries her timbers have been meals for worms, and the few objects which remain on the bottom resemble a deceptive pattern of shapes and shadows on the sand. It took a while before they made sense to me: the object that appeared to be a large stone half-buried in the sand was a cannon; a conglomerate that at first appeared to be a lump of broken coral finally emerged as a collection of broken tiles from the galley. That straight object encrusted with sea growth was actually a cutlass— still in its scabbard. Long dark shapes, on closer inspection, turned out to be fragments of the ship's timbers. And, most amazing, another sword, encrusted with coral, was thrust upright in the sand, as if a lost seaman had cast a final oath, then plunged his weapon through the silent sea.
>
> "A grid of yellow lines had been laced back and forth across the exposed portion of the vessel, and tied off into square sections, marked with numbered floats. Inside the sections, archaeologists were gently fanning away the sand with their hands, finding ceramic shards, buttons, broken green wine bottles, and a small encrusted object—possibly a knife. They sealed their finds in plastic bags marked with the number of the grid section where they had been recovered. Back in the dry-land laboratory, the finds would be correlated with the grid sections and studied in relation to one

another. Gradually, as the archaeologists continue methodically to dig deeper and deeper, the life of the vessel will take shape."

I have never forgotten the fragility of this scene, so jarring in contrast to the ways of those charged with overseeing it. After the dive, I found myself strictly *persona non grata*. I couldn't get straight answers from those in charge. That evening, I gathered together a roomful of graduate students who were working on the site. I asked them to use their imaginations, to let themselves go and talk freely about the possible directions of marine archaeology in the future. Though it may be hard to believe, these young people could speak of nothing but the threat posed by treasure hunters. I persisted. What about the really deep wrecks? Can we use sophisticated new hardware to get at them? What do we need to do a comprehensive ocean bottom survey of cultural resources? No response. To me, this was worse than being kept away from the *Fowey* site. After all, these were some of the best young minds in the field; and yet, they too had been given a case of myopia with all the symptoms that keep the treasure wars raging.

I didn't report those observations in *Smithsonian*. This wasn't a treatise on infectious paranoia. The message was—and remains—that shipwrecks are fragile. To get the most out of them for the public good, the wasteful treasure wars between treasure hunters and archaeologists have to end in a creative compromise. If this doesn't happen, the public itself, which seemed to be so much on the minds of those in charge of the *Fowey*, will be elbowed out of the process as interlopers among Dethelfsen's "temple virgins."

It is true that some treasure hunters have abused historic wrecks. This was especially true in the 1950s and 1960s when the availability of SCUBA gear made it easy for anyone to invade the ocean. Most of this damage, particularly to the hard-hit galleons off Florida, was done by wildcatters and looters who were more closely related to vandals than to disciplined treasure hunters or archaeologists. Unfortunately, their actions came to represent all treasure hunters. The lines were drawn in a kind of absurdly unrealistic way: The treasure hunters, even those like Mel Fisher, Burt Webber, and Kip Wagner, were lumped under the "Bad Guy" umbrella while the archaeologists, even the incompetent ones, were all "Good Guys." The rationale drawn at the academic level reinforced this distortion. It was said that treasure hunters and professional treasure salvors had no scientific conscience, no method other than destruction, no motive but profit. Yet most of the treasure on display in the world's museums has come from treasure hunters. They sold some of the goodies to investors to raise working capital, but the pieces sold were duplicates of others kept in their own collections. The coin market, for example, is flooded with Spanish coins of all kinds; these days, museums are reluctant to accept them even as gifts, so many are in storage around the world. The archaeologists argue that each coin is special and vital to a total historical overview, despite the existence of tens of thousands of duplicates. There is no real scientific basis for such a claim, but it serves to sharpen the differences between treasure hunters and archaeologists. It's as if biologists claimed that, in order to make a proper study of Peregrine falcons, every Peregrine falcon in existence had to be collected and examined. Extend that logic to every item found on a shipwreck. For example, the nails that held together a galleon numbered in the thousands; treasure hunters often sell a portion and place others on exhibit or donate them to public collections. Archaeologists argue that every nail is important, that it is heresy to sell them even to finance further excavation, in which even more important artifacts might be found.

In a world loaded with historic relics, the archaeologists are, in effect, laying their own claim on all treasure. Imagine the professor of nautical archaeology in his conservation lab with several thousand ship's nails, a few coins, a few gold bars, some crates of musket balls, and countless ceramic shards. Given this trove, the professor is in the research business for years to come; he is sitting on his own loot, and so long as it remains with him in his lab, he is in business. He catalogs the material and publishes the catalog. He studies some of the material and publishes the study. The academic qualifications committee at his university looks at the published work and, since he has proved he is advancing knowledge in his field, he is awarded tenure, chairs, grants—he makes a living from those artifacts. To have such antiquities circulating in the public domain destroys his exclusivity. It is therefore in the professor's best long-term interests to keep everyone away except his fellow professors.

Most archaeologists would deny any such motives, and they freely shift the onus onto the treasure hunters as being persons who squander the public's heritage by selling off artifacts. There are some cases in which archaeologists have made new discoveries from duplicate artifacts that were locked away in a vault by one of their predecessors, but these instances are rare. The person who originally collected the items likely studied them thoroughly and archaeologists do not make a name for themselves by studying someone else's collection. The game, which leads to bigger and more prestigious research grants and higher salaries at more prestigious universities, is simply not played that way. The archaeologists, who say they want to collect these artifacts to keep them from disappearing from public view, lock the duplicates away in study collections that then gather dust. A few items are displayed, and the rest are relegated to a warehouse, out of public view.

In the end, it's a battle for turf, and it's a war that increases in stridency each day. Like most territorial disputes, the treasure wars have come to Washington and the halls of Congress. The warriors have been meeting head-on in front of our national lawmakers since 1979, when Representative Charles E. Bennett, the Florida Democrat, introduced his first "Shipwreck Preservation Act."

So far, Bennett's proposed legislation has failed to pass Congress. His latest version is bill H.R. 3558, "The Abandoned Shipwreck Act of 1985." On October 29, 1985, the treasure warriors clashed again in Washington over the merits of the Bennett proposal.

The Congressional Firing Line

In the hearing chamber of the Longworth House Office Building, Congresswoman Barbara Mikulski, the diminutive Democrat from Maryland, was finding it hard to bring the meeting to order. The flood of reporters, flashing strobes, and the 50-foot-long bank of video monitors added to the confusion—and there was enough of that already among the witnesses who had come to testify on Bennett's proposed legislation. The head of the House subcommittee on Oceanography, Mikulski, was a newcomer to the treasure wars. She'd been warned that the witnesses were a seasoned crew; many of them were bitter enemies. In fact, there was so much bad blood and poison ink in the background that even the feisty Mikulski, who had slugged it out with the best of them in the smoke-filled back rooms of Baltimore politics, couldn't be entirely prepared to handle the hostilities in this chamber. It gave her an eerie feeling, as if there were lightning in the room, looking for someone to strike.

Scanning the witness table in the front of the room, Mikulski saw a pantheon of the heroes of the treasure wars, definitely a front-page crew, she thought. There was Mel Fisher, in a leisure suit, the ubiquitous gold coin around his neck, still radiant with the success of his discovery of the

$400 million mother lode of the *Atocha* on July 20, 1985. Beside him sat Robert Marx, a treasure hunter and self-taught marine archaeologist, author of 31 books, and excavator of the sunken city of Port Royal, off Kingston, Jamaica. He had flown in from Indonesia, where he claimed to have found a wreck so rich that it made the *Atocha* look like a sunken slum. Marx wore no gold chain, only a pained expression, as if he'd rather be diving.

Hovering in the background was Dr. George Bass, the discoverer of several Phoenician wrecks more than 3,000 years old off the coast of Turkey. Bass, the founder of the Institute for Nautical Archaeology and self-proclaimed "father" of underwater archaeology, came waving the flag of academia and a resume longer than his arm. Bass might look harmless, but when it comes to treasure hunters, the Texas A&M University professor reveals long, sharp knives.

Dr. Robert Ballard was a striking contrast to Bass: tall, slender, pale, and with the far-away look of a true explorer. Ballard had electrified the world a month earlier by finding and filming the most famous shipwreck of our time, the R.M.S. *Titanic,* sitting upright on the bottom, two and a half miles down in the eternal night of the Atlantic Ocean. He brought to the hearing chamber the ensign of Woods Hole Oceanographic Institution, the official innerspace academy of the underwater world. Neither treasure hunter nor academic, Ballard described himself as a "technologist," one who adds heat to the treasure wars by inventing gadgets that make it easier to locate deep wrecks.

Well, Mikulski mused, the issue before the subcommittee was a lot bigger than any single treasure warrior or discovery, no matter how important it may have been. The Abandoned Shipwreck Act had far-reaching implications. Bennett's first version of the bill, introduced in 1979, underscored the idea that historic shipwrecks (which he defines as those 50 years old or older) were cultural resources, finite and fragile, and no less enlightening to future generations than Mount Vernon, the great pyramids of Egypt, or the Wright Brothers' *Kitty Hawk* flying machine. Author of eight historical books and head of his own museum, Bennett wanted to protect shipwrecks the way we now protect some landlocked historical sites. And, given the thousands of ships beneath the navigable waters of the United States that meet his definition of historic wrecks, his 1985 proposal would create more public lands than Theodore Roosevelt's 1908 dedication of 150 million acres of national park land.

Sweeping though it was, this latest proposal was more temperate than the 1979 bill, which had asked that the federal government take title to all historic vessels out to the 200-mile limit of the Outer Continental Shelf. He based it on the principle of "escheatage," or the confiscation of property in the absence of any claimants. Escheatage is exercised every day by the government. If someone dies without a legal will or heirs, leaving assets in banks or other financial accounts, the government will take title to those assets through escheatage. Why not do the same with shipwrecks, Bennett reasoned. A federal bureau would be established to run the program at a small cost to the taxpayers: "I could fund it myself with a few friends," Bennett once said. The bureau would move at its own pace to survey its escheated trove of offshore treasures. If it took generations or even centuries to survey all those wrecks and determine which of them were truly historic, so what? The wrecks weren't going anywhere, and meanwhile the public would be on notice that any attempt to recover drowned artifacts was a violation of federal law. The bureau would presumably only do business with lettered marine archaeologists.

Except for the academics, who favor any bill that puts a lock on the sea bottom for their own purposes, the 1979 proposal was swamped by opposition. The concept of escheateage, which in British common law refers to property reverting back to a manor's lord after the death of a serf, seemed hardly appropriate in the United States as a way to accomplish ocean exploration. Treasure hunters, commercial salvors, and sport divers saw the Bennett plan as a disincentive; private investment in historic shipwreck salvage wouldn't be allowed and would be forced outside of U.S. territorial waters. Furthermore, the bill appeared to be a less than objective response to Bennett's long-time nemesis, Mel Fisher, who had successfully fought both the State of Florida and the federal government in court for control of the *Atocha* and *Santa Margarita* treasures. Fisher's victory didn't sit well with Mr. Bennett. Besides, the notion of bureaucratic oversight of thousands of sunken vessels seemed the worst kind of overkill, and over the next six years, successive versions of Bennett's bill all carried the unsettling shadow of a federal Big Brother policing the oceans.

A Shift to State Control

By 1985, the bill had been modified significantly. It placed the states in control of historic artifacts in their inland and offshore waters out to three miles, their territorial limit. It further allowed public access to non-historic vessels. The shipwrecks specifically covered by the proposal were those "substantially buried in the bottom," or in coral, or those eligible for listing in the *National Register of Historic Places*. The bill also set aside Admiralty law, affirmed by the federal courts as the prevailing rules governing shipwrecks, which allows private individuals to claim a wreck site by applying to a federal court. Under Bennett's proposal, each state would write its own regulations. Anyone who wanted to track treasure and recover it would be forced to do business with the state agencies administering those rules. In essence, this was a federally mandated return to the system employed by the State of Florida which, for two decades, had generated so many legal conflicts between the State and salvors.

Mikulski's opening remarks stressed the legal aspects of treasure. Admiralty law, which allows salvors to keep what they find, may not be at all appropriate to the goal of preserving our cultural heritage, she said; historic shipwrecks "need to be treated in a different manner." With more wrecks being located and new technologies leading to discoveries in places once thought too difficult to reach to need protection, a dilemma had arisen between archaeological tradition and entrepreneurial energy. The question, Mikulski said, is "whether our law is as contemporary as the technology we're using."

Bennett led the parade of witnesses. His tone was clipped, cutting, and it was clear that most of his remarks were directed at Mel Fisher, the gentlemen who had been bumping his proposal off its pedestal since 1979.

"We've probably all heard and read of some treasure salvor locating an historic shipwreck," he began. " 'How wonderful!' we say. 'Just think of the knowledge that can be gained. . . .' But nothing in present law guarantees that. No one except the treasure salvagers will necessarily gain as things are now. You see, in the haste of many salvage operations, the shipwreck site may become a shambles—wrecked again if you will."

Bennett, in an oblique slap at the treasure hunters, added, "They are not *all* looters." His bill, he noted, merely substitutes "archaic salvage law [which optimizes the recovery of artifacts from the sea in exchange for financial reward] and puts in its place a law which will preserve historic wrecks and their contents for their historical value, as well as allowing for financial rewards in carefully-handled recoveries under state regulations."

Changing the laws of salvage, removing historic wrecks from the domain of Admiralty proceedings, is only half of Bennett's proposal. The other half, Bennett explained, "is assertion of ownership in state governments so that they do not have to go 'hat in hand' to those who excavate the historic shipwrecks."

Of course, there is no record of a state ever going "hat in hand" to a salvor. If anything, just the opposite is true. In the case of Mel Fisher, first the State of Florida and then the federal government came to him literally armed and demanded that he surrender all of the artifacts he'd found, keeping them locked up in Tallahassee for years. A series of federal court decisions in Admiralty suits filed by Fisher's attorney put an end to their claims on the trove. "With the Admiralty Court decisions," Bennett said, "salvagers are effectively on their own—to do just as they wish, with only their consciences or pocketbooks to lead them."

Bennett admitted that, over the years, the courts have consistently denied title to abandoned shipwrecks to the states. Therefore, he proposed that the federal government assert its right to title and then transfer title to the states. "We know that people such as Mel Fisher capture the nation's imagination—imagine actually finding a ship from the 17th-century. But once that fascination is gone, what is left?" he asked. "If the answer to this question is only a ransacked piece of junk and expanded billfolds, the answer is wrong."

It should be noted that a number of first-rate scholars, including the former head of marine archaeology for the Canadian park service and the curator of the museum of the Hispanic Society of America, are studying the artifacts recovered from the *Atocha* and *Santa Margarita*. Mel Fisher has established a conservation facility in Key West to preserve the artifacts from the two ships and has built a museum to house them.

Firestone Favors Bennett Plan

Florida Secretary of State George Firestone testified next. In 1983, Firestone worked with salvors on what was then called a "participatory" shipwreck excavation and preservation plan. The plan included the public, private salvors, and academics. Firestone testified that the Bennett proposal represented a possible solution to the legal monster that has dogged the state for nearly a generation. The problem, he told the subcommittee, is the tangle of court cases at the federal and state levels that have complicated attempts to impose preservation guidelines on artifact recovery.

"For instance, once an Admiralty arrest is filed [a claim to a wreck site], the shipwreck becomes in effect a small outholding of federal authority within state submerged lands," he explained. "Thus, the state's ability to manage its public lands for multiple use activities is hampered because federal Admiralty law preempts the state's management laws."

He said that a salvage operation may stir up sediment that can damage a living coral reef, or a shipwreck might lie under a producing oyster bed, or be so close to public swimming areas that salvage would be a hazard. Yet, if the salvor has placed the site under Admiralty by filing a claim with a federal court, the state's ability to respond to the impact of the salvage operation is severely limited.

Firestone said the 1983 contract worked out with one of Mel Fisher's subsidiary companies, Cobb Coin Company, incorporates archaeological guidelines developed by the state and the salvors. The contract, renewable at Cobb Coin's option in perpetuity, has worked well, he said, and will not be impacted by the passage of the Bennett bill. Yet other cases haven't been so satisfactory. Since 1983, he said, at least 15 federal Admiralty arrests have been filed on historic sites in Florida waters. This has led to dual jurisdiction (federal and state) over the bottom area the wrecks lie on, and very often the state is not made aware that a claim has been filed.

"Dual jurisdiction," he said, "has resulted not only in confusion and loss of archaeological information on which future management decisions should be based, but also in considerable expenditure of state resources on attempts to resolve these needless conflicts." The state, he explained, is being edged out of the picture. The only way to stop this is to give the state ownership of the shipwrecks in its waters and handle all claims in the state courts. "If Congress does not resolve this issue, and if federal Admiralty courts continue diminishing state involvement, the final result will be commercial salvage of shipwreck sites with no concern for historical significance. The only winners in this jurisdictional conflict are the commercial salvors. The losers are the taxpayers who pay for these lawsuits, and more importantly, the citizens and visitors of Florida who are deprived of their use and enjoyment of historical resources on public lands."

"Guys in Three-Piece Suits"

Robert Marx, who in the past opposed versions of the Bennett bill, favored it during the 1985 hearings. Marx's track record is as spectacular as Fisher's, but in a different way. After a stint with Real 8, Kip Wagner's treasure hunting organization that started the treasure gold rush in Florida in the early 1960s, Marx worked for foreign governments all over the world. He has engaged in the sale of artifacts to keep his digs going. When I interviewed him in 1983, he said: "I just don't like guys in three-piece suits telling us how to do archaeology." He stressed the small number of professional marine archaeologists worldwide, saying "they just don't have the time to do what needs to be done." He was annoyed at the purist position of other archaeologists. In 1982, for example, *Skin Diver* magazine published a picture of Marx holding some ancient gold coins, "and some of my colleagues thought I ought to get out of the business because of that," he complained. He was adamant. The purists, he said, "stir up bloody trouble for themselves." Besides, he asked, "what have they written in the way of research? I see very little in the journals. What I do see is a lot of blasting each other, blasting the states for their laws, and blasting the treasure hunters." As for the selling of artifacts, he talked about a project he had once worked in Brazil where the artifacts were auctioned. "What's wrong with that? You do need money to keep going, and the object is to keep going, to get at the history."

Though he scorned his colleagues for their pedantry and declared that, "If all of us [marine archaeologists] worked year 'round, we couldn't make a dent in all the sites there are out there," he maintained that something had to be done to control historic sites. He didn't favor the Bennett proposal when it came up again in 1983: "I'm not into politics," he said. Marx did, however, help write Jamaica's antiquity laws, through which the government retains 75 percent of all artifacts found in its territorial sea. Now, two years later, he was asserting the need for the Bennett bill, claiming it might make some order out of the chaos.

"I'd like to state, in the most forceful way possible," Marx told the subcommittee, "that I have learned that no one, no matter how lucky or skillful, can ever make a reasonable living from the commercial salvage of ancient shipwrecks. I have been one of the most successful salvors in the field and have recovered millions of dollars worth of treasure and artifacts, yet after paying all the costs involved in the search, recovery, and preservation of the artifacts, not to mention the shares paid to financial backers, governments, and the divers, I have not made a proper living from this work.

"I have supported my family with money made from my 31 books, hundreds of articles, filming and selling documentaries, and lecturing. The only people who make any big money in this field are those who get gullible people to invest in wildly-hyped, highly-publicized treasure hunt schemes which grossly exaggerate the actual amounts of treasure."

He said that the Admiralty rules of finders-keepers shouldn't apply to historic shipwrecks. "It has always been my belief that shipwrecks and other underwater finds belong to all mankind and not just to the first person who claims them." And, if the finder doesn't possess the means to properly gather data from the wreck, "he should only work on the site with people who are qualified."

Marx said Bennett's bill would save commercial salvors, not drive them out of business. "In fact, I personally find that, with things as they now stand, that is, with anyone able to run out and file an Admiralty arrest on a site, it is both uneconomical and impractical to do this kind of work. If things continue as they have for the past few years not only will I personally not do any further shipwreck work in U.S. waters, but I know other reputable salvors who will follow suit. Then, the fate of the remainder of our ancient shipwrecks will be left in the hands of those who find the profit motive and opportunities for free enterprise higher callings than cultural values or archaeological and historical integrity."

'Amateurs' and the 'Goodies'

George Bass has favored the Bennett bill from its inception in 1979, even though Bass's work in nautical archaeology is done mostly in foreign waters, where he is responsible for excavation of three of the oldest shipwrecks yet found. He has worked with both archaeologists and treasure hunters, and he will insist at every opportunity that he is the father of underwater archaeology. While this is debatable (Bass was introduced to underwater archaeology by Peter Throckmorton, Art McKee, John Potter, and a few other men who deserve a share of that credit as well) he is one of few academics active in the field, with a broad line of funding through his Institute for Nautical Archaeology at Texas A&M University.

During the October, 1985, hearings he came out for the Bennett proposal, as expected, presenting arguments he has often made in the past.

"An archaeological site in a jungle, on a mountain top, in a desert, or under water, is an archaeological site," he told the subcommittee. "Underwater sites are protected as such in Europe, Africa, Asia, and Australia. Why not in the United States?"

One of his pet peeves is the notion that amateurs or paraprofessional archaeologists can be taken seriously. "A salvage group with one or two archaeologists cannot conduct serious archaeology any more than a large hospital with one or two physicians can practice serious medicine," he said. "And an 'amateur' archaeologist has no more business directing an excavation than an 'amateur' dentist would have practicing dentistry." This analogy may not be terribly appropriate even if, as Bass claims, archaeologists study as long as physicians do, "but are less well-paid."

His presentation to the subcommittee outlined the classic position taken by archaeologists and other academics in the treasure wars: that wrecks are safe where they lie, that, being on the bottom, they aren't subjected to deterioration from storms or wave action. Therefore, the history embodied by the wrecks will be preserved until public agencies or private institutions can fund their excavation. Bass also pointed out that he and his colleagues hadn't found the need to sell any artifacts to pay for their excavations over the past two decades. "Archaeological colleagues in France, Australia, and other countries are doing similarly first-rate work without selling artifacts," he pointed out. "Slivers of wood from the *Mary Rose* in England admittedly are being sold as souvenirs to help pay for its salvage and conservation, a unique exception to the rule.

"Treasure hunters are said to deserve all the profit they can make because they risk their lives and have lost team members. I am dismayed that nearly every article I have read on the controversy between treasure hunting and archaeology has emphasized the loss of life of treasure hunters, but *not one* has mentioned the death of the most promising nautical archaeologist in the world from a diving accident four years ago. He died only weeks before receiving a doctorate from Cambridge University and before the publication of his second book. Others of us have seen friends and colleagues crippled by bends and embolisms, but we believe our daily risks are totally irrelevant to any rights to sell what we excavate."

Bass admitted that treasure hunters are correct when they point out that American archaeologists do not have a good record in surveying and excavating shipwrecks in the Americas. But, he said, there were no archaeologists in Greece or Turkey 200 years ago, and "I believe we are fortunate that not all Greek tombs were robbed or that not all Greek temples were burned for lime, as happened to some. We must think of the future; one day there will be sufficient archaeological expertise in this hemisphere to do the job—if any worthwhile wrecks remain."

As for the sale of duplicate artifacts, Bass claims there is a need to preserve *every* artifact recovered in a research collection. "Treasure hunters say there is no harm in selling duplicate artifacts. Using newly devised techniques, we recently began the long-term restudy of seemingly identical artifacts we excavated more than 20 years ago, and have learned enough to write new chapters and new articles on them. In fact, this restudy is causing us to revise some of our conclusions about the nature of Byzantine commerce."

When treasure hunters say that there are thousands of wrecks, enough for commercial salvors and archaeologists to work, Bass bristles. "Why should archaeologists have them all? There are thousands of land sites. Why not given them to pot-hunters? Why not let some 'free-enterprise' treasure hunters have some Egyptian pyramids and half the classical temples on earth—there are plenty to go around. In fact, wrecks are disappearing at an alarming rate. I have conducted underwater surveys off the Italian coast and found nothing. Shipwreck site after shipwreck site had been stripped bare by souvenir hunters and professional looters. Some of these sites once had held remains of Phoenician ships, so the world has been thwarted in attempts to learn how the most famous of ancient mariners constructed their vessels."

Bass made a compelling, and at times eloquent, case before the subcommittee. But the long-range consequences still pose many questions: Are we willing to legislate the domain of underwater history exclusively into the hands of professional archaeologists? Will they actually get out into the field and recover the history thus entrusted to them? Are there more moderate—and ultimately more productive—ways to go?

Shipwrecks as 'Sanctuaries'

Among those in the hearing chamber that day who perceived at least a partial alternative was Dr. Nancy Foster, chief of the Marine Sanctuaries Program at the National Oceanic and Atmospheric Administration (NOAA). Dr. Foster is a fiercely intelligent young woman with a flair for catching the public eye. During the past few years, and in the face of budget cutbacks, she has managed to keep yet another historic shipwreck in the news, the U.S.S. *Monitor.* This famous Civil War ironclad went down in a storm in 1862, after the dramatic first confrontation of steel-plated warships, its duel with the Confederate ship C.S.S. *Virginia (nee Merrimack).* With its low, metal-plated hull that looked like a clothes iron surmounted

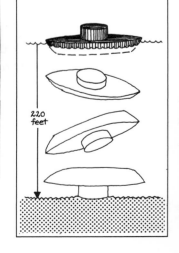

The Loss of the *Monitor*

One of the most famous ships ever built, the U.S.S. *Monitor* revolutionized naval warfare. The first true iron-clad, it presented a low-slung armor-plated profile that looked like an old-fashioned flat iron surmounted by a revolving "cheesebox" gun turret. Its celebrated defeat of the Confederate iron-clad C.S.S. *Virginia (nee the Merrimack)* marked a turning point in the Civil War—and the beginning of the end for wooden warships.

Despite its glory, the *Monitor* suffered an ignoble fate. Under tow to Charleston, where she was to be part of a Union blockade, she parted her towing cables after midnight December 31, 1862, some 16 miles southeast of Cape Hatteras, North Carolina. Leaking badly in a rising storm, mountainous waves engulfed the vessel. She heeled over and sank with the loss of 16 hands.

This fateful event was depicted in a Currier & Ives print published on the cover of *Harper's Weekly* in 1863 (*top facing page*).

Its rediscovery came in 1974 when a Duke University team found the *Monitor* upside-down, resting on its gun turret below 220 feet of current swept, shark-infested water (*bottom right, facing page*). The photomosaic view (*bottom left, facing page*) shows the vessel as she looks today on the bottom. Arrow indicates position of the gun turret. Subsequent investigations reveal the hull to be fragile, badly worn and corroded, and in danger of collapse.

In 1984, one of the *Monitor*'s anchors was recovered by archaeologists (*right*). But the bulk of the ship remains in its watery grave.

The *Monitor* has been declared an official marine sanctuary by the National Oceanic and Atmospheric Administration (NOAA), giving it status similar to that of a national park or monument. Meanwhile, plans to recover the vessel have been seriously considered, a job that will cost millions of dollars with no guarantee that the ship will remain intact during excavation. Once recovered, preservation, study, and display will be equally expensive. NOAA, working with the National Trust for Historic Preservation, is seeking to raise private capital to undertake at least some phases of excavation. One day we hope to bring back to life the ship that launched our modern navy.

Top left: The Wreck of the Iron-Clad Monitor, courtesy Naval History Division, Navy Department. Bottom Left: Photo mosaic, courtesy National Oceanic and Atmospheric Administration. Bottom right: Monitor map wreck site, courtesy National Oceanic and Atmospheric Administration. Top right: Monitor anchor, *courtesy National Oceanic and Atmospheric Administration.*

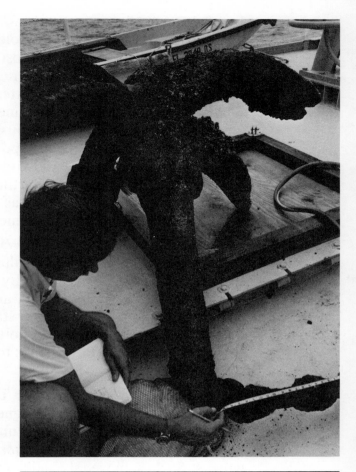

by a "cheesebox" gun turret, the *Monitor* represented a revolution in naval engineering. Its construction wrote the beginning of the end for wooden warships. It was discovered almost by accident in 1974, when one of Dr. Harold Edgerton's deep-sea cameras snagged an obstruction 220 feet down, about 16 miles south of Cape Hatteras, North Carolina. When a team from Duke University retrieved the camera and developed the film, they saw an amazing picture of the "cheesebox" gun turret laying upside-down on a current-swept bottom. The shape of the turret was unmistakable; they knew immediately it was the wreck of the *Monitor,* missing since that stormy night in 1862. A few artifacts were subsequently recovered and displayed, and the lost *Monitor* was declared a federal marine sanctuary, in effect making it a national monument protected by federal law.

When Dr. Foster arrived in Washington a few years later, she immediately perceived the publicity value of the famous warship and backed several probes of the wreck site. By 1984, its huge anchor was lifted to the surface; newspapers, magazines, and television networks worldwide carried pictures of it with Dr. Foster standing alongside. The *Monitor* remains on the bottom, the millions of dollars needed to properly excavate it are simply not available. But, thanks to Dr. Foster, the ship is never far from the headlines.

She told the subcommittee that the NOAA-administered Marine Sanctuaries Act, originally designed to protect and manage natural resources such as the Pennekamp underwater park at Key Largo, Florida, had been used to cover the *Monitor* and might be applied to other historic wrecks. Such a move, she said, would accomplish two things. First, it would place historic man-made resources "in the same management framework as coral reefs and fish habitats" protected by federal authority. Second, like the *Monitor,* vessels protected by the Act would achieve national recognition as "valuable and fragile marine resources."

Dr. Foster, a marine biologist by profession, endorsed the Bennett proposal as a "first step" to larger designs, designs handed down by the federal government. Her suggested application of the Marine Sanctuaries Act actually goes farther than Bennett's plan and is more all-encompassing than anything put forward by the academic community.

"The downside of any archaeological excavation and recovery, besides its cost, is that it can never be repeated," she explained. "It can only be done once. So the decision must be made how to obtain the maximum potential from the resource."

'Pickles in a Barrel'

Use of the Marine Sanctuaries Act to protect historic wrecks certainly would have the effect of drawing out the various phases of any such decision, since it places the entire process within the glacially slow framework of the federal bureaucracy. This could create problems for some sites. For example, despite what Bass and other academics say about shipwrecks being safe on the bottom, serenely awaiting recovery at some date far in the future, the *Monitor* site is swept by stiff currents. The hull plates are steadily corroding and because it is resting upside down on top of the gun turret, there is a danger that the hull will eventually collapse and be scattered. By no means is the vessel "safe as pickles in a barrel," to apply the phrase used by J. Barto Arnold, a marine archaeologist and member of the Texas Antiquities Commission.

NOAA and Dr. Foster are acutely aware of the dangers posed by the *Monitor's* turbulent gravesite, but they have elected, out of necessity, not to excavate until the money to do the job is safely in the bank. Once excavated, the conservation and preservation process, along with perpetual upkeep, will cost untold millions far into the future. In the meantime, NOAA has turned to the National Trust for Historic Preservation to help raise the necessary funds from private sources. The National Park Service, the Smithsonian Institution, and even the U.S. Navy are part of this very worthwhile endeavor. Still, the vessel remains on the bottom, far offshore, virtually inaccessible, and in constant danger of disintegration. The question must be asked: If NOAA and its partners, holding the resources of the federal government, can't afford to raise and preserve the *Monitor,* who can? If NOAA is short of cash to recover one of the two or three most famous ships in U.S. naval history—indeed world history—who can? And who can find the money to recover ships that, while important, have far less public recognition than the *Monitor?* How can we expect state governments to fund management of sunken cultural resources, as proposed in the Bennett bill? And there is a tougher question yet: Can we expect the federal government, which under current President Ronald Reagan has attempted to kill the Marine Sanctuaries Program for the past five years, to do a radical turnabout in policy and use tax dollars to fund underwater archaeology? Clearly, the answer is no. Neither the federal government nor state governments can cut social programs and funds for education and, at the same time, pump money into historical research. It just won't wash with the taxpayers and voters. Thus, Bennett's plan and

Dr. Foster's escalation of it seemed politically doomed in today's atmosphere of economic belt-tightening.

Fisher: 'Fair National Policy'

Mel Fisher's testimony was accompanied by his own proposed shipwreck legislation. His objection to the Bennett bill, which he has opposed since its inception in 1979, is that it ends in the direction of nationalization of the salvage industry. The bill, he said, has gone so far afield that it attempts to protect natural resources "although there are plenty of federal and state laws to do that." It is too broad, too vague, Fisher said, and he expressed the fear that enforcement may clog the courts for years to come.

"If the real purpose of the bill is to protect historic shipwrecks, then the bill I'm proposing will do that while protecting the rights of all those who would enjoy our seas," he told the subcommittee. "If we are really serious about protecting historic shipwrecks, we will concern ourselves with how they are worked, not who *owns* them."

Among other problems, Fisher said the Bennett plan places barriers in front of private salvors. What is really needed are more workers in the sea, he said, not fewer.

His proposal, he declared, will result in "consistent and fair national policy, administered by the federal Admiralty courts as the Constitution intended, and not a proliferation of state laws which will only benefit looters." Responding to the archaeologists directly, he noted that every country with a "hands-off" policy toward historic shipwrecks has encountered unprecedented looting. Laws that threaten treasure hunters and treasure salvors will have no effect whatever on criminals, he said; looters will continue to loot, even in countries such as Saudi Arabia, where those caught stealing artifacts may have their hands chopped off by the authorities. Even George Bass has lamented the incredible restrictions on historic salvage enforced by Greece and Turkey, restrictions which made it all but impossible to recover treasures from the sea without direct government control at each stage of the operation. Fisher feared that, while the Bennett bill seemed almost innocuous, it opened the door to absolutism, to interpretations which no one in the chamber that day could truly foresee.

His proposal set out specific guidelines to be administered under Admiralty law by the federal district courts. The purpose of the bill, according to Fisher, "is to secure for the present and future benefit of the people of the United States, the protection of historical shipwrecks on the seabed and in the subsoil of the lands beneath navigable waters within the boundaries of the United States and its territories." Even his oldest and staunchest enemies realized that this was not exactly self-serving nor self-aggrandizing; his proposal was no less reasoned than the plans of those who opposed him.

A Presidential Committee

The main points of Fisher's bill would have an "archaeological committee" appointed by the President from the ranks of the National Park Service; have the committee operate under Admiralty law; would include any unique vessel, regardless of its age, as an historic wreck; would pay salvors for excavating wrecks; a "cultural heritage protection clause" would require salvors to submit by January 30 of each year an inventory of items salvaged in the preceding year; the list would be given to the Archaeological Committee, who would in turn compile a "wish list" of items from the inventories, and salvors would use these as a basis for giving the Committee about a fifth of their finds; if a salvor refused to donate a representative cross-section of items, the Committee could take him to court or buy the artifacts at fair market value; the Committee would set up guidelines for all historic shipwreck excavations, and all data recovered from shipwrecks would be made available to the Committee and to the public; the guidelines would cover site mapping, data records, recording of salvage areas, structural remains and major artifact clusters, artifact tagging and handling, unique and precious artifacts, artifact preservation, conservation, diver safety, project supervision, reporting requirements, and exchanges of archaeological data.

This proposal came as a bit of a shock to Fisher's old foes. They had expected him to sloganize, to wave the flag of free enterprise. He had done that in the past. But not today. It had been a long and heart-breaking road to the *Atocha* mother lode and traveling it had left deep scars. Those who had accused him of being a con man, of falsifying the early *Atocha* finds in order to lure gullible investors, were strangely silent, perhaps even a little resentful.

In the glare of the publicity, Fisher remained impassive. He had won his own private treasure war, and he had made his statement before Congress. For all anyone knew, it might well be his last. His sense of inner peace, only vaguely sensed beneath his stoicism, infuriated his detractors. He took no delight in it. Mel Fisher, at long last, had accomplished what he set out to do, and in the hearing chamber that day there was a feeling that it was now up to the other treasure warriors to make the peace Fisher had found for himself.

The *Titanic* and 'Technologists'

Among the stellar assemblage of witnesses, one man captured everyone's undivided attention. A month earlier, in the cold reaches of the North Atlantic, Dr. Robert Ballard had electrified the world with the discovery of R.M.S. *Titanic.* Like all explorers who bring legends to life, a magical aura surrounded this young scientist. Ballard cast a spell over the hearing chamber; reporters fell silent, lobbyists ceased their eternal whispering, and the members of Barbara Mikulski's subcommittee clung to his every word.

Yet Ballard didn't bring solutions to the issues at hand, only warnings and more questions. He was not counted among the official treasure warriors. As a "technologist," he represented one of the small cadre of whiz kids at the Woods Hole Oceanographic Institution who are pushing the hardware of deep sea research into the 21st century. In turn, their discoveries add fresh weapons to the on-going power struggle over treasure. But as he described the ghostly visage of the *Titanic,* resting upright more than two miles down in the Alpine-like country that backs onto the world's largest mountain range, the Mid-Atlantic Ridge, the all-too-human bickerings of treasure hunters and archaeologists faded into the gloom. The eternal night below the sea, he said, was a "fitting place for this greatest of sea tragedies to rest," along with the 1,522 souls that perished with her in 1912.

Ballard said he was concerned about the future sanctity of the wreck—very personally concerned, since it was he who had brought to light the very technology that might threaten the ship's survival. It was now possible, he told the subcommittee, to produce live, real-time television tours of the ship, to show the world for the first time in 73 years the magnificent ballrooms of the luxury liner. This technology is advancing rapidly; soon the whole of the deep ocean will be open to manned exploration. This advance of technology, he said, is the real challenge to the future of the *Titanic* and other deep wrecks.

Of course, this technology didn't spring up overnight at Woods Hole. It was a long time in the making, and much of it came straight out of the Pentagon. Still, it is now in the public domain and, like some devastating new weapon, requires judicious oversight. Ballard said his counterpart on the French team that helped find the *Titanic,* Jean-Louis Michel, agreed with him on this point. The pristine condition of the ship reinforced this view: the world's legendary "unsinkable" liner had proven a lot more vulnerable than her designers had imagined. Now, in her loss, she was as fragile as the day she sank.

The first serious attempt to locate the *Titanic* was put together in the 1960s by the Canadian Broadcasting Company. A copy of the CBC's findings was reportedly used by novelist Clive Cussler to help research his best-seller *Raise the Titanic!*

Ballard came onto the scene in the late 1970s with a proposal to use the deep-diving research vehicle *Alcoa Seaprobe* and the smaller submersible *Alvin* to find the ship. But funding was hard to come by and the project was shelved. In 1978, he tried again, using *Alvin* and a special color television system built by RCA. Once again, the funding didn't materialize.

Two years later, Texas oilman Jack Grimm financed his own multi-million dollar search, then tried again in 1981, with the submersible *Aluminaut.* Grimm and his team used side-scan sonar and recorded three possible targets, but foul weather ripped away their magnetometer, making it impossible to distinguish between rock formations and the *Titanic's* steel hull. Grimm, who hoped to make a television special about the discovery of the wreck, was disappointed. He apparently made his records available to Ballard and the Woods Hole group. Grimm believes his generosity was responsible for the discovery of the ship in September 1985. He was incensed when Woods Hole refused to give him the exact location of the vessel. He had no intention whatever of doing any salvage: "I just want to make a movie," he said. Woods Hole has not yet released the location to Grimm or anyone else.

The oilman's data, which reportedly included a video image of the ship's propeller, was at Ballard's disposal when the U.S. Navy took an interest in the *Titanic.* It gave Woods Hole a $2.8 million, five-year contract to develop a new deep-diving robot, known as *Argo.* The Navy also allowed Woods Hole to use its research vessel, the 245-foot *Knorr,* which is a floating laboratory designed to accommodate the *Argo.* Soon after the *Titanic* discovery was announced, Admiral Bradford Mooney, chief of the Office of Naval Research, said the Navy would be backing many probes of the wreck site. Apparently, Jack Grimm has been elbowed out of the picture entirely.

Ballard didn't discuss the Navy's input nor was any mention made of the precise security classification surrounding *Argo*. Ballard's testimony, while general, was thought-provoking.

'Pyramids' of the Deep

"I am neither an archaeologist nor treasure hunter; I am a marine scientist and explorer. I am not here to enter the debate as much as I am here to point out that the technological genius most Americans are so proud of has entered the deep sea in full force and placed before it a new reality," Ballard said. "In short, the great pyramids of the deep are now accessible to man. He can either plunder them like the grave robbers of Egypt or protect them for the countless generations which will follow ours.

"Unlike the shallow reefs of Florida, which reduce a wreck to an unrecognizable mound of encrusted coral, the deep sea is a preserving environment. Ships in the deep were, in many cases, sent to the bottom without having sustained any major structural damage. They either took on water during a storm and sank, or, like the *Titanic,* had a hole punched in their hull.

"In the deep sea, shipwrecks enter a world of total darkness which makes the growth of plants impossible. Without plants, few animals can be found, creating a desert-like world with an organism here and another one there. The freezing temperatures of the deep sea further inhibit biological activity, as does the extreme pressure. The pressure at the *Titanic* site is over 6,000 pounds per square inch. Far from land, the rate of sedimentation in the deep sea is measured in an inch or so per thousand years.

"Some would say, 'So what? If the deep sea is a great preserver of man's history, what good does it do us if it is left in total darkness, beyond the reach of man's inquiring mind?' My answer is, it isn't, and each day we are moving at a faster and faster pace to make it easily accessible to the general public. The technology we used to find *Titanic* is the vanguard of the very technology man will use to find, document, and revisit pieces of history preserved in the deep sea.

"Known as 'telepresence,' this technology in cruder form has been with us for many years. Going to the movies, turning on the television, or picking up the phone are all forms of telepresence. The ability to project your thoughts, your eyes, and eventually your hands, is each day becoming an increasing reality.

text continues on page 109

Treasure: Glory, History, Romance

The search for treasure is as old as time, and none is more compelling than the treasures hidden beneath the world's waters. Sheltered from wind, rain, and the destructive powers of civilization, lost ships and sunken cities represent past glories—time capsules—that contain the secrets and riches of which dreams are made. Look below the waves that cover more than 70 percent of the Earth's surface and you will find the footprints of advancing civilization on the floor of the sea. There the ghosts of ships, men, and drowned cities combine to give us an enduring encounter with the past. There is a bit of the "Nemo Syndrome" in all of us which carries us on the ceaseless search—the romantic voyage after our dreams and sunken treasure.

Double-edged rapier adorned by chains and coins fashioned in precious gold and silver, the symbols of Spanish colonial power in the New World. Despite three centuries of plunder, the Conquistadors failed to save their economy from ruin and billions of dollars worth of New World wealth was lost in the depths of the sea.
Photo by Rick Frehsee.

What Does Treasure Look Like?

Cast upon a lonely beach or hidden beneath the waves, the look of treasure runs extremes, from brilliant, untarnished gold disks and "money chains," to blackened silver, encrusted ceramics, and barely recognizable mounds of "rubble" that turn out to be the final resting place of a drowned ship and crew. But you can't always know the value of your find. The tiniest potshard may in the end unlock priceless secrets. There are no "insignificant" treasures.

olden "money chains" were worn by
lthy passengers enroute from the New
·ld to Spain. These were aboard the
ta Margarita, destroyed in 1622 during
·rricane in the Gulf of Mexico. Money
·ins were generally seven or more feet in
·th, with each link worth about $100 in
·ern-day dollars. Because they were
·ted in fine soft gold, it was easy to
·el" off each link in payment for goods
· services. But when the hurricane struck
· overwhelmed the galleon, the very same
·ious money chains—heavy with the
·ht of gold—drowned their owners in
· fury of the storm.
·to by Don Kincaid.

Wars have littered the ocean bottom with countless historic treasures. This Belgian-made pistol, *above,* and two live rounds of ammunition were recovered by Atlantic wreck divers from the remains of the German submarine U-853. Destroyed May 5, 1945, by American attack vessels off Block Island, within sight of Newport, Rhode Island, it was the last Nazi submarine sunk during World War II. Only a few hours earlier, the U-853 torpedoed a coal-carrying vessel, the S.S. *Blackpoint.* The pistol was discovered in its holster in the forward torpedo room more than 100 feet below the surface.
Photo by Scott Jenkins.

The awesome beauty of New World wealth
is dramatically seen in this gold and emerald
Bishop's Cross and matching ring, *right.* At
left is a golden bird of prey with an emerald
inset, probably worn on a necklace by a
wealthy Spanish traveller. These pieces were
recovered from the watery grave of the
Spanish treasure galleon *Santa Margarita,*
lost with her sister ship, the *Atocha,* in 1622
during a hurricane in the Gulf of Mexico.
These galleons are two of the richest prizes
ever recovered. After nearly two decades of
searching, they were found by Mel Fisher's
Treasure Salvors, Inc.
Photo by Don Kincaid.

A figurehead which adorned the bowsprit of an unknown vessel, probably of 18th or 19th century vintage, discovered by diver/historians off the shores of Lewes, Delaware. The anonymous wooden ship she once graced had been virtually destroyed by the waves and currents of a hostile seawater environment. The figurehead is on display at a mariner's museum in Lewes.
Photo by Scott Jenkins.

Each ship speaks with a unique voice for its era, and vessels lost beneath the sea are waiting to give us profound insights into who we are, where we came from and what the future may hold in store.

These distinctively exquisite blue and white patterned Ming Dynasty ceramic cups and bowls are part of a fabulous treasure trove recovered in 1979. The adventurous salvor and historian Burt D. Webber, Jr., found them aboard the *Nuestra Señora de la Concepción* nearly three centuries after William Phips, a trader from the Massachusetts colony, salvaged 32 tons of silver from the 1641 wreck which sank on the deadly Silver Shoals, north of the Dominican Republic. Phips became the rage of Europe, was knighted, and later named governor of the New England territory. Webber's rediscovery of the wreck was no less electrifying and made headlines around the world. In addition to the Ming ceramics, the *Concepción* was rich in silver and precious artifacts, now on display in the Dominican Republic. *Photo courtesy Burt D. Webber, Jr.*

The real value of treasure is in the eye of the beholder. This souvenir spoon, for example, recovered by sport divers from the gift shop of the sunken Italian luxury liner *Andrea Doria,* casts a spell nearly as powerful as the glint of gold. *Photo by Gary Gentile.*

Where Do You Find Treasure?

Every ocean, every sea, lake, river and stream conceals traces of human dreams and passion. Yet some treasure troves are richer than others. None was more fabulous and sanguine than the New World spoils of the Spanish Conquistadors. Between 1492, when Columbus landed in the Bahamas and proclaimed his discovery of the "Orient," and 1825, when Spanish colonialism ended in the Americas, billions of dollars in precious metals, gems and art was lost to hurricanes, pirates, human error, and fate. Treasure hunter Mel Fisher, who discovered a $400 million treasure aboard the 1622 galleon *Atocha,* 40 miles from Key West, has estimated that the Spanish lost more wealth along the old trade routes than the total of all American gold rushes combined. From Latin America to Spain, from Manila to Acapulco, the floor of the sea is paved in gold. From the warm clear Caribbean Sea to the wastes of Sable Island, a crescent of disappearing sand off Novia Scotia, the fortunes of lost empires await new ownership and care. Fortunately for most of us, most of the world's sunken treasure lies within a mile of almost any shoreline. To discover a sudden glitter in the sand is no less a thrill for its close proximity and is no less important in piecing together the complex fabric of history.

Some 40 feet below the placid surface of this tropic harbor at Charlotte Amalie, *above,* St. Thomas, in the U.S. Virgin Islands, lies an incredible storehouse of lost 17th century maritime history. Dozens of ships at anchor went to the bottom suddenly when a devastating earthquake rocked these volcanic islands three centuries ago. Today, SCUBA divers find huge mounds of artifacts, piles of ship's materials, old bottles, pottery, ceramics, weapons, and even silver bullion along the harbor's silty bottom. The Caribbean is a vast repository of such treasures, and Charlotte Amalie is only one "X" on a seemingly endless map.
Photo by Carl Purcell.

To explore the unseen highways across the floor of the world's seas and oceans is to seek the footprints of civilization through the fog of time, *left*. Seafaring was the leading edge of advancing culture, and there is hardly a body of water anywhere on the planet that does not hide the "time capsules" of human experience. Using simple SCUBA (self-contained breathing apparatus), the explorer knows that every inch of watery bottom is new territory waiting to be discovered.
Photo by Ned DeLoach.

Everyone Can Make an Important Discovery

A flash of gold in the sand, the glitter of silver beneath emerald waters, the ghostly interiors of long-lost ships—all are within your grasp. Clifford "Kip" Wagner recovered millions in Spanish treasure near his home in Vero Beach, Florida. Beachcombers still unearth coins, china, pottery, ship fittings. In fact, as there are no seas devoid of civilization, so there are no "empty beaches." Along the Outer Banks of North Carolina alone hundreds of wrecked and abandoned vessels, standing in the surfline, cast their relics onto the beach after every storm. And—if you should decide how to learn the art and science of skin and SCUBA diving, to become what Cousteau calls a "Manfish"—even more mysteries will be within your grasp.

Wreck diver Rick Jaszyn, *below,* shows off a gold leaf china dish from a shipwreck off the coast of Massachusetts. Jaszyn and other spirited sport divers are constantly exploring the vast population of shipwrecks off the coast of North America. They give the rest of us a close-up look at that mysterious commodity known as "sunken treasure," which Jaszyn and his colleagues provide in the form of unique artifacts. *Photo by Bill Campbell.*

from the deep, dark, and lonely wreck of the Italian luxury liner *Andrea Doria,* underwater photographer and explorer Gary Gentile, *above,* displays the ship's bell. The 656-foot liner collided with the S.S. *Stockholm* July 25, 1956, 55 miles south of Nantucket Island, and sank beneath more than 200 feet of cold Atlantic water. Gentile has been exploring the *Doria* for years and has recovered and displayed many of the ship's intriguing artifacts. The bell, seen here covered with growth, has been restored to original lustre and serves to bring the starred vessel back to life for divers, historians, and sea buffs everywhere. *Photo courtesy Gary Gentile.*

SCUBA diver, *left,* patiently searches through the wreckage of an unknown freighter in the crystal clear waters of the Caribbean Sea, trying to identify the coral-encrusted fragments of this nameless ship. Each fragment is a clue, and every vessel is a composite of thousands of such clues. Over time, they will be pieced together like a complex work of art to reveal the life of the long-lost ship. *Photo by Ned DeLoach.*

The Tools of Treasure

Centuries ago, Old World rulers sent their slaves diving into the sea after riches. Many ill-fated early divers used cumbersome diving bells and often wound up entombed in them. In fact, man's ability to hold his breath was the key to successful recovery of riches from the seabed. Today modern explorers use television miles below the surface, side-scan sonar that can "see" far beneath the sand, computers that give us exact coordinates and data, and multi-million dollar innerspace submersibles. Other devices, such as the "mailbox" prop-wash deflector which directs a column of surface water down to the seabed and removes tons of—*centuries* of—overburdening sand, are thought to be destructive. But more often the mailboxes and other tools of technology invented by treasure hunters—such as the Venturi airlift—are being used by even the most fastidious scholars. All such technology can be used with the delicacy of a surgeon's hand, the creativity of an artist.

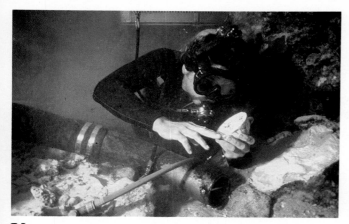

Using a venturi "airlift", *above,* —an underwater vacuum cleaner— a diver uncovers a ceramic cup from the wrecksite of the *Nuestra Señora de la Concepción,* lost in 1641 north of the Dominican Republic. The airlift removes large sections of covering coral and sand. *Photo by Burt D. Webber, Jr.*

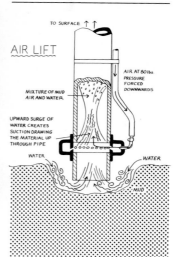

AIR LIFT

TO SURFACE ↑ ↑

AIR AT 80 lbs. PRESSURE FORCED DOWNWARDS

MIXTURE OF MUD AIR AND WATER

UPWARD SURGE OF WATER CREATES SUCTION DRAWING THE MATERIAL UP THROUGH PIPE

WATER

WATER

MUD

Diagram shows a typical underwater venturi "airlift" used to remove overburden such as sand, coral, and other debris from a buried shipwreck. Forced air from the surface creates a vacuum, pushing materials upward through the hollow tube. At the surface, airlifted debris falls into a mesh screen. Much of the debris falls through the mesh, leaving larger objects on the screen to be sifted out. Despite the force created by the vacuum, the airlift can retrieve delicate ceramics and pottery intact. While it is not a perfect solution for removing artifacts from the bottom, an experienced operator is able to use it with amazing delicacy.
Drawing by Kathryn Williams.

Ten fathoms below the sea, treasure salvor Burt D. Webber, Jr., tunes his super-sensitive cesium magnetometer, *above,* a device capable of detecting the presence of metal buried in sand or coral. Webber used the instrument with almost pinpoint accuracy in his search for the *Nuestra Señora de la Concepción* at Silver Shoals Reef. *Photo courtesy Burt D. Webber, Jr.*

A diver, *right,* photographs sections of an underwater grid at the *Atocha* site. The camera moves over the dual-tracked setup. Each photo is logged to match the grid sections to form a photomosaic of the wrecksite. *Photo by Don Kincaid.*

These formidable-looking elbow-jointed tubes, *left,* are "mailbox" prop-wash deflectors. Mounted at the stern of a dive boat, they direct clear surface water through the tubes to the ocean bottom, giving divers good visibility to carry out the intricate task of working a jumbled wrecksite. The mailboxes also can remove tons of sand and debris in short order to expose a ship's remains. Once decried as "destroyers" of fragile wrecksites, they have become standard tools of the trade and are routinely used in many underwater digs. *Photo by Daniel A. Koski-Karrell.*

Pyramids at the Bottom of the Sea

A ship on the bottom seldom reflects its days of glory. Ancient wooden vessels become piles of ballast stone, encrusted anchors, and cannons scattered on and beneath the sands. In tropical waters there are teredo worms and ever-growing coral that will obscure even the largest ships. But in the cold darkness of the deep sea are the new pyramids. In these great depths are the *Titanic,* remarkably preserved, and the ships of the Great Lakes, all in pristine condition. In the Pacific, at Pearl Harbor, Hawaii, the National Park Service has preserved the remains of the ships destroyed by the Japanese sneak attack on December 7, 1941. In the Atlantic, the National Oceanic and Atmospheric Administration (NOAA) is working to recover and preserve the famous Civil War ironclad warship, the *Monitor.* These "time capsules"—and many like them—are in our trust. We must treat them with care, respect, and our best creative talents. We cannot afford to destroy these rare and wonderful pyramids of the deep for future generations.

Innerspace explorers, *above,* use SCUBA gear to descend into the blue and head for the remains of a lost ship resting silently on the seabed. Always the mystery remains: Where did this ship come from? What happened to her crew? What forces destroyed her and plunged her into an oceanic realm far from the world "up there"—the world of sun and sky? Each lost vessel is a pyramid of the deep, a storehouse of wealth, culture and human history. These divers will turn the key to unlock these secrets and help write future history.
Photo by Dr. Robert Leahy.

text continued from page 96

"Exploration of the deep sea is not driving this technology, but it is beginning to benefit from it. The space program with its robots on Mars and Venus, the military with its desire to remove humans from the risks of combat, and the commercial world with [its] evolving television coverage and the proliferation of multiple cinemas, are the driving forces of tele-presence technology.

"I strongly believe that if *Titanic* is left alone that within the next few years, beginning as early as [1986], robotic vehicles will be able to enter its beautifully-designed rooms and document in color its preserved splendor. No salvage operation in the world could duplicate this feat.

"*Titanic* is just one such example. The question is, will we come to plunder or to appreciate? This is a debate which grows louder, not quieter. Technologists, like myself, can only cause this problem and suggest its possible impact. But Congress must take the necessary actions and, in my case, hopefully before the *Titanic* is destroyed."

Parting Shots

In the last analysis, the treasure wars are not a simplistic dogfight between archaeologists and treasure hunters. It would be ideal, in my view, if full-time treasure hunters, or salvors, worked more often with full-time archae-ologists. They have much to learn from each other, and together they have the power to advance the frontiers of technology and scholarship. There is a great deal of history entombed in shipwrecks. Only through a creative compromise between the factions of treasure warriors will it be brought to light—responsibly and safely—before it is consumed by looters and the sea.

One can't ignore the fact that between the treasure salvor and the archaeologist exists a vast middle ground. It is here, among the serious amateurs, that enormous resources can be tapped. In the past it has been the paraprofessional amateur who has been at the leading edge of ship-wreck survey, recovery, and preservation, and who in the past has led the professionals to that spot on the map marked with the mysterious "X."

Archaeologists and technologists, such as Dr. Ballard, can call on large sums of tax dollars or grant monies to continue their explorations. But surely we can't limit the road to discovery to those few avenues. Nor can we arbitrarily brand all amateurs as looters. It simply isn't true. The name-calling is only another sad manifestation of the fighting over turf. And this is what the treasure wars are really all about—the right to go in search of the unknown. Archaeologist Bass assures us that new nautical archaeologists are being produced at a prodigious rate, yet we know we can't produce enough of them in this century for the overwhelming task at hand. It seems naive to assume, too, that one generation will be content to pass over the possibility of making the new discoveries now within our grasp and leave them to succeeding generations.

Further, the acceptance of such an idea leads inevitably to a waste of talent and resources. We refuse to waste talent in medicine, physics, astronomy, biology; why waste the talents of those who possess the skills and desire to pursue the search for the sunken treasures of the past?

It's a distortion to argue that one does not seek the aid of "amateur dentists" or "amateur brain surgeons," and therefore we shouldn't seek the aid of "amateur archaeologists." The truth is that nautical archaeologists are amateurs, too, pursuing an infant discipline, and hoping to impose the scientific method on it through trial and error. The grand field manual of underwater archaeology has yet to be written, and it is ironic that the most prolific writer and worker in the field is Robert Marx, a self-taught marine archaeologist. The so-called amateurs, in fact, have added a dozen or more titles for every book written by a Ph.D. And for every grant-funded or tax-funded dig there are dozens being paid for by amateurs out of their own pockets. These digs are not conducted for loot; they are contributions to history driven by adventure and curiosity. So far, they've contributed the bulk of knowledge we have gained from the sea.

This by no means diminishes the labors of the professional archaeologists. I wish there were more of them, and that they were able to get out into the field more often. But at this juncture, late in the 20th century, we're coming to grips with the realities of historical research. We find ourselves at the threshold of a challenge every bit as awesome in scope as the exploration of our solar system. It should be remembered that the first men to walk on the surface of the moon were not scientists; they were military test pilots who taught us a great deal about space and raw human courage. Given the enormity of the sea, it will take as many hands as there are available to get on with this challenge. To legislate these hands out of existence would be a mistake that would only leave future generations poorer.

A New Awareness

The conflict between archaeologists and treasure hunters raises serious questions about how we will write history in the future. No one disputes the place of archaeology and anthropology and the attempts to apply science to the study of submerged cultural resources. Archaeology in the sea is only a quarter-century old, but already it has become the leading edge of future history—a new frontier of awareness.

This awareness, however, is not without its problems. It presents a kind of moral spreadsheet which requires careful attention.

If you are thinking of participating in the search for sunken history—the real riches to be found—you must be aware of the unsettling realities of the treasure wars. If you believe this kind of sleuthing may be for you, ask yourself the following questions:

- Am I doing it for the right reasons or am I just after the goodies?
- Am I aware that underwater sites are fragile and must be handled with utmost care, so that future generations may enjoy them?
- Will my children and grandchildren be proud of what I have accomplished in my searches of the sea?

Positive answers may indicate that you are on track, and that, hopefully, you will approach your explorations as you would a garden—with care and an open heart. After that, you should know the law as it applies to your quest, get professional input if possible, and head into the blue with a clear conscience.

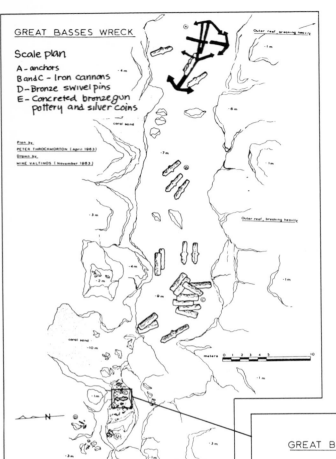

GREAT BASSES WRECK

Scale plan

A - anchors
B and C - Iron cannons
D - Bronze swivel pins
E - Concreted bronze gun
     pottery and silver coins

Plan by,
PETER THROCKMORTON (April 1963)
Drawn by,
MIKE VALTINOS (November 1963)

MAP A

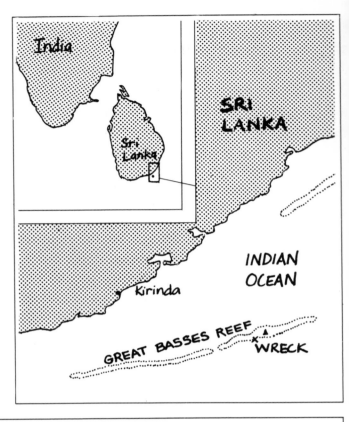

India

SRI LANKA

Sri Lanka

INDIAN OCEAN

Kirinda

GREAT BASSES REEF

WRECK

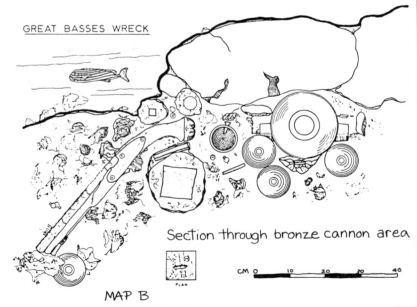

GREAT BASSES WRECK

Section through bronze cannon area

CM 0   10   20   30   40

PLAN

MAP B

The Plan of the Great Basses Reef Wreck: Throckmorton and others became bored with the recovery of Mogul silver and began to make a systematic plan of the wreck site. The "Silver Gully" in Map A shows the reef on both sides with cannons and anchors. Tremendous surge ripped through the gully, making the workday short and mostly frustrating.

In Map B, a cross-section of materials is revealed.

Maps courtesy of Peter Throckmorton.

PART TWO

Casting Off:
How To Get Started

Draped in golden Spanish "money chains" (each link in a seven-foot strand valued at several hundred dollars) a SCUBA diver glories in the sun. He has come a long way and done a lot of painstaking homework to be so "lucky." What do you have in common with the man in the picture? Are you one of the select who will go beyond the pages of this book and into the fantasy realm of treasure?
Photo by Don Kincaid.

CHAPTER FIVE

Your Personal Treasure Profile

The single most important development in the treasure field over the past 25 years—aside from improved undersea technology—has been the emergence of paraprofessional explorers. Members of this group, estimated to number as many as two million worldwide, have discovered 99 percent of all historic shipwrecks, and they have done so absent a profit motive and often at great personal sacrifice.

Today's paraprofessionals are ordinary citizens with extraordinary ambition, drive, and devotion. They represent a cross-section of skills, vocations, education, and economic backgrounds. They are teachers, engineers, secretaries, lawyers, SCUBA divers, conservationists, computer experts, physicians, mechanics, politicians, and artists. Born of the aqualung revolution, this group is every bit as serious as the full-time treasure hunters and far outnumber *working* marine archaeologists, of which there are fewer than 25 in the United States. They are devoted—often avid—researchers who support their own efforts and produce first-rate results.

"They have an interest in doing right," says Charles M. McKinney, former manager of the Federal Antiquities Program at the U.S. Department of Interior. "They do the research, organize, explore. And when you think of what a big job we have ahead of us in the cultural and historical aspects of the ocean, you realize that it's much too big to be left to a tiny group of 'experts.' The paraprofessional has made a measurable impact on our knowledge—and that is going to continue to be very important in the future."

The paraprofessionals often work with local historical societies and conservation groups, waterfront committees, and other organizations involved in maritime history. Their contributions can be seen in virtually every museum in the world. They stage film festivals and traveling exhibits, excavate rivers and harbors, and generally keep up a steady drum beat of publicity. Their enthusiasm equals their output, which is voluminous. Especially productive are the hundreds of shipwreck diving clubs, such as The Boston Sea Rovers, The California Wreck Divers Association, and The Atlantis Rangers, which meets monthly at the University of Maryland at College Park. Generally, these clubs focus on World War I and World War II vintage vessels, as well as a scattering of truly historic ships dating back a century or more. I know from first-hand experience that a group like The Atlantis Rangers can boggle the mind of even the most accomplished maritime historians and put on a display of artifacts worthy of any museum. Critics of these organizations say they are destroying valuable "time capsules" that are better left alone until such time as a real expert, presumably equipped with a water-proof Ph.D., arrives on the scene during this generation or the next, with grant money in hand.

This issue will be taken up again later, and for the moment I prefer to address it by telling of an experience I had early in my oceanic career. We were diving on a classic intact wreck, the *Papoose,* a 600-foot merchant vessel torpedoed in 1943, by a German U-boat lurking in the Gulf Stream off the coast of North Carolina. The *Papoose* was not yet historic and was properly considered a modern vessel. Still, as we swam along her sadly naked hull 120 feet down, it occurred to me that one day she would be a true relic as rare as any galleon. I had been working on a brass dog on one of the portholes, hoping to take it back home with me as a reminder of the ship and its tragic role in the sea, when a little voice inside whispered, "No! Let it be. Let it pass into history."

At 120 feet, a diver has little time for contemplation before having to ascend to the surface. My dive buddy, noticing my hesitation, wrote on his white underwater slate: "*Don't you want it?*" I shook my head negatively. My buddy scribbled on the slate again and showed it to me: "*If you don't take it, the sea will!*" I realized he was right. The site of the *Papoose* was five hours running offshore; she was very vulnerable, very obscure, and my pangs of conscience about taking the brass dog were silly and perhaps a little arrogant. I gave my buddy the diver's "okay" signal, a circle formed by the index finger and thumb, quickly removed the dog, and headed for the surface. As I write this years later, I realize that the *Papoose* is still out there, a little deeper in the sand, a little more obscure, rusting away slowly. In a century or so we will both be long gone. But for years to come I can look at the brass dog and remember, show it to others who will wonder, and in this small paraprofessional way I have preserved a tiny sliver of history.

More Than Money

Those adventurous souls who dream of discovering gold and silver at first find themselves in the bizarre green shadow of greed. This is to be expected. Visions of dark treasure chests overflowing with loot, vast stretches of ocean bottom paved with gold, the flash of jewels at the base of a tropical coral reef—all are tantalizing magnets that spark the imagination. Yet, in most people who search for history, the almost overwhelming and seductive power of pure riches gives way to a deeper—some would say higher—instinct. It might be misleading to generalize on the precise nature of this instinct, except to note that it operates within most treasure hunters. Whatever it may be reaches out to us from some inner well of awareness that has never entertained the notion of cashing in at the bank.

Consider the case of famed cinematographer Peter Gimbel, who in 1981, recovered the Bank of Rome safe from the ill-fated Italian luxury liner, *Andrea Doria*.

Twenty-seven years earlier, only 24 hours after the *Doria* sank to the bottom of the Atlantic on July 26, 1956, after a collision with the liner *Stockholm* 40 miles south of Nantucket Island, Gimbel raced to the scene, cameras in hand, prepared to record the tragedy which lay on the sea bed more than 200 feet below the Atlantic's swells. This area of the ocean is known to modern mariners as "Times Square," because it's a section of the commercial shipping lanes dangerously congested with ocean-going traffic. The *Doria* herself was (and still is) a deep and exceedingly perilous dive; recovering any of her treasure, which was said to be substantial, presented a truly death-defying task. A man of great means, related to the New York family that founded the department store that bears his family name, Gimbel seemingly had little to gain by risking his life. Yet with complete sincerity he spoke of recovering the treasures locked inside the wreck. His initial dive produced only motion picture footage—and not a lot of it. The *Doria* was in agony, groaning, shifting, badly leaking her life's blood—thick black oil.

Shortly after Gimbel's initial exploration, famed ocean explorer

Jacques-Yves Cousteau brought his hardened crew of *Calypso* divers to the site. They quickly sized up the risks. The *Doria* was deep, dark, and cold, and still leaking oil—a death trap. Cousteau was happy to leave her for other more hearty, or foolish, explorers. Over the years, I have received various invitations to explore the ship, none of which I would dream of accepting. Two friends who did accept were crippled by the bends and I recently learned that yet another brave diver among many has given up his life there.

But the *Doria* was a magnet for Gimbel. So was her treasure. He visited the ship many times and eventually produced a television documentary, "The Mystery of the *Andrea Doria,*" which aired in 1975. It sought to explain why this "unsinkable" liner went down while the *Stockholm* survived and limped into port in New York. He speculated, somewhat tentatively, that the *Doria*'s water-tight doors lacked integrity. The documentary was interesting but inconclusive.

Gimbel is an incredibly persistent man who spent two years filming *Blue Water White Death,* his classic treatment of the great white shark. But it was more than persistence that kept him coming back to the *Doria.* He experienced at least one serious diving accident during one of his forays, but now his New York publicists were claiming he had his eye on more than a million dollars in cash inside the Bank of Rome safe, and perhaps another million or so in cash and jewels in the first-class purser's safe. The idea of getting at these safes, buried somewhere deep inside a huge vessel that was by now collapsing in on itself, was at once hair-raising and unreal. The cost of getting to the safes inside the black jumble ·of the wreck was unknown, but certainly it was proportionate to the degree of risk, which was very high. Even if recovered, the fragile paper currency would be mostly pulp, and there was the matter of taxes, attorney's fees, and claims by the ship's owners and insurance companies. In the end, it would wind up costing a lot more than could ever be recovered. Still, talk of the *Doria* treasure was constantly in the news.

In 1981, Gimbel decided to make another, more conclusive, television special, "*Andrea Doria:* The Final Chapter." He departed Montauk Point, New York in June aboard the 180-foot oil exploration ship, *Sea Level II,* with his wife and partner, Elga Anderson, and a large crew. The ship was equipped with a deep water diving bell, a deck decompression chamber, and an underwater habitat that would allow the divers to spend long periods of time actually living and working on the wreck.

During the filming *Sea Level II* weathered two hurricanes; one of them threatened to send the vessel to the bottom to join the *Doria*. Working conditions were grim. By now the wreck was wrapped in layers of dangerous fish nets that constantly threatened to snare the divers. Subsurface currents were severe, and at one point photographer Nick Caloyianis was swept off the hull and onto the sand, well out of sight of the wreck.

"I was on the sand, and it was dark," he recalls. "I had no idea where the wreck was. I was completely lost."

Underwater visibility was extremely poor. Caloyianis could barely see his hand in front of his face mask. He groped through the murk, talking into the tiny microphone inside his mask—his connection to the crew on the surface. His air hose was trailing out of sight; at any moment it might be fouled, trapping him and perhaps cutting off his air supply. After a long, nerve-jarring period of being slowly guided by the surface tender, he at last made it back to the wreck.

"Nothing about the *Doria* was ever easy," he says.

The divers hired by Gimbel from Oceaneering International miraculously recovered the long-sought Bank of Rome safe. The first-class purser's safe remains inside the wreck to this day.

Meanwhile, Gimbel wanted answers to his questions about the *Doria*'s mortality. Led by a diver who used an acetylene torch, Gimbel penetrated 130 feet inside the twisted bowels of the wreck and entered the generator room. There he found a massive breach in the hull. Any further talk of a lack of integrity of the water-tight doors as a primary cause of the sinking became ludicrous. When he swam to the upper levels above the promenade deck he found nothing but a huge void. The entire superstructure—the upper decks above the hull—had fallen away onto the sea bed.

Gimbel, in a masterful stroke of public relations, decided to store the safe in the shark tank at the New York Aquarium. It would not be opened, he announced, until his "Final Chapter" documentary was aired. Part of the show would include the opening of the safe on live network television. In the meantime, the sharks in the tank would watch over the treasure, rumored to have cost about $3 million to recover.

True to the tradition of treasure, snags developed. The television producers who had encouraged Gimbel to produce the film had second thoughts. The documentary went through several edits. And, with each day that passed, the treasure inside the safe seemed to grow smaller and smaller in everyone's mind, especially Gimbel's. The contents were free of insurance claims, but only Gimbel knew how much this adventure had cost in real dollars.

Treasure in the Rain

At last, the documentary was set to air in 1984, nearly three years since Gimbel left Montauk with high hopes. To promote the film he made several public appearances, talked about treasure and danger and why he did it in the first place. For some reason, he appeared a little sad, a little pensive, but his quick smile and sharp wit saved him on more than one occasion.

The documentary received a big build up and George Plimpton was retained to host the show. The safe had been removed from the shark tank and placed outside the aquarium in a huge retaining vat filled with water. Using his best *You Are There* style, Plimpton told the audience what was on the bill. At the end of the show, he said, the world would gaze in astonishment at real treasure—treasure to be revealed tonight, on network television.

I'm no film critic, but I can tell when something has been hacked to pieces. This appeared to be the case with "Final Chapter." The two-hour show was given the effect of a flashing light in a darkened room by cutting away from painfully-edited short segments of film and back live to Plimpton, whose job it was to get the audience excited about the safe. George Plimpton is a writer I have always admired. He is a publisher of great courage, and a man who for the sake of a story sparred several rounds with a former boxing champion, Archie Moore. But this night, his considerable charisma was severely tested.

The documentary ended. Plimpton was back on camera. The skies opened up and dumped rain on the crowd which had gathered around the holding vat. Plimpton opened an umbrella; rain dripped from Gimbel's thick gray eyebrows while a couple of husky assistants attempted to open the safe. It was harder to do than anyone had anticipated and the show was in danger of running overtime—actually being cut off before the grand finale, the treasure. Gimbel was smiling, Elga Anderson was smiling, and Plimpton reassured viewers. "It's coming. Yes, any moment now. Yes, we're getting it . . ."

At last the television camera peered into the dark cavern of the opened safe. Almost everyone had expected to immediately see the glint of gold, the flash of rubies. Instead, amorphous gray matter issued forth, perhaps the remains of ordinary paper. "Careful," Gimbel warned his assistants as the rain increased in intensity.

It seemed like an hour had passed when the gray amorphous stuff ended and the bills appeared. Italian lira! Soggy Italian lira! And soggy U.S. Silver Certificates! Hardly the price of the safe, and no fortune on any currency market. Gimbel was happy—and terribly relieved.

In the fall of 1985, as I began this book, I was informed that I could buy one of those lira notes, price strictly negotiable. Gimbel, it seems, had dried them out and had them individually encased in plastic. A little legend went with each note telling where it came from.

This story, intended to applaud Gimbel's indomitable spirit, illustrates a point stated earlier—that the search for treasure is always about something other than money. It certainly was true for Gimbel. It was the *Doria* herself that obsessed him, that fired his curiosity and his insatiable need to find out what happened in the final moments of her life. Though he always justified his adventures on a business level, Peter Gimbel, in truth, is another seafaring poet, moved by his own inner visions and secrets.

Because It's There

Like Gimbel, most treasure hunters believe that they're going to win despite the long odds facing them. But what will they win? I have known perfectly sincere and intelligent people to follow an obvious dead end because:

1. They could not decide what it was they wanted to win.
2. They refused to let go of their faith that, indeed, there was a pot of gold at the end of the phony treasure map they were following.

The unhappy fact is that no treasure map is real. If it were, its owners wouldn't be offering it for sale. Cousteau once said that virtually all the money made in the treasure business comes after a few drinks and the passing of dollars hand-to-hand across a desk. This is a bit cynical but Cousteau went well out of his way to prove the point. His *Calypso* team wasted an entire summer working an alleged treasure wreck in the Caribbean. The fruits of this labor were a living coral reef destroyed by his divers, a few ho-hum artifacts, and a warning to all that an alleged treasure wreck very often is a wreck salvaged soon after sinking by its owners and crew; its treasure had already passed into legend. The *Calypso* divers were annoyed, but the "Pasha" Cousteau was pleased. *He knew what he wanted to win.*

And he cleverly made another point. As his divers worked harder and turned up less, they became irritable, easily annoyed, disgruntled. They also became greedier. Instead of working together consistently, they went off on tangents, dooming themselves to failure.

Successful treasure hunters work together and share everything. This is a safety valve. It neutralizes greed. And when enough is enough, they know how to back off. They say to themselves, "Yes, the thing I am seeking is worth a lot to me. But it isn't worth as much as my life." After a while one comes to understand that the sea has her own needs and always wants to keep something for herself, even in the face of the most determined treasure hunter. To miss this point is to beg disaster.

CHAPTER SIX

What's Down There: An Inventory

Long before our prehistoric ancestors learned how to live together in primitive villages 30,000 years ago, they were bravely venturing out across rivers and lakes in crude vessels. And having learned that it was occasionally possible to get safely from one shore to another, they took even bolder steps across water: they confronted the seas and oceans that cover more than 70 percent of the Earth's surface. From the very beginning they left their traces hidden in the mountains and plains of the oceanic world. These traces—in the form of boats and men—are still down there waiting to be discovered.

Archaeologists have only scratched the surface. Seafaring has always been on the leading edge of advancing civilization and commerce, but the trail is well hidden. Modern technology has given us a start at tracing it, and in the past quarter century we have begun to uncover many long lost mysteries.

In December, 1984, archaeologists from Texas A&M University uncovered a Bronze Age cargo ship in the Mediterranean Sea off the coast of Turkey. The 3,400-year-old ship is the oldest ever to be excavated. Like virtually every important shipwreck ever discovered, it was spotted by an amateur, in this case a Turkish sponge diver who subsequently told an American archaeologist working in the area that he'd seen an object on the bottom resembling "a bisquit with ears." The archaeologist asked the diver to draw a picture of the object. The result was something that looked very much like a copper ingot, the type known to have been produced in ancient Cyprus. The ship sailed before the Greeks waged the Trojan War; it was carrying cargos of copper across the Mediterranean when Tutankhamen ruled Egypt.

The excavation has so far produced one of the richest historical troves ever found in the sea. A golden goblet has been found on board, and a piece of jewelry in the shape of a bird of prey; it may have been part of a necklace. Amber and faience beads were recovered nearby in water ranging in depth from 145 to 175 feet, about 75 yards off Cape Ula Burun, near the town of Kas. Explorers also found an elephant tusk and a hippopotamus tooth, both forms of ivory used by the ancients. Inside of amphoras were glass beads, an arsenic compound, and a variety of seeds. Divers also found a small personal seal which might have been used by a merchant to stamp correspondence. What a spellbinding encounter with the past, and how lucky we are to view it.

As wondrous as this find may be, it is only an indication of what still awaits us. If archaeologists concentrated on the Americas alone, they'd spend many lifetimes tracing the identities of the ancients who landed here. For example, there is evidence that the Chinese voyaged to America 1,000 years before Columbus. There are written records that indicate that a Chinese Buddhist missionary returned to the court in Peking to report having discovered a land he called "Fu-Sang," 17,000 miles away—the width of the North Pacific. At this writing, divers on the West Coast are searching for the remains of a Chinese vessel said to be lost off the shores of Oregon.

Thor Heyerdahl, in *American Indians in the Pacific,* makes a case for the Indians of the North Pacific being carried by the currents southward along the coast of California, then powered westward by prevailing winds and currents toward Hawaii. Some of the largest dugout canoes ever found in Hawaii are made of Douglas fir, a tree not found on those islands but abundant in the Pacific Northwest. This appears to strengthen the case for the Chinese discoveries. Scholars also have come across evidence that around 3,000 B.C. the Chinese taught the American Indians to make pottery.

Dr. Barry Fell, a Harvard University professor, believes that Celtic mariners crossed the Atlantic about 3,000 years ago from Spain or Portugal, settled in the New England area, and later migrated as far west as Oklahoma. In his book, *America B.C.,* Fell shows that many of the ancient stone buildings in New England, once believed to be of no historical importance, are actually Celtic temples and observatories. He found that an inscription on a strange stone building discovered in 1780, near Mount Hope Bay, Rhode Island, was written in a language called "Tartessian Punic." It says: "Voyagers from Tarhish this stone proclaims." Tarhish is a seaport mentioned in the Bible believed to have been located on the south coast of Spain. Another inscription, found on Monhegan Island, 10 miles off the coast of Maine, reveals a "Celtic ogam" that says: "Cargo Platforms for the Ships from Phoenicia."

Of more recent vintage is speculation that Saint Brendan the Abbot sailed to America with a group of seafaring Irish monks sometime before 600 A.D. Historians believe that Brendan and his crew sailed aboard a 36-foot boat made of wood and leather, a vessel designed to "breathe" with the pounding waves. Brendan was in search of *Terra Repromissionis Sanctorum*, "The Land Promised to the Saints."

These and many more speculations abound. If only we could find a Chinese junk or the remains of Saint Brendan's leather ship. But so far, the sea has yielded nothing. Proof lies somewhere beneath the waves, and sooner or later we're going to find it.

Time Capsules in the Sea

From a scientific and historical perspective the finding of a shipwreck is like no other discovery. Sunken vessels represent a moment in time, a frozen instant of calamity. Each reflects almost completely the society from which it came—a microcosm of life sealed away until we come upon it. With good reason, shipwrecks are sometimes referred to as "time capsules." On land, antiquities are subjected to the ravages of wind, rain, and erosion, and the most serious threat of all, the looter. But ships undisturbed on the bottom of the sea are locked away in an airless environment, preserved like a portrait behind hermetically sealed glass.

Only a few years ago our best scientists believed that the sea was a kind of gigantic disposal. We were taught that the seabed was a lifeless, featureless void, and that everything down there was destroyed by the corrosive properties of seawater. By accident we discovered that just the opposite is true. In 1968, the research submarine *Alvin* was under tow when a cable parted and the vessel sank in 5,500 feet of water off Cape Cod. Lunch boxes were lashed to the sub. Some months later *Alvin* was recovered, lunch boxes still in place. When the scientists inspected the contents, which included meats, bread, vegetables, and sweets, they were pretty soggy—but edible. They had been marvelously preserved in the cold, airless cradle of the deep. The message of *Alvin* was that the deep ocean is a great conservator.

To understand what happens when a ship goes down, imagine being adrift when the vessel begins to break up and sink. You look over the wave tops and see that she is damaged and listing; wind and waves deliver terrible blows, accounting for a greater portion of the damage. Then comes the long slide to the bottom. On the way down the air spaces are crushed by water pressure. Falling through a medium eight times denser than air, loose objects float away, and the ship begins to lose some of its identity as it continues to break up. If your ear is beneath the surface you can actually hear the sound of the ship dying, a sound you're likely never to forget. It is a mournful wail, like the voice of a lone whale in the deep ocean. World War II submariners claimed they heard their victims sinking through the hull of their submarine; they say a steel hull crushed by water pressure "screams" like dissonant violins; a wooden ship is softer, but no less forbidding. The fidelity of the sound is remarkable and it comes from all directions simultaneously, since water conducts sound five times more efficiently and clearly than air.

Ships impact the bottom moving at 30 to 60 miles per hour. The superstructure (deck cabins, masts, rigging, and all decks above the hull) tears away from the ship's hull and will eventually topple over into the sand. The entire catastrophe sounds like a muffled kettle drum. Any cannons on deck will settle into the sand, or fall backward into the hull. The site will be marked by scattered patterns of cannons, anchors, and other heavy objects.

The ship will begin to stabilize in its new environment. A few more objects will fall off the existing structures and form strange shapes on the sand. Heavy cargo will work through the hull as gravity pulls it into the bottom. Years pass. A century later, a wooden ship has become only a suggestion of her former self. She sinks deep in the sand. In tropical areas, living corals will grow over every inch of exposed metal. If she lies in shallow water, say 30 feet or less, currents, surge, hurricanes, and man will work on her with their combined fury. In time, the ship may be scattered over miles of bottom, but the mother lode—the bulk of her cargo— generally remains in place, sinking ever deeper, like a glowing diamond returning to its sources deep in the earth.

Yet despite the hostile environment of the sea, where teredo worms can make a meal of a wooden ship in just a few years, the ship holds her own. Deep water seems to protect a sunken vessel, keeping her structure intact. Cold water, too, is a great preserver. Though scientists now say the victims of the *Titanic* were long ago consumed by sea creatures, I believe it is more likely that they are in a state of preservation that may rival Egyptian mummies. Those with a grisly curiosity can witness this for themselves in the cold waters of the Great Lakes, where the victims of the merchant ship *Kamloops* remain entombed nearly a century after sinking, their soft tissues still intact.

Even tropical seas have been kind to sunken ships on occasion. In waters that are warm and thick with teredo worms, or ship borers, archaeologists and treasure hunters have recovered ships' logs made of delicate paper. Seeds found on wrecks in the Mediterranean have been planted and have borne fruit—centuries after sinking into the sea. Leather, timbers, and even foodstuffs have survived.

No matter what the water temperature, a shipwreck properly exhumed is a history book and a museum all in one. It is this single remarkable fact that makes sunken treasure of any form such a rare and illuminating cultural resource.

The British Sub-Aqua Club, with the British government and private investors, recently raised large portions of the 1545 Tudor carrack, *Mary Rose,* flagship of King Henry VIII. Her recovery off Portsmouth revealed a cross-section of Anglo-Saxon society: silver flatware for the officers of the vessel, rude wooden "trenchers" for the men; gaming boards used by the officers; and arrows still ready to fire, proving that Henry insisted that his crack bowmen use their talents at sea as well as on land. The *Mary Rose* came back to life after centuries on the bottom—a true ghost of the past, but a tangible one.

Whole vessels have been found intact, such as the *Vasa,* a 64-gun Swedish warship which capsized and sank in 1628, in Stockholm Harbor, carrying more than 50 crewmen and passengers to the bottom on her maiden voyage. She was recovered in April, 1961, by a team of salvage experts.

Generally, salvage of an intact wooden ship is impossible after it has been on the bottom for more than 50 years because the timbers are eaten by shipworms. Fortunately, Stockholm Harbor is one of the few places in the world where there are no shipworms. Swedish Navy divers, directed by petroleum engineer Anders Franzen, found *Vasa* deep in the mud. They removed loose objects, then blasted tunnels beneath the wreck using water jets—a very dangerous undertaking because the ship, which displaced 1,400 tons, could have easily shifted and crushed them. Steel lifting cables were inserted under the hull and, using the cables and pontoons, the *Vasa* was lifted to the surface, towed to dry dock, and placed on a special concrete barge equipped with sprinklers to keep her wet until she could be properly treated for preservation. Inside the vessel, researchers found sea chests, boots, tools, beer steins, and weapons. Lying among the cannon carriages, Franzen found a dozen partially-clad skeletons; one wore a sheath knife and a leather money pouch, containing 20 coins, clipped to a belt around his waist.

More recently, we have seen the eerie intact remains of the U.S. gunboats, *Hamilton* and *Scourge,* lost in deep water in Lake Ontario near Niagara Falls, New York, during the War of 1812. In 1982, the National Geographic Society used the cameras of a diving robot to photograph these two vessels standing upright on the bottom, guns in place, swords scattered across the deck beside the remains of the crews.

Even more awesome in its state of preservation is H.M.S. *Breadalbane,* a British barque, built in Glasgow in 1843. This 123-foot vessel and its crew of 21 were dispatched from England in one of the greatest rescue attempts ever assembled—a constant convoy of ships and men sent from England to the Arctic in search of two lost ships, *Erebus* and *Terror.* In August 1853, *Breadalbane* was at Beechy Island north of Baffin Island in the Northwest Passage when ice closed in, shearing away her bottom and sinking her in 330 feet of water. In 1980, famed Arctic explorer, Dr. Joseph McInnis, after three years of searching, found *Breadalbane* upright and intact. "Everything is nearly the way it was when she went down," Dr. McInnis says. "Historians will love it, as will anyone who has ever wondered exactly what it was like aboard a ship that probed the Arctic more than a century ago."

An Inventory

A great riddle remains: How many ships are waiting for us beneath the world's seas and oceans? And, putting aside for the moment intangible historical values, can we make a reasonable estimate of their monetary values?

Unfortunately, these questions may never be fully answered. Shipping records are limited and those prior to 1900 tend to be extremely scanty and not altogether reliable. Advanced technology may one day give us a better inventory than we now possess, and hopefully someone will think it sufficiently important to actually do the necessary research—a job that will encompass many years and many separate disciplines. In the meantime, we can piece together an outline of the community of lost ships.

Prior to the advent of modern navigational gear at the turn of the century, worldwide ship losses averaged 1,000 to 2,000 a year. Modern electronic navigational devices have cut the annual losses significantly. Figures are based upon sinkings of relatively big ships—those of 100 tons or more. To get an idea of what a 100-ton ship looks like, recall the wooden-hulled World War II torpedo boat, or the 50- to 65-foot motor yachts at the local marina. Most boats are a lot smaller, apparently too small for record-keeping purposes, and we can only guess at how many of those have disappeared.

John Jedrlinic, a U.S. Navy historian, says pre-1900 sinkings were epidemic. With its flair for war, Europe destroyed its navies as if they were cheap playthings. In 1822, for example, at a high point of the Napoleonic conflicts, more than 2,000 ships were lost in those bloody European waters. "There's no way to get exact totals," says Jedrlinic. But, indications are that during France's siege of the high seas between 1781 and 1822, 20,000 sailors were lost.

Wars always add greatly to the ever-growing inventory of lost ships. Dr. Robert Scheina, official U.S. Coast Guard historian, says Allied naval forces lost 6,000 vessels in World War I and more than twice that number in World War II. To place some economic value on these statistics, Scheina suggests that if we could have salvaged all the oil tankers lost during World War II, we would have had more than enough reserves to overcome the 1973–74 Arab oil embargo.

Since the end of the war, losses have been reduced to about 250 ships annually, even with vastly improved radar and safety gear. As for the continued loss of smaller vessels, "the number is at least ten times greater," Scheina says.

Not even the venerable marine insurance company Lloyds of London knows the full extent or value of the world's lost ships. It's necessary to piece together reports and personal accounts, in different languages and in different lands, to trace the outline of the inventory.

There are as many ways to judge the worth of sunken vessels as there are vessels on the bottom. They carried cargos of every imaginable commodity, from coffee to gold bars, to the tons of precious mercury used by German naval architects to ballast their U-boats. Most ships qualify for insurance payouts, and salvage claims amount to billions of dollars annually. But the so-called "treasure wrecks"—both old and new—are the stuff of which fantasy and fortune are made.

British marine historian Rex Cowan estimates that there are 250,000 potential treasure sites pre-dating 1900 in the waters around England. There may be twice or three times that number along the Mediterranean coastline. Cowan agrees with Captain Nemo, who said there is more wealth at the bottom of the sea than there ever was or will be on dry land.

'Wrecks on top of Wrecks'

In America, marine archaeologists have come to a general agreement that there are a minimum of 100,000 pre-1900 wrecks in American waters. Don Kincaid, an underwater photographer who has spent more than two decades photographing and searching out treasure, believes there is a wreck every quarter mile—"wrecks on top of wrecks"—from Florida to the Canadian border. "Every marina, every boat yard, every bay and inlet, riverside dock and jetty has wrecks piled on top of wrecks," Kincaid says.

Kincaid and others who patiently search beneath the sea must determine which of these are important and valuable: "I could spend my whole life working wrecks between Key West and Miami and I probably wouldn't scratch the surface."

Measuring Market Values

What magnitude of resources or wealth do these vessels represent? Again, there is no precise measure. Mel Fisher believes that the loss of gold mined in Spain's New World colonies may equal all the gold mined during the Klondike and California gold rushes combined. This is a mind-boggling claim, yet consider the fact that the artifacts recovered from the *Atocha* and the *Santa Margarita* have been appraised at astonishingly high levels. A bosun's pipe has been appraised at $120,000, and there are seven-foot "money chains" with each of its gold links worth about $52, exclusive of the antiquity value.

Rex Cowan, working in England, has helped in the recovery of equally fabulous troves. When I interviewed Cowan in 1984, he spoke of the recovery of 350,000 silver coins from the Dutch East India ship, *Hollandia,* which wrecked in 1743 off Sicily, near Cornwall. His work on the *Campen,* lost off the Isle of Wight in 1627, produced 8,000 silver coins. On today's market, each coin is worth about $350. "As you can see, when you start multiplying, the figures are staggering," he says.

Cowan admits that the value of any treasure depends on many factors, such as the quality of the objects, rarity, demand, and a dozen other intangibles. "Frankly, there is no way to assign absolute value to any-thing," he says. "The only fairly good measure is in the precious metals, and their 'melt-down' value. This means that conceivably we can melt the coins into a sizable brick and sell it on the bullion market. But, depending on your dealer and the conditions of the markets, the worth of precious metals can be discounted 40 percent or more." He reached into his pocket and placed a Pillar Dollar on the table. Minted by the Spanish, it was the first silver dollar to be used in the Americans. "There are a lot of these around," Cowan explains. "Every coin dealer and every museum in the world has scads of them. So it's not rarity we're dealing with. It's just the fact that this coin came up from the sea after a very long time. There is a challenge connected to it, a mystique. You don't destroy such things. If anything, you highlight them for what they are, and they are not, strictly specking, monetary units."

A number of researchers have attempted to place values on the trea-sure lost along major trade routes. For instance, John S. Potter, Jr., in his classic *The Treasure Diver's Guide* (Bonanza Books), gives us the following figures. Potter calculated these values in 1960, when gold was just $32 per ounce. It's now worth ten times that. Silver too, has risen from slightly more than $1 to more than $6 per-troy-ounce. There's evidence that Pot-ter's figures were conservative, even in 1960, and there may be far more treasure in these areas than he listed:

- Spanish armadas—Peru to Spain via Cape Horn (1500–1820): $8 billion carried, $400 million lost
- Peru Merchantmen—Peru to Spain via Cape Horn (1534–1810): $2 billion carried, $50 million lost
- Manila galleons—Acapulco to the Philippines (1570–1815): $1 billion carried, $50 million lost
- The Spice Route—Europe and the Far East (1502–1870): $2 billion carried, $50 million lost

Robert F. Marx gives a remarkable round-up of lost vessels in his classic work, *Shipwrecks of the Americas* (Bonanza Books). This huge reference book, covering the years from 1492 to 1825, is an excellent starting point from which to categorize and assess the value of lost ships. He documents 3,125 ship losses, from Columbus' flagship *Santa Maria,* wrecked in 1492 off Cap Haiti, to the 1812 loss of the *Barbados,* with its multi-million dollar cargo of precious metals hidden in Canadian waters off Sable Island.

One of the busiest shipwreck excavators in the world, Marx spends most of his time tracking treasure for foreign governments. He shakes his head when he considers the sheer numbers of wrecks waiting for a finder. "There is so much out there that all the marine archaeologists in the world, working full time, couldn't make a dent in the population," he says. And Marx is speaking only of *known* sites, ships and treasures with a history behind them in someone's archives. But to even attempt to fix a number of all shipwrecks would be impossible, he says. "We are never going to find them all."

However, Marx's figures give an outline on the numbers of shipwrecks of importance in this hemisphere during a period of approximately 300 years. Following are some samples:

- Canadian waters—108 known wrecks (1583–1822)
- U.S. Gulf Coast, including Mississippi and Texas (but excluding Florida—393 wrecks (1743–1824)
- Florida—263 wrecks (1521–1825)
- Mexico—127 wrecks, including most of Cortez's fleet, which was burned and sunk at San Juan de Ulua in 1519 (1511–1824)
- Lesser Antilles—345 wrecks, including sites at Anguilla, St. Maarten, St. Barthelemy, Saba, St. Eustatius, St. Kitts, Nevis, Barbuda, Antigua, Aves, Guadeloupe, Dominica, Martinique, St. Lucia, St. Vincent, Barbados, Grenadines, Grenada, Tobago, and Trinidad (1628–1821)
- Bermuda—85 wrecks (1500–1824)
- Bahamas—269 wrecks (1500–1825)
- Cuba—186 wrecks (1500–1825)
- Dominican Republic—186 wrecks (1500–1825)
- Jamaica and Cayman Island—900 wrecks (1504–1825)
- Puerto Rico—29 wrecks (1515–1822)
- Virgin Islands—97 wrecks (1523–1822)
- Central America—90 wrecks (1526–1819)
- South America—147 wrecks (1504–1815)

Using only these figures as a guide, it is easy to account for billions of dollars in lost treasure.

There are many more shipwrecks to add to this list. Nearly every day we find a new treasure ship or a trail of documents leading to one. And the list is by no means confined to ancient wrecks. Modern salvors working modern wrecks have made fortunes that would shame even the conquistadors. Two such bonanzas involved war losses by the British in this century.

The first strike came from the *Laurentic,* whose owners, White Star, also owned the *Titanic.* Over a period of years White Star saw all of its liners go to the bottom. The *Laurentic* was bound from Liverpool to Halifax during World War I when she struck a mine off Malin Head, Donegal, and went down with 250 tons of gold bars that were being sent to Canada to repay war debts. Her grave was not a peaceful one. She was 120 feet down in an area notorious for its stiff currents and frequent storms. Captain G. C. D. Damant, of the Royal Navy, took charge of the recovery under a government contract in 1917.

Damant's divers worked deep inside the ship where the gold was stored. They blasted away an outside cargo port to gain entry and cleared, by hand, tons of debris that had piled up in the pitch-black passageway. As work progressed, *Laurentic* began to cave in and sink deeper into the muddy bottom. The steel decks fell in on each other, so that the passageway to the gold room was turned into a deathtrap of wires, plates, and protruding steel girders. After a while, the area was no more than two feet high, hardly enough space for the divers to crawl through in the blackness. Slowly, but consistently, the way was cleared with guncotton explosives. But the debris piled up so quickly and dangerously that Damant was forced to change his entire salvage plan. Rather than burrow through to the gold room, he decided it would be safer to blast through *Laurentic*'s five decks and straight down into the storage room. Meanwhile, the ship continually shifted and settled, threatening at any moment to collapse.

Seven years and 5,000 dives later, Damant's crew had recovered all but 25 gold bars, returned to the government at a cost of only three percent of its market value—and with no loss of life. It was one of the most challenging and successful recoveries ever. Damant, interviewed in retirement some years later by Cousteau associate James Dugan, quipped: "Today I would do this business of gold salvage differently. You should have it down there as long as you can. It gets more valuable. Then get it up and send it to America." (*Captain Cousteau's Underwater Treasury*, Harper & Row Publishers, 1959).

More recently, salvor Keith Jessop pulled off what has to be considered a salvage miracle in very deep water. In 1981, using the most advanced diving systems, Jessop and his team recovered 5.5 tons of gold from the British cruiser *Edinburgh*. The *Edinburgh* was the victim of a World War II German U-boat and was sunk in 900 feet of water in the Barents Sea, off the Russian port of Murmansk. The Russian gold was payment to Great Britain and the U.S. for certain war debts and was authorized for shipment by Joseph Stalin. Salvor Jessop wound up with $30 million of the $81 million haul; Russia and Great Britain divided the rest.

Such huge fortunes are indeed impressive, and so is the technology required to get at them, to say nothing of the risk to life and limb. Yet the most compelling treasures, those most personally rewarding and the stuff of which dreams are made, almost invariably come as if we were guided to it by sheer luck or fate. To find a single gold doubloon on the beach is no less thrilling than the exploits of Captain Damant or Keith Jessop.

CHAPTER SEVEN

The Sea-Going Investor: High Rollers of Romance

The search for sunken treasure seductively lures men and women from virtually every level of society. Once thought to be the exclusive turf of the wealthy "playboy adventurer," the relatively new series of investment partnerships, the pervasiveness of modern media, and a geometrically expanding system of personal networking has afforded many of us a chance to turn our own personal *Treasure Island* into something more than a daydream. There would be even more opportunity if the Securities and Exchange Commission (SEC) allowed direct advertising by treasure hunting companies in newspapers and magazines. The unwritten theory behind this SEC prohibition is that such glittering temptations are not good for us, that it would create an irresistible underground of gamblers who could not be easily taxed or policed. It is certainly a comfort to know that the Commission is so concerned about keeping us from such perdition.

It may also be that the investor in treasure is more vulnerable than the average Wall Street swinger, and therefore needs this extra ounce of protection. The point is a highly debatable one. What is not so debatable is that the treasure seeker has a special constellation of priorities that appear to sail lightly around the straightline objectives of the "real world" marketplace. The first priority is the thrill of the chase rather than the compulsions of the bottom line. Second is the once-in-a-lifetime opportunity to take a hand in one of the most unique pursuits available to any of us. Profit is, of course, a primary factor not to be taken lightly, and I do not wish to convey the false notion that all treasure investors are hopeless romantics, because they are not. In fact, they tend to be ultimate realists who define their values in seemingly unconventional ways. To them, any object rescued from the deep—be it bankable gold or a rusted flintlock—holds relatively equal value in the long view of history and one's personal contributions to the process. It is not unheard of that silver and gold will on occasion be swapped for pewter and brass. And in this complex of values is the single biggest difference between the Wall Streeter and the treasure investor: The investor in securities takes his reward in cash. The treasure seeker takes his profits in artifacts, and if he wishes to convert them to cash, he must market them on his own. In most cases the conversion never takes place and the artifacts remain as heirlooms.

Limited Partnerships In The Sea

You won't find it listed on the "Big Board" or any other securities exchange, but the adventurous investor who seeks to strike it rich in that most unusual commodity known as undersea treasure can, with a little persistence, find an opportunity to buy in. Be advised, however, that putting your money into an on-going or start-up treasure dig is for rugged entrepreneurs only—the individualist who isn't afraid to buck prevailing Wall Street wisdom and who values excitement over the traditional prudence of blue chips.

Just how risky is treasure? Jerome U. Burke, whose family founded Underhill Associates, a general brokerage firm with five branch offices, compares it to an investment in wildcat oil and gas exploration, a field in which 90 percent of all potential wells turn out to be dry. "You've got to be a risk taker," Burke says. "But there's always that chance of making a very big killing—and, of course, there are certain tax considerations and advantages."

Since 1980, Burke has been putting together unit trusts or "limited partnerships," as he prefers to describe them, to help finance Mel Fisher's various explorations. Up until the July, 1985, *Atocha* strike there was room to buy into these partnerships at $1,000 per unit; now, Burke says, "People are standing in line to get in."

Burke views treasure through the lens of his 27 years on Wall Street. While he is not about to minimize the risks, he is of the opinion that other more traditional investments are equally risky. He points to index futures and options, penny stocks, and oil and gas wildcatting as no less of a long shot. And when it comes to the frenetic speculation in commodities such as soy beans, pork bellies, precious and non-precious metals, lumber, sugar, and wheat, "You're better off at the race track," he says. Oil and gas are typical blind-side risks in which one can never know for sure what's on the far side of the drill bit. "With treasure you know—or you certainly should know—*exactly* what's on the manifest," he explains. And in the galleon trade, the almost certain presence of additional unregistered contraband is the unknown but ever-present factor that hikes the overall value of the find.

There are a variety of reasons why people invest in treasure. Some are dazzled by the potential and believe, often naively, that they can get rich quick. It is the get-rich-quick investor who is almost sure to be disillusioned.

"It's best to be in for the long haul," Burke says. That's the nature of the market—uphill all the way. "It's okay to be in it strictly for the money. It's just a long time coming." By way of example, he points to his client, Fisher, and his often disenchanting 16-year search for the *Atocha* mother lode. "He's the best in the business," according to Burke, "and he's been sort of like Babe Ruth: He's struck out a lot, but he also hits a lot of home runs."

The happiest treasure investor is one whose motives transcend money. The collector, the historian, the adventure-oriented person who enjoys having a hand in the making of romance and history sleep best at night. Those in search of an unusual tax shelter also enjoy their treasure investment. Burke raises about $3 million to $4 million annually for Fisher's salvage company, Treasure Salvors Inc., from 1,500 or so investors. He says those who get the most out of their investments are patient, motivated, "fun" individuals who, like Burke, are not the typical Wall Street "hard money guys."

Small Investor Partnerships

Underhill's limited partnerships are made up primarily of small investors who get in at $1,000 each. Each partnership is allowed under SEC rules to raise up to $500,000 in small unit increments. Before 1980, when the SEC relaxed its rules on such arrangements, the units of the partnerships were required to be in much larger dollar amounts; it amounted to an arbitrary form of economic discrimination which excluded small investors and favored larger ones. Trouble was that it hurt treasure hunters and limited the economic horizon. "After all, there aren't that many people around who are willing to plunk down $30,000 or $40,000 a crack on a treasure hunt," says Burke. "And even if there are, their lawyers and accountants will take them out of it." The units of the $1,000 increment partnerships are exempt from SEC registration, and the relative lack of red tape makes them attractive.

The general informality also goes well with the adventurous nature of the chase, but the investor must always be prepared to lose it all. The Fisher partnerships, for example, are time-sensitive, and expire in one year. An investor who was in the chase in 1985, when the *Atocha* mother lode came in, can expect to receive 1/10,000 of that year's haul, making a $1,000 investment worth up to $40,000. On the other hand, those who bought shares in the lean years may lose their money, or at best recoup only a small portion of it.

The High Roller Route

There are partnerships for investors with money to spend on higher stakes. Using the Fisher example again (since his operations are the IBMs of the treasure market), there is a 30-unit partnership in which each partner has to put up $150,000. Known as the Treasure Company, the deal was established to help find and salvage the *Atocha* and *Santa Margarita.* Each investor will receive a full 10 percent of both treasures. The Treasure Company group got to write off 100 percent of its investment and took a 10 percent investment tax credit.

The difference in scale between what the small investor will make compared to the high-rolling Treasure Company are readily apparent: The $1,000 player may receive up to $40,000 in treasure from the 1985 strike; Treasure Company partners have already received nearly $5 million in treasure. Cark Paffendorf, head of Vanguard Ventures, Glen Cove, New York, and syndicator of Treasure Company, says there is already enough coming back to pay off the investors, and about $21 million will be coming in when both the *Atocha* and *Santa Margarita* are completely salvaged—a job which promises to take several years. The rough profit on such a payback for each $150,000 investor will be $800,000! Most of the investors are holding the profits in a trust set up by the partners to qualify for long-term capital gains treatment.

Jerome Burke points out that the Internal Revenue Service will not tax the distributions held for five years or more. After five years, the treasure receives long-term gains treatment. Burke is offering a small investment partnership in 1986 with 12,000 units. He expects it will quickly sell out.

Since the *Atocha* find, Burke has been swamped by inquiries from other would-be and established treasure hunters who want him to finance their operations. He shuffles daily through a ponderous stack of mail as if it were leftover confetti. "All this stuff—it's from everywhere. Everybody's got a wreck." He is not very impressed by what he sees. "Most of them are a bunch of nuts! Bunch of wild men."

Burke remains staunchly behind Fisher. "He's the best. He's been at it the longest and his record is already history."

He wishes there were more Mel Fishers to go around. If so, there would be a bonanza in it for Burke, whose commissions range from eight percent to ten percent ("not out of line in the 'new issue' business") and more opportunity for investors who are bombarded almost daily by media reports of fabulous new treasure finds. As it stands today, however, Fisher and his partners are the most visible, most vocal, most time-tested investment vehicle around. The operation is well structured, easily contacted, and totally dominates the field with 1.2 million shares outstanding.

Forming Partnerships

There are much smaller partnerships which form to find particular wrecks. One such organization is Maritime Analysts Group, Inc., of Edgartown, Massachusetts. Headed by Martin Bayerle, a former New York area dive shop owner, the outfit is seeking investment capital to salvage the White Star liner, *Republic,* which sank in 1909, 50 miles south of Nantucket Island. A portion of its cargo was $3 million in U.S. Gold Eagle coins (150,000 troy ounces), all newly minted. Bayerle, whose group located the wreck in 240 to 260 feet of water, estimates today's market value of these coins at $400 million to $500 million. Bringing up anything from such deep water is a mammoth undertaking, and Maritime Analysts is working with the Canadian salvage firm of Wolf Sub Ocean, Ltd., Dartmouth, Nova Scotia. Bayerle realizes the salvage work will be expensive, and is working out limited partnerships with $150,000 individual antes and a $5 million cap. In return, the partners will receive 10 percent of the treasure's gross value.

Bayerle has no manifest for the *Republic,* but has instead reconstructed the gold market in 1909 as a way to trace the Gold Eagles. The group has a salvage permit and does not have to split any of the find with the state. A five-year trust is set to hold the finds for long-term capital gains treatment. He says the coins will be sold piecemeal, so as not to flood the collector market and bring down their antiquity value.

Another salvor, Barry Clifford, also operating out of the Cape Cod-Nantucket area, is seeking investment input to salvage the pirate ship *Whydah,* the first pirate ship ever found, which went to the bottom in 1717, in 18 feet of water, within sight of the beach at Wellfleet, Massachusetts. Clifford has also located the so-called "Hell's Gate" wreck in New York's East River, a gold carrier which he claims was bearing bullion worth $500 million.

The *Whydah,* an outlaw vessel, carried no manifest, so there is really no reliable way to pin down the true value of its cargo. The hull is buried beneath 25 feet of sand, and sampling of finds have been recovered. The vessel belonged to "Black Sam" Bellamy, a pirate who roamed the Caribbean and gained a reputation to rival Blackbeard.

Clifford has a state salvage permit, and he must share 25 percent of his finds. In the meantime, he is seeking investment and eventually hopes to open a "Black Sam" pirate museum to display the finds.

The discovery came purely by chance. He first heard of "Black Sam" as a child when his uncle, a masterful storyteller, told him the legend of the *Whydah.* He became obsessed by the story. Years later, while working another wreck, Clifford came upon the log of Captain Cyprian Southack, a salvor sent in 1717, by Massachusetts Governor Samuel Shute to find the pirate treasure. "I knew my life was about to change," he recalls in a January 1985 interview by David Fairbank in *Parade* magazine. "I'd finally found the missing link."

In the fall of 1982, Clifford made his first strike. Thirty years after his uncle told him about "Black Sam," he sat on the edge of his uncle's bed. "This time it was my turn to tell him a story."

Clifford may convince investors that the *Whydah* is worth what he claims, but it's likely that he will be forced to sell some of the treasure to finance further research and salvage. There are people who would object to this method of digging in the ocean, insisting that nothing be marketed. Such a policy, however, would delay the salvage for many years, increasing the chances for the wreck to be looted or waste away in a big storm. Until "Black Sam" and his nautical bones are uncovered, we will have to live with Hollywood's version of piracy—an image equal in distortion to Hollywood's almost unbelievable character assassination of Captain William Bligh, of *Mutiny on the Bounty* fame.

Knowing the Numbers Helps You Score

Burt D. Webber, Jr., Rehrerburg, Pennsylvania, operates in the upper reaches of the treasure world. He won considerable fame for his work on the 1733 Spanish Plate Fleet wrecks off the east coast of Florida in the

1960s and early 1970s. He made it to the hall of fame in 1977 and 1978 when his Phips-I and Phips-II expeditions to Hispaniola's Ambrosia Banks (now called Silver Shoals because of all the treasure lost there) turned up nearly 30,000 Spanish coins and nearly a ton of bullion. Webber had successfully excavated the wreck of the Spanish galleon *Nuestra Señora de la Concepción*, which Sir William Phips had partially salvaged in 1687, some 40 years after the vessel was lost. Phips became the New World's first great treasure salvor, was knighted, and later became the Governor of the Massachusetts Bay Company. Webber's expedition was no less impressive. Unlike Phips, however, he deliberately maintained a low profile and passed on most requests for interviews to a New York public relations firm. Today, he still maintains a serious, understated and business-like demeanor, and he laughs when he recalls press reports claiming that his *Concepción* strike was worth $800 million. On a more serious note, he's concerned with what he calls "flimflam" values placed on treasure, and he believes that the hoopla which is passed under the noses of investors may one day undermine and perhaps destroy the credibility of treasure hunting.

"These false values are bad for everyone," he says. In his calm, gentlemanly style, he refuses to point fingers at any of his colleagues, and he does not wish to diminish the importance of a necessary dose of fancy that makes the treasure world go around. What concerns him most is the fear that the flimflammery will eventually wreck even the most sincere efforts to find and recover sunken riches.

"Every potential investor should know that no treasure has any value until it's appraised. This is especially true of large volume finds, where you have thousands of artifacts, coins, and bullion. Treasure is worth only what you can get for it, and huge volume saturates a market and knocks down prices."

Webber conducted a two-year market research study on treasure values, and he kept coming back to the same position: Treasure is worth only what someone is willing to pay for it. "We got about 31,000 pieces of eight from our digging," he says. "They sold at pretty high prices at first. But after we had sold 12,000 of them, we found a saturated market that forced us to wholesale the coins at $45 each. That's better than a melt down price, but still not very good."

He says treasure investors are generally unaware that values are based on the prices paid for the first items placed on the market. For example, the first gold coins sold out of a total trove of 30,000 may bring in $50,000 each. "You try to do that for all 30,000 but it can't be done. Yet treasure hunters tell their investors that each of those coins are worth $50,000. A lot of investors, when they discover what's happened, tend to back off. They get disillusioned; more than a few times they go to court. Honestly, one day the whole system is going to blow up."

Buying a Piece of History

The big ticket values are used to draw in investors. These days, for instance, hardly anyone values a treasure under $500 million. Many have taken the lead from the *Atocha,* originally valued at $400 million, but more lately revalued at $238 million. Wild fluctuations in the market makes investors nervous, the overall effect being pretty much the same as huge up and down spikes on the New York Stock Exchange.

To promote the sale of his *Concepción* finds, Webber set up a traveling exhibition and worked with the upscale department store chain of Nieman-Marcus to sell "limited edition treasure chests." Each black walnut chest contained 15 coins, several books on the expeditions, and various catalogs. They were priced to sell at $5,000 apiece.

"We went through the best outlets and couldn't sell them at that price," he says. "In time, the same coins that sold for as much as $800 apiece were discounted down to $275.

"Our concept was not to sell the professional coin dealer, because the professional cares nothing at all for the charisma. His only concern is the coin itself, its rarity, and that sort of thing. We wanted to reach the general public, and that is a pretty hard market, too."

The history of treasure investing shows that people "will buy a piece of history," Webber explains. With romantic visions dancing in their heads, people will pay inflated, pumped-up values. "Sure, you can sell romance—but not forever. Sooner than later the market catches up and your prices go down."

Webber financed his Phips-I and Phips-II operations through the limited partnership route, with units selling at $15,000 to $20,000 each. This kept the partnership small, and gave him a close connection with his backers. He says he cannot work with the Fisher-style $1,000 time-sensitive partnership concept. "There are too many people in for too short a time with pie-in-the-sky notions. I need big investors for the long haul, investors as serious as I am."

Webber is as much a market analyst as a treasure hunter and historian. He claims to have pioneered the limited partnership concept in the treasure field, perhaps one reason why he tends to be skeptical of its ultimate worth as a commercial venture.

Treasure hunters tend to be highly competitive, and undoubtedly some of Webber's criticism of the $1,000 ante partnership is colored by his one-time race with Mel Fisher to find the *Atocha*. But Webber's style would not support the small investor's dreams, and he believes that the Fisher-style partnerships may look good on paper but, realistically, there is a downside. "What's the end product? What will the investors actually receive? Sometimes I think he's (Fisher) leaving himself open for 20 years of lawsuits by people who are going to contest the real value of the payback. I couldn't afford that kind of down-the-road problem. I'm just too serious about what I do to be exposed like that."

His deal with the Dominican Republic, in whose territorial sea the *Concepción* lay buried, was put together through official diplomatic channels, and it was one of the few treasure contracts to be completed without litigation. It was a clean 50-50 split between Webber's firm, Continental Exploration, and the Dominican government. No artifacts were sold, and the Dominicans claimed all of them, valued at about $3.6 million. The government also took the higher valued gold and silver of an appraised $4 million haul. He is proud of the efficiency of the deal and the lack of acrimony. "It's one of the reasons I prefer to go with people I know, people I feel comfortable with. The corporate route can get out of hand."

He says that treasure hunting has yet to prove itself as a real business. "I'm talking flat-out returns. It's hard to find a real profit from any of these operations, and one of the reasons, as I said, is that we don't have true values on what we bring up from the ocean."

"Let me point out that if you went to the Harvard Business School's library you won't find one case study on treasure hunting. We haven't come full circle yet. It's all too new. For now, investors really cannot look to returns in actual cold hard cash. Money can be made—I believe this. But you have to realistically value the product and turn down all the hype."

Webber suggests that treasure hunters value their precious metal finds on melt down prices—the price paid for gold and silver on the Comex, absent the fickle multiplier of "antiquity value." This system would lead to a major decline in treasure prices, he says, but it would put the industry on a more conservative and accountable footing.

"These guys who operate on hype are going to be the ruin of us all," he says. "I want to be completely honest with my investors. I tell them: Look, you're buying a piece of history, something unique in all the world. Don't come to me looking to make a killing, because you are going to be disappointed."

Different Strokes, Different Folks

Webber's point is well taken. There is a lot of hype in the world of treasure—everything from outrageously inflated value to impossible promises and, of course, the ubiquitous phony treasure maps. But, at the same time, there is a wide range of real opportunities, and the tips listed at the end of this chapter should assist you in finding them.

Let's examine two entirely unique treasure seekers with different goals and philosophies. One is Jud Chalmers, who is squarely situated in the "high roller" category. Yet Chalmers is a realist, quite levelheaded, perceptive and motivated by romance and profit. The other gentleman is John Amrhein, an historian and writer dedicated to the search for history and not the least beguiled by the possibility of striking it rich.

First, meet Jud Chalmers.

I was introduced to him in 1983, while in Key West on assignment for *Smithsonian* magazine. Chalmers is the president of Coral Investments, Jacksonville, Florida, and he's just the sort of man Hollywood might cast in the role of the rugged individualist treasure hunter. Tall and beset with craggy features, his pale eyes fix on you like a hawk; he is likely to be the one who spots something shiny in the sand while others would most likely never notice. Middle aged, he's fit, charming, and worldly. He says he made his fortune long ago in life insurance, land development, oil speculation, and communications.

He has backed Mel Fisher since 1965. He owns and leases sea-going workboats to Treasure Salvors and flies back and forth between Jacksonville and Key West aboard his own Grumman Gulfstream. He travels to Key West primarily to dive with the Fisher crew. "That's a big part of why I'm in this," he says. But another reason has to do with his special fascination with gold, its historical mystique, and its particularly finite quality.

Chalmers is prototypical of the wealthy men I have known in this field: part dreamer, part hard realist, and fully fortified on both sides of the line.

At the time I interviewed him he asked not to be named in the story I was writing. "A lot of people out there see that you're doing this sort of thing, and the next thing you know, you've got some nut parked on your doorstep." I honored his request, because it is true that, like those who track Jerome Burke, men like Jud Chalmers attract a paparazzi following, wearing him down with requests for money to excavate their own treasure wrecks. I could tell that Chalmers sympathized with them on one level, but truly was bothered by them. When the *Atocha* strike was made in July, 1985, his name appeared in newspapers and magazines around the world, and I thought it was time to say in print what he told me in April, 1983.

"I was drawn to treasure by the romance. I admit that. I visited Mel in 1965, and we went diving together. I had dived and looked for treasure before, as a complete amateur. I went aboard the *Virgilona* (one of Fisher's search boats) and found silver the first time out! Didn't know what it was, and I tossed it away. Mel was annoyed. He said, 'You aren't going diving with us again!'

"Well, it was a challenge. I had ideas, got more involved, made 'contributions,' lived my own fantasies."

This was the first part of our interview. I had heard others say similar things about treasure and their involvement with it, and it would be easy enough, all things considered, to keep Chalmers out of print. But later on that same day, as I sat alone scanning my notes, he walked up to me with a kind of airy boldness in his step, and sat across from me on a metal folding chair.

"I don't want to give you the wrong idea," he began. "I invest in the man. I invest in integrity of purpose. . . . Mel impressed me, so I invested. It wasn't a write off. I want to make that clear. If I didn't think there was some profit to be gained, I wouldn't have done it. But, yes, it keeps me young. If I didn't love diving, I probably wouldn't be into this. . . ."

Here was a man of unquestioned business acumen justifying his investment, as if to make more substantial the lure that hooked him in the first place.

He said several times that when he sees an opportunity, he does as Confucius says and does his "duty." But never, he said, would he sell. "Who knows, maybe someday a scholar will want to study my gold—I collect only gold, because it fascinates me. I would make the collection available for study, but for now I have it, and one day my grandchildren will have it."

Possessing this collection isn't like owning a Rolls Royce, which he might enjoy showing off. "It embarrasses me sometimes to show those golden objects to friends. They only see them as so many troy ounces. They really don't see the magic and the history, so mostly I don't show my stuff."

There was a long pause. I was busy writing all of this down and working my tape recorder. As an afterthought, Chalmers parted with, "Gold is really attractive to me, but if I didn't have other income, I probably wouldn't be in this. It's high risk—but worthwhile. I think ahead. And I believe if I appraised everything I've collected against what I've invested, I'd come out with a profit."

How to Spot Scams

One hundred and eighty degrees away from Chalmers is maritime historian John L. Amrhein, the man who will most likely be credited one day for discovering the origin of the famous wild Chincoteague ponies. Now living in picturesque Salisbury, Maryland, which is only a short drive from where he believes the ponies first came ashore, Amrhein illuminated the pony legend through his discovery of a Spanish warship, *LaGalga*, which wrecked on Assateague Island during a September storm in 1750. Assateague and Chincoteague are neighboring islands along the east coast. According to Amrhein, *LaGalga* was a 50-gun vessel that now lays hidden beneath the sand of a federal wildlife refuge. Federal authorities, despite pleadings by the Smithsonian Institution and other interested parties, refuses to allow excavation of the wreck, claiming it will disturb the wildlife sanctuary. In the meantime, Amrhein involves himself in various pleadings by salvors for permits to excavate wrecks. He specializes in investigating phony pleadings on non-existent wrecks. Because the cases he is now pursuing as *amicus curie* (friend of the court) are all live actions, he will not disclose them. He prefers to allow the law to take its course before naming names. As a result, Amrhein's discussion of the scam of phony treasure companies is general.

"It works like this," he begins. "You have a company that goes into court asking for a claim on, say, five wrecks. The company officials have a few affidavits, a little history, and an apparent willingness and resources to do the job and give the state its share. Now, how many judges know the difference between a real claim and a phony one? Maybe one in a thousand, tops. So the game is on . . ."

The company really does have five wrecks where it says it does, Amrhein says. "But they're just empty hulks—something the ocean has plenty of. But it may be enough to obtain salvage rights. At this point, the company goes looking for investors, flashing its research, which is weak, and showing the investor the salvage permit. Most people, seeing the permit, think, 'Hey, if a federal judge is willing to hand out a permit, there *has* to be something there.' That's where he's wrong. There doesn't have to be anything there. In most cases, a permit can be had on appearances."

Such practices go on all the time, he says, and extend from the oceans to phony overnight historical societies.

"Anyone who is going to put up money should insist on certain things. It's very important to get background on the salvor; just what sort of guy is he? Any track record in the field? Any run-ins with the law? These are essential to know, especially if he acts too secretive, is one of those 'just between you and me' types. Granted, there's a little phoniness in all treasure hunts. It's part of the romance to blow things slightly out of proportion. But the sort of thing I'm talking about is legal fraud."

In addition to checking on the salvor, Amrhein suggests that investors get exact locations of wrecks, double-check the source of all documents if possible, and get the advice of local maritime historians. Losing your money to a con man is bad enough, Amrhein says, but losing your pride and feeling stupid is even worse.

He agrees with Burt Webber about the inflated claims of value. "Make it a rule to be skeptical first," he says, "especially when salvors talk about hundreds of millions of dollars. The numbers are too big, the claims too sweeping. Ask the salvor how much it's worth at melt down prices. Do not accept multiples based on historical importance. They're usually debateable. Be a hard-nosed buyer. Remember, the man wants you to invest.

The treasure's been there a long, long time, and it isn't going anywhere. Time is on your side."

Amrhein encourages investors to look for artifact-rich wrecks rather than vessels purported to be carrying negotiables. An investor can, for example, get an appraisal on a musket and donate the item to a local museum or historical society, and deduct it from income taxes.

"I'm one for small-scale operations," Amrhein says. He wants to know who he's dealing with and what he can expect from them. "I don't think I could sleep knowing that I made promises to people about big dollars coming out of the ocean. The truth is, you just can't be sure about it. The corporate route makes you sound very positive, but there are abuses all the time and you've got to be careful. For myself, I'm into the history and the fun. If profit comes, great! But it isn't my game."

Tips on The Trade

Inside the treasure business there are several highly respected researchers upon whom treasure hunters depend for vital data. Some of these men and women go public with their achievements, and some write books, such as Dr. Eugene Lyon and his fascinating book, *The Search For The Atocha*. But others remain deliberately anonymous, after the fashion of ghost writers with famous clients. A few years ago, one busy New York ghost writer, Harold Prince, said the public buys his clients' books because of their reputation. "If I put my name on it, nobody would buy and I'd be out of business." Treasure researchers work on the "Prince Principle," allowing glory to accrue to those who pay for it and go public with the results.

I have discussed this section of the book with several well-known researchers, all of whom thought it a good idea to place a few Webber-like caveats on these pages. True to type, however, they declined to be named or formally credited with the following list of tips for would-be investors:

1. Most treasure contracts tend to be informal deals made between a select group of people. The outsider should be exceedingly cautious before deciding "to climb into bed with strangers," as one source put it.
2. Investors should back away from any treasure deal with serious legal overtones. For example, a state may have claims against a treasure, and there may also be hidden litigation by individuals. Litigation of any kind will jinx almost any deal.

3. Because investors are inclined to think big, it is often difficult to make them see reality and swallow the real risks of any treasure hunt. Therefore, never invest when your imagination is running full-blast. Wait it out, be sober, play devil's advocate, and be critical.

4. The cargo manifest is vital. It tells an investor what is supposed to be out there waiting for him. If no manifest is available, the risk factor doubles or triples; to proceed without it may be a leap into the dark.

5. A manifest is only the beginning. Insist on seeing all available documentation. Even if it takes weeks or months to wade through it, you simply must do it to convince yourself that the expedition is real. You need the name of the vessel, its registry, date of sinking and location, and salvage conditions at the site. Without this crucial information, you are probably being sold a bill of goods.

6. Never trust a treasure map. It is a sure sign of a con man. After all, why would anyone sell a treasure map? And even if it is real, what proof is there that the treasure wasn't salvaged years ago?

7. Do not be seduced by treasure galleons. They are not all that rare. It is estimated that hundreds of them may be hidden beneath the navigable waters of the United States.

8. Does the salvor have the necessary papers, such as a salvage permit and other legal documents granting full or partial title to a wreck? If not, wait until such documents are forthcoming before you are forthcoming with your hard-earned dollars.

9. Try to circulate in the treasure field. Get to know people whose names appear in local news reports of treasure finds. Remember, there is no ready market available and the investor has to size up his prospects on his own. Since most shipwreck recoveries are closely held operations, it is important to get inside in a realistic way. Some salvage jobs are quick—they may be started and finished in a year or two. After the treasure, if any, is found, the group may dissolve. Don't be caught in a disappearing act.

10. A solid treasure hunter is many things: salvor, ship handler, historian, marine technician, diver, researcher, lawyer, and engineer. Be certain your investment buys these capabilities, and that these talents are indeed on board.

11. Don't butt in on secretive treasure hunts. As one insider says, "It will give you a witches' brew of problems." Instead, go for the

open, public hunts, especially ones in which you can take a direct hand.

12. If you invest for the purpose of gaining a tax shelter, make sure you understand the details and are certain that the dig qualifies for tax deductions. You cannot write off a "hobby." It must be a real business venture to satisfy the IRS.

13. Sometimes you can trade information for a piece of the action. If you are good at research, or have exclusive information of any kind on a shipwreck, a salvor may agree to give you a percentage of the haul if you lead him to the mother lode.

14. Be skeptical of values. Like Burt Webber, be conservative and think of melt down values. Unless you are a professional antique dealer, you are in no position to place a value on artifacts. If you have the data on what is to be salvaged, seek outside appraisals.

15. Be wary of greed. It has a way of reaching out to all of us. It can destroy all you've worked for and leave you cynical and broke.

16. If money is what you're after, determine the value of the cargo and be certain it's authentic. In general, the net worth of a wreck has to be at least $30,000 to make it worth diving on. This is a very low figure, but treasure is an inexact art and those who contributed to this list agree that $30,000 is a reasonable figure to start with.

17. Be able to read between the lines of the deal. Are the treasure hunters 100 percent sure that treasure is where they think it is? What makes them so sure? Make them prove its existence in concrete terms that you and your accountant can understand.

18. Invest only what you can afford to lose. If you violate this rule, not only will you probably lose your investment, but you will create havoc in other areas of your life.

19. Do not participate in hush-hush underground deals that appear to be on the outskirts of the law. The risk isn't worth it. Remember, it's one thing to lose your money; it's quite another to go to jail. Learn to recognize the looter, and stay away.

20. The happiest investors are those who do it for reasons other than monetary return. Never go for gold alone and you'll probably be a winner.

PART THREE

At Sea

Throughout this book we have been examining *sunken* treasure and the unavoidable (and perhaps unfortunate) fact that it is mostly hidden from view. But, like most things, hidden is a matter of degree. Those ships lost in the abyssal deeps—the *Titanics* of the world—are very likely to remain out of sight until Woods Hole or some other scientific organization comes along with the money and the technology to bring them to us on our home television screens. In the meantime, there is an enormous population of relatively shallow shipwrecks; these extend from the surface down to less than 200 feet, and to the competent SCUBA diver they are generally accessible.

The introduction of SCUBA (self-contained underwater breathing apparatus) to America in the 1950s has inspired millions of people to experience first-hand the riches of the deep, to go beyond the obscurring curtain of water and see for themselves the marvels of the deep. This section of *Tracking Treasure* invites you to explore the islands of the Caribbean. But to really know them and their long-hidden secrets you may need to get wet. It's time to consider your own role as a potential SCUBA-equipped innerspace explorer.

At this point you may be wondering if SCUBA is worth learning? Can anyone do it? Is it safe?

The answer to these questions is generally yes. To begin with, almost any healthy individual can learn to dive, and in so doing open up a vivid new world of excitement. Short of physical conditions such as heart disease, uncontrolled epilepsy, fainting spells, and claustrophobia, the average person can learn how to practice safe, sane SCUBA. In most instances you will need your physician's clean bill of health to launch into SCUBA training. No SCUBA instructor wants a "floater" on his hands who simply decided to ignore a physician's advice. So, in general, you will need to prove your fitness before you begin training—a requirement entirely in the SCUBA student's best interests.

Besides being reasonably healthy, the new SCUBA diver should be a confident swimmer, level-headed and not inclined to panic. The student must also maintain a proper respect for the power of the sea and the elements. Heroes need not apply!

Depending on your choice of a training agency, of which there are several, all quite good, the road to gaining a SCUBA certification card (without which you can not buy air for your tanks) may be as short as a one day "resort course," which is widely available in the Caribbean and leads to a limited and temporary certification, or possibly as long as 16 weeks of intensive pool instruction, classroom work, and open water checkout dives. The longer course is by far the best and leads to full-fledged standing as a diver. With your certification in hand (a "C-Card"), an incredible new world of exploration opens up to you—a world which most people think of as being no less alien than outerspace, but which you as a competent ocean explorer are now privileged to visit at will.

You will not be alone. There are approximately three million certified SCUBA divers in the United States today—not a huge group when compared to skiing or aerobics. But SCUBA is not merely a sport. It is truly unique. This relatively small group of individuals represents a kind of elite corps who, in addition to having fun, are charged with the unwritten responsibility to explore our oceanic world and to teach others about it. Every centimeter of subsea soil is new ground, and each visit teaches the diver new lessons.

It sounds great, but what about costs?

Happily, SCUBA instruction is within reach of most of us. A course may run anywhere from $50 to $350. However, the cost of basic diving equipment—air tanks, regulators, buoyancy vests, masks, fins, dive knives (to cut yourself out of entanglement—not to fight sharks!), and a good wet suit for chilly climes—can add up pretty quickly to an investment of more than $1,000. Fortunately, prices vary and there is no immediate need to buy anything except a face mask, snorkel, and swim fins, which add up to less than $75 in most cases. You can rent equipment until you can afford your own, and most courses offer rentals at very reasonable rates. Sooner or later the motivated diver will want personal gear, but even then there is no need to buy it all at once. (Like diving itself, equipment purchases should proceed prudently.)

Is a certain "type" of person best suited to diving?

I think the answer is yes. Those who view SCUBA as a tool to greater understanding, and not an end in itself, make the best dive buddies. Over the years, I have encountered (to my chagrin) a certain macho type whose greatest satisfaction is to be seen on the deck of a dive boat literally encased in underwater gadgetry. If pressed, some will confess that the actual experience of exploring the sea means less to them than the bizarre thrill of giving the superficial appearance of a Navy underwater demolitions expert. Such people should never go into diving. Time and again I have seen them get into trouble—sometimes very serious trouble involving innocent people. Personally, I am waiting for the day when there will be a special dive resort for these crackpots, a resort perhaps aptly named "Puerto Macho," where each dive comes within a hairline of disaster. But that is another story. Closer to the point, if you are possessed of a healthy curiosity and an adventurous spirit which draws you to the sea, then I suspect diving is in your future.

Certainly diving is not for everyone. Any number of reasonable factors may add up to a decision to remain on the surface. Just as there are good reasons to dive, staying high and dry comes with good reasons, too, not the least of which is ordinary caution.

For those who elect to stay on terra firma, there are the beaches—thousands of miles of rich shoreline along our coasts. Beachcombing is the oldest form of treasure hunting—every bit as productive and satisfying as SCUBA. I have therefore included in this section an original compilation of the best treasure beaches in America.

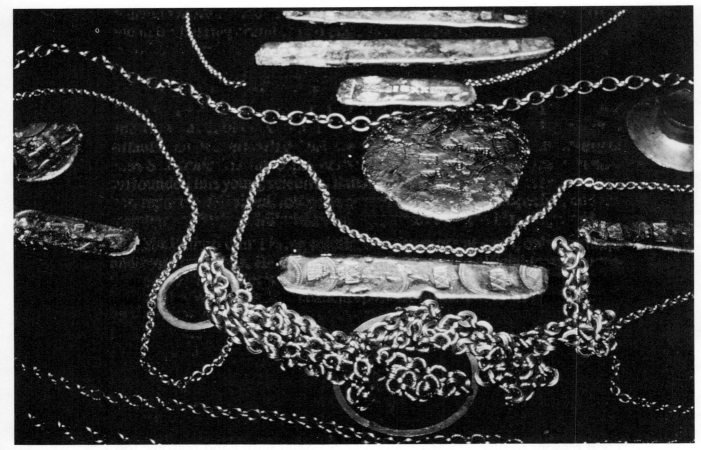

Golden bars, disks, and "money chains" lost by the Spanish during centuries of colonization and exploitation of the New World. At one time, these items were highly sophisticated art and religious objects fashioned by Inca, Aztec, and Toltec craftsmen. But in their overpowering lust for wealth, and to shore-up Spain's sagging economy, the Conquistadors melted down whole collections of art, turning statuary into raw bullion. Though the original art is tragically lost forever, these relics of lost civilizations represent billions of dollars in investment potential to today's sea-going entrepreneurs.
Photo by Carl Purcell.

CHAPTER EIGHT

Treasure Islands: An Introduction to Caribbean Treasure

Treasure has become synonymous with warm breezes, emerald seas, sails billowing against clear tropical skies. This image owes much to the enduring popularity of Robert Louis Stevenson's *Treasure Island,* the classic tale of a boy's search for pirate gold "buried somewhere on an island far away," and Hollywood's amplification of that story.

Was Treasure Island real? Stevenson gives us only a vague clue. The ship in which the story's youthful hero, Jim Hawkins, puts to sea is called the *Hispaniola,* which today is the combined island nations of Haiti and the Dominican Republic, located in the Caribbean. Hispaniola was an important treasure center in the New World, but there is no evidence to suggest that the author ever spent time there. His story was pure invention and grew out of a map which he drew randomly to entertain his little stepson, Lloyd Osbourne.

Toward the end of his life, Stevenson, who had always been in frail health, could no longer endure the winters of his native Edinburgh and moved to the Pacific Island of Samoa—half a world away from Hispaniola. Yet the name lingers like a mist and focuses the tropical treasure mystique directly on the Caribbean. Today, almost every island in that unique oceanic community claims that it was the very one Stevenson described in his story. This will remain a disputable claim for the foreseeable future, but it has left us with an immutable notion of where treasure *ought* to be. And, as it turns out, Stevenson was absolutely correct.

Thanks to the Spaniards, the New World sailing routes through the Caribbean offer the most opulent repository of treasure the world has ever known.

The Spanish Conquistadors arrived soon after Columbus' voyages, and by 1519 had defeated and enslaved the Aztecs with black powder and smallpox. In Peru, Pizarro destroyed the Incas. For more than three centuries the Indian slaves mined gold, silver, and precious gems to save the Spanish Crown. When this proved insufficient, the Conquistadors melted down the collected art of the New World to make more bars of gold and silver. In the first four decades of Spain's rule, crown records showed that more than $200 million worth of booty had been shipped from the New World. Unofficially, precious goods smuggled back by dishonest Spanish sailors were likely worth twice again that amount.

The plunder went on non-stop. King Ferdinand and Queen Isabella established the greatest bureaucracy ever conceived to keep it going, the House of Trade, *Las Casa para la Contratacion y Negociacion de las Indias.* The *Casa* maintained absolute power and absolute corruption. It is from the meticulous records kept by this bureaucracy's *escribanos* that much of what we now know of Spain's Indies trade is drawn.

The fleets left Spain in the spring and sailed down the coast of Africa, provisioned at the Canary Islands, then sailed west with the trade winds. Two months later, they arrived in the Caribbean and separated to pick up cargo from the principal colonies.

The New Spain fleet coasted around Mexico's Yucatan peninsula and headed north up the coast to Veracruz. At Veracruz the riches of the New World mixed with the wealth of the Orient, shipped from the Spanish-held Philippines aboard the Manila galleons. The Manila galleons unloaded their Far Eastern treasures—fine Chinese porcelain, carved ivory from Ceylon, silk—at Acapulco. The wares were transported overland to Veracruz on the backs of slaves. From Veracruz, the fleet sailed with the currents of the Gulf of Mexico, north to Texas then down the west coast of Florida, landing at Spain's most powerful outpost, Havana, Cuba.

Another fleet, the *Galleones de Tierra Firme,* called first at Cartagena, Colombia and then went on to Portobello, Panama to pick up treasure from Central America. These ships also loaded riches from Chile and Peru, shipped to Panama City aboard the South Seas Fleet and carried across the malaria-ridden Isthmus by slaves, before sailing to Havana to meet the New Spain fleet. From Havana, the fleets sailed together back to Spain. The general timetable for one of these round-trips was seven to nine months.

But the voyage home was incredibly perilous. The ships sailed north from Havana across a rough passage of open water to Florida, where they entered the powerful north-flowing Gulf Stream. They navigated up the Straits of Florida, with the Florida Keys to the west and the dangerous Bahama Banks and reefs to the east. If all went well, they made it to Cape Hatteras, North Carolina, then turned east and into the deep, open Atlantic.

Many, many times, all did not go well. The sudden, violent storms and fierce waves spawned by the Gulf Stream drove merchantmen and galleons alike onto the jagged teeth of the shoals of the Bahamas Banks and East Florida.

If the reefs didn't snare the heavily laden, slow-moving galleons, freebooters often did. Some of the infamous "buccaneers" were legitimate naval mercenaries, called privateers. Spain's enemies in the Old World— England, France, and the Netherlands—encouraged the privateers by giving them safe harbor and the protection of friendly naval forces. The privateers were heroes at home; they kept millions of pesos of New World treasure out of Spain's coffers, cutting off funds for the European wars. Their names are famous: Sir Francis Drake was a privateer, so were Captains Henry Morgan, William Kidd, and Edward Teach. After the end of the War of the Spanish Succession in 1714, England agreed to stop supporting these privateers. Some, including Morgan, Kidd, and Teach (also known as Blackbeard), having tasted the good life bought with Spain's blood money, became pirates—outlaws condemned and feared by all.

Scholars disagree about how much treasure reached Spain and how much was lost, but the documented losses alone certainly amount to billions of 20th century dollars. Not even the imaginative Stevenson could have calculated its value—and it is a value that is constantly changing.

Daniel A. Koski-Karrell, a marine archaeologist with extensive experience in the Caribbean, says the value of lost New World treasure is constantly being revised as new data comes up from the sea. Only in the last few years, he says, have we begun to calculate the enormity of colonial underground economy. More than four billion pesos were mined and registered at the Royal Mints, but recent galleon excavations reveal that perhaps more than two billion pesos moved through the Caribbean as contraband.

Actual ship losses may be higher than once believed, Koski-Karrell says. A few years ago, scholars such as John S. Potter, Jr., estimated galleon sinkings at two percent to ten percent of the Caribbean armada; newer evidence places the losses at more than 20 percent.

Koski-Karrell notes that Potter did not factor the "collectors' value" into his calculations of the value of lost treasure fleets. This represents a multiplier of ten and turns a $6 peso on the bullion market into a $60-plus item on the collectors' market. Using Koski-Karrell's slide rule, a single gold coin could be worth approximately $3,250.

"These figures are constantly moving," he says. "For the future, I don't see them moving any way but up."

He singles out two galleons out of the thousands that went to the bottom—the *San Jose,* sunk in 1708 off Cartagena with 11 million pesos (making her the richest galleon ever lost), and the *El Nuevo Constante,* a medium-size vessel heavily salvaged by the Spanish in the 1700s, but which produced $250,000 in bullion for modern salvors off the coast of Louisiana during their very first day of exploration.

"When you see things like that," Koski-Karrell says, "you realize that there's a lot more than we thought. If you do the basic multiplication with all the variables, the *San Jose* alone is worth something like $2.5 billion."

U.S. Virgin Islands

St. Thomas

These and other mind-boggling numbers noted in this book should give you a working knowledge of the current market value of shipwrecks. But over the years, I have learned that most people who are lucky enough to come upon any form of treasure—from gold bullion to brass buttons—would never think of cashing it in. It is a precious gift from the sea, so rare as to be priceless. As it happens, such gifts are most likely to be found in the vast treasure storehouse of the Caribbean. It's likely to appear when you least expect it. One part of the world where this is true is in Charlotte Amalie Harbour, St. Thomas, in the U.S. Virgin Islands.

Charlotte Amalie is one of the loveliest ports in the Caribbean. The green hills behind the harbor are dotted by white stucco and red tile roofs, and at night they create a string of lights that resemble a glowing necklace. The harbor is wide and accommodating, sheltered and deep enough for big luxury liners to find a haven among the fleets of richly appointed yachts that sail the trade winds from St. Thomas out to the Sir Francis Drake

Channel, and on to Virgin Gorda and northeast to Anegada, the island of shipwrecks, in the British Virgin Islands.

It seems hard to believe that three centuries ago an offshore earthquake (not uncommon in this volcanic island chain) caused the waters to flow out of the harbor to fill a massive subsea void opened up by the quake. Dozens of ships were at anchor—galleons returning to Spain, Dutch vessels laden with cargos of rum and sugar cane, British privateers, darkly sullen, observing keenly the ebb and flow of traffic and plotting future adventures. In a single cataclysmic moment, the earth trembled and the ships were trapped. As the water receded, they sank into the silt and mud bottom at crazy angles, beams bursting, keelsons snapping, masts and rigging smashed and wound into a mad jumble. Soon afterward, a tidal wave swept into the harbor, drowning men and boats, erasing the symbols of ambition and empire.

I was introduced to this submarine wonder by Charlie Peet, who some years earlier had come to St. Thomas to head up the Virgin Island Water Safaris sailboat charter service at the Yacht Haven Hotel and Marina. Charlie, who lived aboard a large motor yacht that served as a kind of floating museum for his recovered artifacts, spoke fluently and vividly of that long ago earthquake as if he had been there to witness it.

"Everything out there went down like *that!*" he said, snapping his fingers. He had been exploring the harbor on his own for years. "It's too murky for most divers. But I can assure you, it's an absolute museum on the bottom."

Twenty-four hours later, and 40 feet below the surface, any skepticism I had vanished as quickly as those ancient vessels had. Charlie and I swam slowly and easily along the bottom. Charlie held a line attached to a small john boat on the surface, in which he planned to stow our recovered artifacts. Visibility was awful. The conditions proved once again that there is no such thing as a gin-clear commercial boat basin. I was startled when we bumped into a large mound that looked like a huge gray anthill. Charlie pointed at it and motioned with his free hand that we should gently fan away the silt. Within seconds, the water was a storm of sand and silt as the overburden streamed away. Though he was merely inches from me, Charlie's features were blurred, except for his excited eyes on the other side of his face mask. When the silt settled a bit, we saw a huge artifact mound— the biggest I have ever seen before or since. Bottles, endless bottles; very old bottles, blackened by the sea, some broken, others solid as the day they were made 300 years ago. The vessel in which they were cargo was now far below the mud and sand and completely invisible. Yet somehow this trove of thick sea-going glassware had remained neatly conspicuous on the bottom, as if the ship's crew had deliberately stacked them there, neat and tidy, and only a bit encrusted by sea growth. Methodically, almost fastidiously, Charlie made his selections, gently replacing those items which did not pique his curiosity. He tried to explain what he was doing by talking through the regulator clenched between his teeth, but his words were incomprehensible. All I could make out was a deep rumbling and the sound of air bubbles exploding through the regulator exhaust ports. He carefully placed his choices in a red net bag, which he quickly took to the surface and stowed in the tiny john boat. Then he was on the bottom again. The mini-excavation continued for an hour or so before the inevitable chill of submergence overtook us and our air supply began to give out. Before we surfaced, however, we swam another 100 yards in a circle; artifact mounds were everywhere.

On the warm sunny dock we rinsed our finds in fresh water. It occurred to me that these bottles had remained unseen for centuries, and now here was Charlie Peet and some stranger from the Frozen North bridging this huge gap of time and bringing the past back to the world of sun and sky. It was a heady sensation. One bottle was a glowing amber color with raised letters spelling *P.F. Heering.* Charlie inspected it lovingly. "The distant cousin of *Cherry Heering,*" he said. "Beautiful, isn't it?" Indeed, it was beautiful, but no more so than the rather crudely made Spanish grog bottles which bore no lettering or inscriptions of any kind; it was time that imbued them with a certain magic. One rather large and well-constructed bottle bore the inscription *A. Haake.* Charlie, who had collected hundreds of samples from the harbor, said *A. Haake* was a new one in his experience. Perhaps it was the name of a wealthy shipowner who insisted on personally monogrammed grog bottles. "I think that one may be worth something," Charlie said.

A small crowd had begun to gather around us, mostly locals who lived at the marina. A bystander explained that one of the bottles was obviously from a Spanish galleon; the Spaniards, he explained, fitted the necks and lips of their glassware just so. I showed this person my *A. Haake* and his face brightened. "Haake," he said. "Big land owner in these parts." Then he said something I'll never forget. "I'll give you $700 for it." Charlie gave me a look, a very enigmatic look, indeed. "Thanks," I said. "You're awfully generous. But, really, I think I'll keep this one." The man chuckled. "Suit yourself." Then to Charlie, "You ought to talk to this fellow. Be seeing you."

I now return to the point I made at the beginning of this little saga—two points, really. First, the Caribbean is alive with such treasures. Second, *A. Haake* may be worth $700 (I later learned the gentleman was one of the wealthiest men on St. Thomas and an avid ceramics collector), but the bottle was priceless to me. That is how it is with treasure.

Charlotte Amalie is a good starting place for treasure seekers visiting this part of the Caribbean. The following destinations are offered as equally intriguing possibilities for exploration in the U.S. and British Virgin Islands.

The Mangroves

To the east of Charlotte Amalie is Secret Harbour, so named, according to legend, because of the clandestine activities which occurred there in the days of the pirates. In the nearby Mangroves was a secret meeting place, close to the sea yet sheltered, with water only about waist deep. Gold and silver were traded for opium and other commodities and, on special occasions, women were passed from sailor to sailor in the customary etiquette of the day. There is no reliable written evidence of these bawdy exchanges, and most of what I have learned is word-of-mouth from West Indian friends and my own brief exploration of the Mangroves. Fragments of old clay pipes, grog bottles, and old brass have been recovered, but no bullion that I know of. I am sure it is there; probably quite a lot of it spilled during drunken debauches. Also, a slow, careful inspection of the shallow coves at Secret Harbour occasionally turns up fragments of flintlocks and brass decorations and ship fittings. Any finds will be of great interest to local historians. (*See illustration, page 248.*)

Cow and Calf

Less than a half-mile south of Great St. James Island, off the eastern tip of St. Thomas, is Cow and Calf, a pair of stark volcanic outcroppings standing against the open sea. Cow and Calf are not solid monolithic formations; below the surface they become a series of caves, tunnels, and grottos separated by long avenues of ochre and sand 40 feet below the surface. Within this complex network, carved by ancient volcanic action and the constant movement of the sea, a diver will discover "rooms" partially secluded from the open water and vividly decorated by pink corals, violet "glass sponges," sea fans, and schools of silvery fish that swim in and out as a single ribbon of life. The effect is abstract and haunting.

Armando Jenik, owner of Ocean Adventures, St. Thomas, tells a strange tale about Cow and Calf that becomes believable once you have seen the place. A friend of Jenik's, who wishes to remain anonymous, bumped his camera on a wall inside one of the "rooms," tripping the shutter and strobe. He paid no attention to this accidental happening until his film was developed several months later. One frame revealed an odd sea chest, sea-blackened but intact. The pirate Bluebeard, who operated in these waters, is said to have actually hidden chests in these rooms, which were later recovered by members of his various cut-throat crews. The amazed photographer returned many times to Cow and Calf hoping to find the object which appeared so plainly on his accidental slide, but without success. I have listened to several bizarre explanations, including the theory that the photograph is the result of telekinesis, that Bluebeard's ancient "energy" pervades Cow and Calf to create optical illusions reproducible on film, similar to photos made in old English castles showing a ghostly presence against a black background. Well, anything is possible and photos are not supposed to lie. But I tend to believe that the image on the slide *was* a sea chest and perhaps only one of several hidden in this incredible undersea haunted house. Only time, and plenty of persistence, will tell.

British Virgin Islands

R.M.S. *Rhone* off Salt Island

Ships can be like people in that they sometimes become better known after death. So it is with R.M.S. *Rhone,* one of the most famous shipwrecks in the world. Built in 1865 by the Royal Mail Steam Packet Company, this advanced design 310-foot propeller-driven ship was utterly destroyed two years later by a Force-12 hurricane, one of the most vicious storms ever to sweep through the Virgins. The *Rhone* has been known to the inner circle of explorers for years, but she received worldwide recognition in the 1970s when she became the underwater set for the Hollywood box office thriller, *The Deep.* She still looks like a ship—a most unusual characteristic for most wrecks—and she is somehow haunting, downright tragic, yet compelling to the limits of imagination. Had she been a few yards on either side of the rocks when the hurricane struck, she would have been swept onto a sand beach, and the loss of life would not have been so fearsome. The sea must have wanted her very badly. The *Rhone* is now a British national monument and nothing can be removed—though there is plenty still left in her coral-adorned remains. However, she is one of the best underwater museums anywhere, *the* classic wreck, easily accessible to divers, snorkelers, or those who are happy using a glass-bottom bucket for observation. The stern is in 30 feet of crystal clear water, and her huge rudder stands only ten to 15 feet below the surface. The bow lies at right angles in about 70 feet of water. You need not be a naval architect to see that the *Rhone* is sheer marine artistry. Her 18-foot prop is a pretty sight, and along its length the explorer may examine the gear box and the engine room with its huge engine block now encrusted by vivid orange fire coral. Deeper down lie the boilers, a water pump, plates, and grating. The mid-section reveals a winch that looks ready to work and a full set of open-ended hand wrenches, also seemingly ready to use. There is an open sea chest, still all in one piece, but now lined with soft sponges. On the sand near the iron hull is a mast and an eerie, empty crow's nest. The bowsprit is 150 feet long from tip to davits, and a solitary cannon is pinned beneath the wreckage. The *Rhone* is for looking. *Do not remove any wreckage;* every centimeter is protected under British law! Now, having issued this caveat twice, I wish to relate a true and personal story of how a tiny fragment of the *Rhone* happened to come into my possession.

A few years ago, while sailing through these islands on assignment, I made a special point of visiting the wreck site. We anchored our work boat several hundred yards off Salt Island and motored in aboard a Boston Whaler filled with diving gear, lead weights, cameras, tons of assorted equipment, and three crew members besides myself. Toward the end of our *Rhone* shoot I was coming up off the shallow stern section when I felt something hard in my left hand. This was very odd, since I was suspended in water, well above the ship. At first I thought a piece of my own gear had come loose. I closed my hand without looking and surfaced. The sea was rough that day and, as I floated near the Whaler to wait for the rest of our company to surface, I opened my hand carefully; what I saw truly startled me. Somehow a brass belt buckle in the shape of an ornate wreath was staring up at me from my palm. I could hardly believe it, let alone explain its presence. I saw Carol Craig, our first mate, in the Whaler and I swam toward her through the chop, my fist tightly closed over the buckle. "Carol, give me your hand," I shouted. I placed the object directly into her palm and closed her fingers over it. "Don't let go," I instructed her. "Not until we're back to *Dulcinea,*" our yacht, named after Don Quixote's elusive mistress. About an hour later, we sat around examining the belt buckle; there was a series of numbers etched into its reverse side, probably the general issue number of the sailor to whom it belonged. Obviously it came from the protected *Rhone,* perhaps stirred up by all our activity and the surge of the sea. A good many bizarre things have happened to me at sea, and this one ranks fairly high on my list. It was altogether spooky, as if we had been visited by some strange spirit. The buckle itself was small, about the size of a silver dollar, and its design was lovely. But should I keep it? After all, the *Rhone* was protected, and if it was part of the monument I probably should have recommitted it to the sea. "No," Carol said after I had asked for everyone's opinion. "It's so small and fragile. Toss it back and it's gone forever." That night I thought it over. She was right. I had received similar advice from older and saltier hands. There are times to leave things lie, and there are times when you should take—especially when the item you are taking comes to you by pure chance or fate. "Wear it," Carol said. "Wear it and you bring that sailor back to life."

In the end, it stayed with me. I am still searching the British Admiralty records to match the number on the buckle with a name of a lost sailor. If I find him, I'll look for his descendants, and the buckle will be handed over to them as a gift from the sea.

Anegada Island

If you visit the Virgin Islands primarily for treasure, Anegada is the place to be. This coral and limestone atoll at the northeastern end of the Virgins, known as "The Sunken Land," is a true oceanic perversity which has trapped more than 200 ships. Unlike its volcanic island neighbors, Anegada is 13 miles long, three miles wide and only 28 feet above sea level. In effect, it comes out of nowhere to snare even the wisest mariners. Anegada Passage, a primary sailing route between the Caribbean and the Atlantic, places twin perils before the mariner: either striking the virtually invisible island itself or running up on the shallow 20-mile shoal of elkhorn coral known as Horseshoe Reef. Hardly a more profitable location could be found for the pirates of old. The infamous Edward Teach, known as Blackbeard, used it as one of his favorite hideouts, shared by his various and ever-changing selection of 14 wives. The pirate captains Kirke, Bone, and "Prince Rupert of the Rhine" also ran profitable sorties out of Anegada. Prince Rupert, in fact, once told his

European sponsors that he could operate forever out of this location, since its treasures, he said, were "uncountable." He was right. Centuries later, large numbers of artifacts are continually being recovered along Horseshoe Reef and Anegada's powder-white beaches. Of course, the island remains a notorious ship killer, and any attempt at a landfall without expert local knowledge may add today's explorers to Anegada's more than generous list of victims.

Among those who can get you there and back safely is Bert Kilbride, master of Virgin Gorda's Saba Rock, patriarch of the "Kilbride Clan" (there are no less than 15 of them) and director of Kilbride's Underwater Tours. A former construction engineer, he is one of those mature men who, at some crossroads of a half-forgotten past, decided to escape the Frozen North to pursue a special vision of himself and the lure of treasure. During the 1950s, he realized he was headed for a radical change of lifestyle. "I said to myself, 'Bert, you could wind up a drunk in Miami.' So I figured to heck with that. I made the leap—and it worked." Today he runs a profitable business, writes history, searches after treasure, and pursues his dreams on a full-time basis—an energetic personality that's all too rare in the languid atmosphere of the tropics.

It had been a standing journalistic ambition of mine to interview Kilbride, who had made a reputation for himself as one of the deans of Caribbean treasure. He had pulled together a lot of information about the wrecks of Horseshoe Reef, which he can describe in detail and analyze *ad infinitum*. Finding him and pinning him down, however, was no simple task. I had been sailing through the Virgins for nearly ten days before I was able to raise him on the marine radio and set up an interview.

I landed at Virgin Gorda and rowed out to Saba Rock, where he made his headquarters. One look at him was enough to convince me that Kilbride was the quintessential adventurer and explorer whose life could not be separated from his work; like his old friend, Mel Fisher, he had become synonymous with treasure.

Kilbride, a compact and powerfully-built man of 65, looked 20 years younger. The figure of a gold sea nymph dangled from his neck, and as he spoke he fingered the object the way some people finger worry beads.

"Sorry I was hard to get," he said. "The *Defiance* has been keeping me pretty busy." The *Defiance* is a British privateer thought to have been carrying an immense fortune when it ran up on Horseshoe Reef in 1652

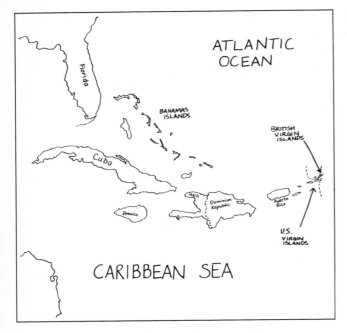

Shipkiller

The bottom of the Caribbean Sea is paved with treasure and the remains of lost civilizations. Nations of the Old World built outpost empires among these islands and used slaves for agriculture work and other heavy labor, while British, French, and Dutch pirates preyed unrelentingly upon the treasure trade of the Spanish Conquistadors. Over the centuries vast fortunes slipped away from greedy hands and came to rest in the silent green depths. Uncharted reefs claimed untold numbers of ships and sailors. One of the most dangerous of these reefs is the sprawling ring of razor-sharp coral heads surrounding the island of Anegada, located at the northeastern end of the Virgin Island chain. Known as Horse Shoe Reef, this death trap extends a full 20 miles to the south of Anegada and has claimed more than 200 vessels between 1750 and 1929. The reef is especially dangerous because Anegada, sometimes called "The Low Land," is only 28 feet above sea level, making it almost impossible to see in any but the clearest weather. At present, the British are working with treasure hunters, salvors, historians, and archaeologists to unlock the mysteries hidden in the coral. No artifacts may be removed from Anegada or any other sites in the British Virgins.

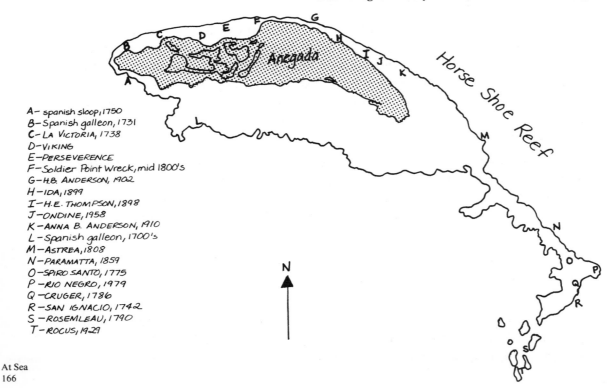

A— spanish sloop, 1750
B— Spanish galleon, 1731
C— La Victoria, 1738
D— Viking
E— Perseverence
F— Soldier Point Wreck, mid 1800's
G— H.B. Anderson, 1902
H— Ida, 1899
I— H.E. Thompson, 1898
J— Ondine, 1958
K— Anna B. Anderson, 1910
L— Spanish galleon, 1700's
M— Astrea, 1808
N— Paramatta, 1859
O— Spiro Santo, 1775
P— Rio Negro, 1979
Q— Cruger, 1786
R— San Ignacio, 1742
S— Rosemleau, 1790
T— Rocus, 1929

The Wreck of the R.M.S. *Rhone*

The Royal Mail Steamer *Rhone*, used by Hollywood as the underwater set of "The Deep," is the most famous shipwreck in the British Virgin Islands. In real life, the 310-foot propeller driven ship was destroyed October 29, 1867, at Black Point Rock, Salt Island, by one of the fiercest hurricanes ever to ravage the Caribbean. The disaster unfolded on the morning of the blow, as Captain Robert F. Woolley held the *Rhone* against heavy swells just outside Great Harbor, Peter Island. The barometer dipped to 27.95 inches. Gale force winds were building. Another ship, R.M.S. *Conway*, stood nearby. Captain Woolley signalled that both vessels would be safer at Rhode Harbor, Tortola. Because the *Rhone* was considered more seaworthy, the *Conway's* passengers were transferred aboard. At 11 a.m., the hurricane smashed across the islands from the north at Force-12 on the Beaufort scale. During a brief lull the *Conway* made a dash across the Sir Francis Drake Channel but was hit by a second blast and driven onto the rocks of Tortola. The *Rhone*, meanwhile, lost its 3,000-pound anchor and 300 feet of anchor chain. With its engines churning, *Rhone* plowed into the channel hoping to gain steerage way. But the hurricane bore down with a second blast, this time from the south. The ship was trapped and was carried helplessly onto the rocks at Salt Island, where she heeled over, broke in two, and sank instantly. Fifty feet on either side of the rocks would have carried her onto the relative safety of a sandy beach. Only one of the more than 300 passengers survived, along with a few crew members. Captain Woolley was washed into a skylight and then carried overboard. His body was never found.

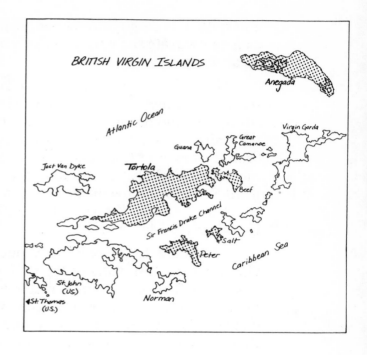

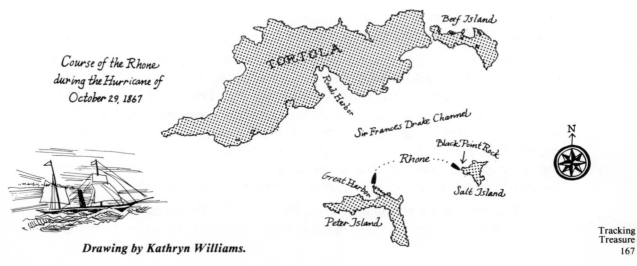

Course of the Rhone during the Hurricane of October 29, 1867

Drawing by Kathryn Williams.

and spilled its cargo into the sea. Kilbride was working with British officials to excavate the wreck, which was only one of many he was working on at Anegada.

His home has become a showplace for the relics he has brought back from the sea such as a silver dinner set for 16, plus delicate porcelain cups, silver trays and bowls, all recovered from the *Rhone* before she was placed off limits to collectors by the British. Other *Rhone* items included a small bronze cannon in fine condition, an eerie religious figurine which struck me as being cabalistic, several conventional statues, and some darkly polished Stone Age implements found in the waters off Virgin Gorda. These last items reflected Kilbride's fascination with palentology and the natural history of the islands.

"There's a lot of prehistory out there," he said, motioning toward Gorda Sound. "All sorts of things have been dredged up from as deep as 1,000 feet. This used to be a much deeper sea, you know." He explained his theory that the eastern Virgins were at one time affected by radical climatic changes, and that the granite rock formations, such as the famous Baths at Virgin Gorda, were not indigenous and were deposited here millions of years ago by great glacial movements.

This was fascinating information, but I had come to talk treasure. Kilbride invited me to join him and some of the "Clan" at the Bitter End Yacht Club, a world famous stopover at Virgin Gorda for the boating crowd. In the easy going opulence of the Bitter End, treasure talk seemed as natural as sails, rigging, and long-legged women.

"There's one thing I want you to understand," Kilbride began. "I'm not a profiteer. I'm in it for the history, for the challenge of being the first to lay eyes on something that's been lost for centuries."

Kilbride had excavated 65 wrecks of varying nationalities at his own expense and never really made any money at it. He stressed the difficulties of turning any sort of profit on a full-scale dig. True, a treasure hunter might turn a few rare coins or other artifacts into cash, provided he could find a buyer. But on the long term, full-blown excavation requires monumental time and money, to say nothing of manpower. The notion of covering all expenses and turning a profit, he said, borders on the extreme fringes of belief. Even so, investors were eager to get involved.

"There's never a problem finding investors," Kilbride explained. Most of them were affluent, secure "people who can afford to write it off." He showed me several typical treasure contracts, all of them very straightforward documents emphasizing the enormous risks involved in such investments. One contract called for an initial $25,000 investment which gave the purchaser 1/800 of a share of all recovered treasure. Kilbride did some quick calculations on a cocktail napkin and showed me that under this agreement the treasure hunter would have to bank $20 million before the investor broke even.

"They're well aware of the odds," he said, "and they know it's not for everybody. You don't find widows dropping all their savings into this sort of enterprise—and you wouldn't take their money anyway. The people who come my way are excited by the hunt. They think it's fashionable to tell their friends that they've got a piece of the *Atocha* or some other dig."

As for liquidity, Kilbride said treasure had a funny way of remaining as solid as a bar of silver. The truly negotiable finds, such as specie and bullion, generally wind up in a safe at the bank, where it acts as collateral for cash needed to continue the digging. Hopefully, this stash gets bigger over time. When it's big enough, the investor may begin to claim portions of it.

From the spacious veranda of the Bitter End, I looked out past tiny Saba Rock, imagining the invisible line that divided the aquamarine waters of the Caribbean from the deep cobalt of the Atlantic. There, on that plane of open sea, was Anegada and its vast storehouse of mystery. I had drawn up a brief list of treasure ships known to be hidden by the reef, and I showed it to Kilbride for confirmation. Here is a sampling:

La Victoria, sailing from Puerto Rico bound for Spain, wrecked in 1738 with a cargo estimated on today's market to be in excess of $5.75 million in gold and silver.

San Ignacio, wrecked in 1742 at the southeastern end of Anegada in very shallow water with a cargo of gold (estimated at $1.5 million) and a great number of crude diamonds of inestimable value.

The so-called "Great Spanish Galleon," still unidentified, lost sometime in the 1600s. Records are very sketchy, but it's understood that the survivors buried a considerable treasure at a place referred to on a 1775 chart as "Ye Treasure Point." The trove has never been uncovered.

Other Anegada wrecks on the list were the galleon *N.S. de Lorento y San Francisco Xavier* (1730); *Victory,* a Spanish warship (1738); and an unidentified sloop returning with the fruits of a salvage operation on the

Nuestra Señora de Soledad, a treasure ship lost off Cape Hatteras, North Carolina.

Kilbride knew all of them, and a lot more besides. "There are hundreds of *known* wrecks in these islands, and plenty that aren't known. Anegada represents a big share of them, but you can chart them almost continuously as far south as St. Croix."

He reeled off a list in rapid-fire order: The *Bark,* carrying French settlers, sunk in 1647 near St. John; the *Graham,* a British merchantman sunk on the south side of St. Croix in 1769; *Neptune,* a Dutch vessel lost in the nearby harbor of Tortola; *Ortello,* a slaver lost in 1783 at Tortola; *La Trinadad,* a galleon carrying $6 million in silver and gold, lost in 1738 off Beef Island.

You may sense that Kilbride and other treasure hunters are inordinately overtaken by the demands of their most unusual trade. Obsession is the operative word, and it is a necessary characteristic of anyone who's made a life of treasure hunting. Without it, one may never leave the classroom or the archives, and there's the danger of becoming as obscure as the past itself.

Kilbride's summation of why anyone in their right mind would take it upon themselves to track treasure has always seemed essentially humanistic, a quality understood by those with the curiosity and the tenacity to actually live the life. After a long evening at the Bitter End, he leaned forward and half-whispered, "How many adventures do we get in this life anyway? Think about it. Treasure and history. They're like food. We need it to live."

The Netherlands Antilles

This corner of the Caribbean, which extends from the northern coast of Venezuela eastward to the Windward Islands, was first explored, mapped, and colonized by the Spanish prior to 1500. Subsequent invasions and exploitations by the British, French, and Dutch added greatly to the region's storehouse of treasure. In the wake of this historical evolution, the Dutch have even been so thoughtful as to leave us a 17th-century underwater city at St. Eustatius, in the Windwards. Nearly four centuries after Oranjestad sank below the waves, it is still yielding significant reminders of the past.

But the challenge is considerable. The maritime logs are not as detailed as those in the United States, especially in Florida, where treasure is part of the ambiance. The Dutch Caribbean offers enticing bits of hard information and a lot of blank spaces waiting to be filled. In this sense, these islands appeal to those who love a mystery.

The most promising are St. Eustatius, St. Maarten, Bonaire, and Curacao. Like the other islands mentioned in this book, these are known to me; I have visited them over a period of years, and I've done a little of my own investigation. There are no guarantees in the treasure chase, but at the same time no story told here qualifies as fiction; they are real and told in hopes of stimulating further exploration.

Bonaire

This tiny island off the coast of Venezuela has long been a favorite of the SCUBA crowd. Its clear water, ease of diving, living reefs, and marine life keep it high on the list of most desirable Caribbean destinations.

Bonaire appears under various names on the oldest maps drawn of the Western Hemisphere. In September, 1499, when it was discovered by Juan de la Cosa and the famed Florentine navigator, Amerigo Matteo Vespucci, Vespucci called it *Isla de Palo Brasil,* the Dye Wood Island. Fifteen years later the Spanish had exported almost all of the native Caiquetios, an Arawak tribe still living in the Stone Age, to its slave camps at Haiti. By 1526, a permanent Spanish government was commanding the island. Being 62 miles north of Venezuela placed it nicely along the Spanish trade routes, and there is evidence suggesting that a substantial amount of treasure shipping passed under its lee. The question is, how many of those treasure galleons never made it past this low ancient island of Bonaire? And, where are they?

Bonaire has not gained a popular treasure island image. Divers visit to explore the rich marine biosphere; the idea of history on this island never goes any farther back than World War II, when this Dutch area of the Caribbean was crawling with Nazi U-boats. The Flamingo Beach Hotel, that *Don't Stop the Carnival* jewel of a place where so many divers go, was once a camp for German prisoners of war. No one seems to recall the New World conquerors and the spoils of the empire they left behind in these waters. In fact, I do not recall ever seeing a physical reference to the Spanish occupation anywhere on the island. As a result, there are few historical records on the area. After three visits I've concluded that Bonaire has more to it than meets the eye.

For example, in 1678, a fleet of French warships and two privateers went down in a storm on nearby Aves Island. Out of 18 vessels, only two survived, and one of them was the privateer. As far as I know, none of these vessels have been surveyed or investigated.

Earlier still, in 1610, the Spanish capitana, *San Felipe,* and a smaller escort vessel went down in sight of Bonaire. There was some salvage, using Arawak slave divers, and some recovery. This 850-ton, 42-gun vessel has not been seen since. So there is a lot more of *San Felipe* below the surface.

A ship reported to be carrying treasure was the strange playboy Spanish schooner, *San Carlos-II.* It seems that *San Carlos-II* may have been a hired vessel run by private owners for the Crown. Over time, it gained a reputation suggesting independent piracy. The ship went down (at a date not determined) east of Aves Island. The rumors of treasure are probably true and might be checked against a manifest in Seville. In any case, her approximate location is a mystery.

The records that do exist describe "unidentified Spanish vessel carrying pearls, Ave Island," and no date. Then there are specific names, even dates: *John & Stephen,* Irish merchantmen, lost August 10, 1776; *Mariposa,* Spanish merchantman, lost 1819, Aves Island; *Morning Star,* American merchantman, bound for New York out of Curacao.

No one that I know of has come to look for any of these ships, and few on the island ever speak of them. My chum Wendell, up in Rincon, once remarked, "The ships, they be gone, mon!"

But not entirely forgotten, Wendell.

I know of two local sites that may be of interest to the motivated treasure seeker. Experiencing them requires more than merely casual interest. They are offered as potential exploratory work, without a single guarantee of gold.

The first is a ship that has been known simply as the "Mystery Wreck." Research by Ellsworth Boyd, a Maryland marine historian, has turned up the name and origin of this steel wreck that has intrigued visitors for years. Built in Glasgow, Scotland in 1874, the *Mairi Bhan* (Gaelic for "Bonny Mary") was bound from Trinidad to Marseille with a load of asphalt when she sank off Bonaire December 7, 1912. A three-masted bark, the *Mairi Bhan* is 240 feet long with a beam of 37 feet. She now lies in deep water, ranging from 130 to 220 feet. Her wreckage is strewn down an underwater slope that rolls off at a 70 degree angle. She must have been driven ashore in a storm, dashed on the ironshore, and tumbled backward down this steep hill. There is a lot of wreckage to see. About midway down the slope is a large iron mast, slicing across the drop-off like a sword. Following it down to its end, at about 130 feet you see the ship's iron ribs. She has that 19th-century transitional look about her—a long proud bowsprit, the lines of a sailing ship, the metalwork of a steamer. At the bottom of the slope, away on the white sand and just before the scene is obscured by darkness is the ship's crow's nest, upright in the sand. It is an impressive sight—all the more so at 220 feet below the surface.

As I said earlier, this is not a project for the casual visitor of the deep. At 130 feet, I felt a very pronounced nitrogen narcosis. I noticed, however, that our crew drifted down to the 200 foot level; they looked like strange underwater creatures, and the popping of the strobe by our cameraman resembled a lightning bug. One of the photographers was in the crow's nest, his strobe flashing in slow motion, the air bubbles sounding like steel bells. Time seemed to stand still, and I was no longer aware of time or depth or the 45 minutes of seat-of-the-pants decompression we had to go through before we could surface. Given the depths involved, I agree with the local divers who will not take anyone to the *Mairi Bhan* unless they are fit, experienced, and sane.

You may wonder about that last attribute. There are sane and safe ways to see the *Mairi Bhan.* For example, a diver need not go very deep to see it. By controlling buoyancy and hanging in mid-water at 50 feet you can perceive the broad outlines. The ship is close to a northwest point of land just south of the Bonaire Petroleum Company. The water is deep and clear; horizontal visibility may be in excess of 110 feet on a good day. At 50 feet you can see the mast and parts of the rigging. A few yards farther out on the seaward side it's possible to catch sight of the long bowsprit and the deep basin where the crow's nest came to rest. At 80 to 100 feet more details are visible, and at 130 feet most of the hull is yours. You can make good detailed photographs with a Nikonos.

If the water is particularly clear, even a snorkeler can observe portions of the wreck from the surface. There is the mast and sundry wreckage strewn down the slope. The dim outline of the hull may be visible, but it would require remarkably clear water to make out the entire length of the ship.

Having said this, I issue a caution: Do not undertake the *Mairi Bhan* on your own. Go with local divers or the hotel's dive guides. All have excellent knowledge of the area and are alert to the tricky aspects of the site. Bonaire divers are a sane, safe, and competent breed. Use them!

A far less demanding site is at the southwest corner of the island, directly across from the salt ponds of the Antilles International Salt Company. On the shore side, at the head of the beach, you'll see a 200-year-old shipmaster's house, a grim line of stone slave huts, and two tall obelisks, painted blue and orange. These obelisks were used by the ship captains of old to raise sight of the low-lying island out of the sea and as markers to guide them into port. The old salt works have been in the same place for a long time, and the ships docked near the obelisks carried the precious salt back to Europe. While the ship was tied up in port to take on cargo, the sailors dumped the inbound ballast and replaced it with salt. Very often, the inbound ballast consisted of cannons and cannon shot of various shapes and sizes. The bottom here is littered with this refuse—it has become an ancient burial ground for the obsolete weapons of the Old World. And there were other discards—coins, grog bottles, jewelry, and bodies. The fish have taken care of the bodies, but the rest is still there just below the surface.

An old tourist map of Bonaire, printed by the remarkable Caribbean publisher, R.J. Dovale, shows the beach as a good place to go snorkeling. Dovale knew his history, was familiar with the loading docks, and believed that holiday visitors might find some relic to take home with them. Over the years, however, the area has been downplayed. Perhaps the salt works remind the visitor too much of the Frozen North. Or, it may be that storms have made the beach somewhat difficult to negotiate. Big rollers occasionally come crashing in, and there are large fish in the area. As with the *Mairi Bhan,* I caution the explorer to go with local guides who know what to expect. Under good circumstances (a calm sea), a survey of the bottom from 10 to 110 feet will produce a fascinating collection of objects. Generations of maritime lore is down there, safely tucked away. If you go to it with respect, armed with knowledge and good guidance, your reward will be a close-up personal encounter with the past. That, too, is treasure.

Curacao

Like Bonaire, the neighboring island of Curacao is a yet-to-be uncovered treasure area. Many vessels out of Columbia and Venezuela on the South

American mainland ran afoul of the island but, unfortunately, precise data is scant. The clues that do exist are enticing.

The remains of the old settlement of Willemstad, on the west side of the island, were blown into the sea in 1808 by a fearsome hurricane. Records indicate that whole buildings, churches, and portions of a fort were flung into the Caribbean; a fairly large graveyard is said to have been swept away. To date, it is still there, unseen and unsurveyed in relatively shallow water.

Among the ships lost on the island's reefs are: *Good Hope,* registry unknown, en route from France, lost in 1780; *Escape,* also of unknown registry, en route from Martinique, lost in 1802; H.M.S. *Firefly,* a 12-gun British frigate, lost in 1807; *Penelope,* British merchantman, lost in 1809; *Ceres,* a Dutch merchant vessel, lost in 1817; and the American schooner *Cecila,* lost in 1822 off the western tip of the island.

These are the *known* vessels. Many more are waiting to be found. A few years ago I was a little reluctant to recommend Curacao as a destination for underwater research. The island's dive facilities were indifferent at best. Today the situation has changed dramatically with the appearance of Peter Hughes' Underwater Curacao, located east of Willemstad. Hughes is perhaps the Caribbean's most successful dive entrepreneur. His success is based on providing a high quality operation—plenty of boats, excellent diving gear, competent staff, and an empathetic attitude toward those who are looking for the unusual.

Curacao is a sophisticated island community with good libraries and extensive ship registers. Solid research can be undertaken. Hopefully, the fragments of the treasure puzzle in this part of the world can be searched out and eventually pieced together into a coherent picture.

The Bahamas

The seemingly endless islands and banks of the Bahama archipelago are among the richest treasure grounds in the world. It is second only to Florida in shipwreck excavation. In fact, wreck salvage has been a thriving industry here for nearly three centuries. Many discoveries have been made, but a lot more will follow as wreck excavation activity is imported into the islands from the United States and Europe. Marine archaeologists from Texas A&M University are getting started in these waters, and teams from other institutions are bound to follow. As for treasure hunting, it always was and always will be one of the primary lures. The value of Bahamian treasure is virtually inestimable, but modern scholars agree it amounts to billions of dollars on the metals markets.

Spectacular finds are by no means limited to well-financed salvage groups. Many present day Bahamian families made their millions chasing Spanish gold, and there are verified accounts of local fishermen coming up with remarkable treasures. In 1978, I met a conch fisherman at Great Abaco Island who had accidentally come upon a cache of Spanish silver coins in less than six feet of water at the northeastern tip of the island. The coins filled a small bucket. There must have been more than 100 of them. The ever-productive Robert Marx tells of a fisherman in Grand Cay who discovered several gold and silver bars and several hundred gold coins. As might be expected, the fisherman refused to disclose the location. And, in 1933, fishermen working a reef on the north side of Green Turtle Key brought up a safe containing $100,000 in American gold coinage. When I was at San Salvador Island, Columbus' first port in the New World, an elderly woman who called herself Hannah showed me a gold ring and a Spanish *reale* she had picked up on the beach. She said similar finds had been made by a group of children after a storm in 1975. There are other tales, of course, and when placed end-to-end they form a variegated chain of treasure spilled in these waters over more than four centuries. No Bahama island, it seems, holds a monopoly.

Besides wreck materials, explorers are studying what is loosely referred to as "Atlantis," below 10 feet of water off the west coast of Bimini, and what appears to be the remains of ancient stone buildings beneath the waters of Andros Island. I have visited both, and they are exciting. Bimini's Atlantis is a series of rectangular stone formations close to shore. It is certainly not the image of Atlantis we get from the Greek philosopher Plato; instead, the Bimini formations (sometimes called "Bimini Road") appear to be the remains of a very old loading dock. The remarkably large stone slabs are nearly equal in size (about ten-by-six feet) and may have been a foundation for an above-water structure. The clean sandy area around it may be rich with artifacts, though this remains to be proven. The submerged structures off Andros may be of Mayan origins; they are not as modern in appearance as the sunken city of Oranjestad, off St. Eustatius. The Andros remains reveal no westernized artifacts, no cannons or bottles. It is, if anything, much older than Oranjestad.

Though you may explore all you like, a permit is needed to salvage or excavate a site. These permits are issued by the Ministry of Transportation and are good for five years. The conditions are that the finder keeps 75 percent; the Bahamian government is entitled to the rest, off the top. Small accidental or incidental finds go under the honor system. But *beware!* Bahamian law is very strict, and there are horror stories of foreign divers spending a year or more in jail for unauthorized salvage.

More than 3,500 wrecks are known to exist in the Bahamas. The following is a small sampling.

Bimini

The "English Wreck": This vessel was discovered in 1968 by Captain Skeet La Chance deep in the sand a mile and a quarter north and slightly west of North Rocks Light. Not long after finding it and making a tentative identification, storms and wave action covered the ship again. Four years later, La Chance "rediscovered" it. Its ribs can be found at the edge of the Moselle Bank in 17 feet of very clear water. Israeli explorer Shlomo Cohen claims to have found artifacts at the site. Cohen reported a substantial amount of pottery is strewn about the area. Other relics have been uncovered but the finders have been somewhat reluctant to describe them.

Sapona: This is a steel-hulled World War I ship originally named the *Lone Star.* It grounded during a hurricane in 1926, $1^1/2$ miles east of Turtle Rocks, off south Bimini. The wreck is above water, its huge screw still in place. During prohibition she served as a secret storehouse for bootleg liquor, and during World War II she was an ignominious bomber target. A lot of old ordnance is on the sandy bottom, and you must be very careful in handling it. *Sapona* is far from a gold and silver treasure wreck, but it can be a fair storehouse of military items for those with a specific interest in World War II ammunition. For those seeking reminders of the prohibition era, there are old whiskey bottles which appear on the sand after rough weather.

Santa Elena: This Spanish frigate went down November 12, 1719, $1^1/2$ miles from Bone Fish Hole. She is down in 48 feet of water. *Santa Elena* was reportedly carrying gold and silver specie which was estimated by treasure hunters in the early 1960s to be worth $1.2 million on today's market; the figure may be multiplied by a factor of ten or more. The Spaniards may have accomplished some salvage using West Indian divers. The site is still worth investigating.

San Juan: This Spanish treasure ship and four escort ships went to the bottom in 1586, between Cape Florida and the Bimini Islands. The wreckage is strewn on the shoals between Castle Rock and Great Isaac, evidence that the vessels were destroyed by a violent storm. The jumble of wreckage ranges from very shallow water (eight feet or less) down to about 75 feet. Some salvage was attempted, but it appears that most of the treasure, valued as high as $10 million in gold and silver, was not recovered. This indicates that the glittery stuff was in deeper water. It's probably still there.

British merchantman *Active,* en route from Jamaica to London, was wrecked in 1794, during a storm at Cat Cay, south of Bimini. *Active* carried typical West Indies cargo and there was some money on board. Early attempts at salvage were only partially successful, and most of the wreck is still there. No exact location or value is available at this time.

Grand Bahama Island

"Memory Rocks Wrecks": This area stands offshore north and west of the northern tip of Grand Bahama. It has been a ship killer for centuries and the bottom here is rich in artifacts. It has been difficult to identify the remains of these vessels; many are strangely mixed together, and there are wrecks on top of wrecks. In 1966, however, the Spanish origins in this population of lost ships was confirmed by Norman Scott's American-based salvage company, Expeditions Unlimited. Working under contract to the Bahamian government, Scott's team recovered 16th and 17th-century Spanish coins minted at Potosi and Lima, with dates ranging from 1693 to 1697.

"Silver Point Wrecks": There are at least three lost ships at Silver Point, which is located a half-mile west of Lucaya at the farthest southern point of Grand Bahama. No positive identification has been made. Like the ships at Memory Rocks, the debris is churned up and widely scattered. So far no silver or gold has been recovered. However, a generous sampling of ceramics, glass fragments, bottles, brass nails, and ballast stones have been found. Locals say the area has been mostly salvaged, but each new storm brings new materials to the surface.

"Lucayan Silver Wreck": At a point slightly south and west of Silver Point is what is left of a much-salvaged wreck of undetermined origin. Some marine historians believe it was one of Dutch admiral Piet Heyn's fleet, possibly a ship called *Van Lynden.* Others say it is a prize vessel captured by Heyn. In 1964 and 1965, American treasure hunters Jack

Slack and Gary Simmons recovered thousands of Spanish silver coins in huge 200-pound conglomerates. Using an air lift, they scoured the bottom, recovering conglomerates and individual coins at the rate of 300-per-hour. The coins bore mint marks from Potosi, Bolivia, and Mexico. The earliest date found was 1584, and the latest, 1641. Just after January 1, 1965, newspapers began reporting that a $9 million treasure find had been made at Grand Bahama—a trove of more than 10,000 coins. The American salvors who had tried to keep the find secret now faced worldwide press coverage and innumerable claim jumpers. The Bahamian government marched onto the scene, demanding its share of the find. Huge sums of money were committed to overhead costs to continue work on the site. Meanwhile, the rare cobb coins, which had been appraised at $225 apiece in New York, tumbled in value when it was learned that 10,000 were on hand. The antiquity and rarity factors simply nose-dived. The numbers and percentages now looked bleak. The Bahamian government owned 25 percent, and an organization known as the Bahamas Oceanographic Society had 20 percent. The agent hired to sell the coins also had 25 percent. The Americans had virtually no equity left in the dig and faced substantial overhead bills. Finally, they decided to sell out for a nominal sum. When it was over, 16,000 coins were recovered—all silver. In his book, *Finders, Losers,* Slack speculates that the wreck contained too much silver not to have also carried gold. As it now stands, the presence of gold is pure speculation; or, as some have suggested, it may have been there but was salvaged years earlier. It's known that veins of silver coins still turn up after a storm—a few at a time. Close inspection may prove rewarding.

Gorda Cay

This popular diving area is located at the edge of the Northwest Providence Channel off the southwestern finger of Abaco Island. The reef area here is rich in artifacts, but getting at the best of them may be next to impossible. Underwater geography is the key: the reef stands in only 10 to 20 feet of water before dropping off steeply into the great cobalt blue depths of the channel. This is certainly the limiting factor of the so-called "Gorda Cay Treasure," presumed to be from a Spanish ship that wrecked here in 1660. Some historians believe it was the *San Pedro,* an extraordinarily wealthy treasure ship which fell victim to a storm. In the 1950s, 70-pound silver ingots were recovered bearing markings of the Royal Mint at Santa Fe de Bogota, dated 1652. A quantity of coinage was also recovered, along with sabres, pistols, and other materials. The ingots and coins are believed to be only traces of the mother lode; the main haul was most likely in the stern section, which broke off and disappeared into the deep Channel. However, patient fanning of the powdery white sand of the shallows continues to reveal a variety of artifacts—and an occasional piece of eight. The mother lode probably will never be found.

Great Abaco Island

This large island is only now beginning to capture the enthusiasm of treasure hunters. Many ships have come to ruin here, but pinpointing them will require time, money, and persistence. One of the reasons Abaco has been somewhat overlooked has to do with the kinds of ships that were lost—not a single galleon appears on the records. The Spanish treasure ships dashed themselves to pieces on the numerous surrounding cays; none made it past the fringing reefs, or at least none that I can find. But since treasure is a relative thing, formed in the eye of the beholder, the following list of Great Abaco victims may appeal to the reader whose fancy is beyond precious metals: American merchantmen *Lilly,* en route from Georgia to Nassau, and *Adventure,* en route to Havana, lost December 5, 1803; American ship *Hiram,* en route to Havana from New York, lost 1808; American merchant ship *Twin Sisters,* en route to Havana out of Baltimore, lost February 18, 1812; American vessel *Carlton,* en route to Havana, lost April 16, 1812; Scottish merchantman *Irmelinda,* sailing from Clyde to Nassau, lost November 9, 1812.

In 1817, seven vessels were lost near the island. Among them: American ship *Louisa,* bound for Havana; Bahamian merchantman *Do,* bound for Nassau; American ship *Industry,* en route to Boston; *Adeline,* vessel of unknown registry, en route to Havana out of Savannah; American ship *Robert Potter,* en route from Norfolk to Havana; American ships *Natchez Belle* and *Frances Mary,* both en route from New York to New Orleans.

No fewer than 16 large ships have disappeared completely at Great Abaco between 1821 and 1824—"Bermuda Triangle" mysteries.

The Bahama Banks

These vast oceanic formations encircling the Bahamas are at once hypnotic and merciless. No wonder so many New World ships disappeared close to safe harbors at Nassau, Andros, Great Exuma, San Salvador, and the Turks and Caicos islands. Many of these ill-starred vessels come down to us under the ghostly heading of "unidentified." These nameless voyagers, groaning under the weight of their treasures, went up on the Banks and were never seen again. Glib science-fiction buffs like to ascribe these disappearances to Little Green Men; but the reality of the Banks is far more convincing.

We do not know even now how many "unidentifieds" are out there, both old and new. But consider a tiny sampling of the old treasure ships we can pin down: *Santa Clara,* lost October 6, 1564, at El Mime Shoals; the *Nuestra Señora de la Concepción,* lost on the Silver Shoals in 1641, with millions in her hold, and found in modern times by master treasure hunter Burt Webber; three nameless privateers wrecked with all their loot in 1644, at Arcas Reef near the Old Bahama Channel; the fabulously wealthy galleon *Nuestra Señora de la Maravillas,* wrecked in 1656, on the Little Bahama Bank 20 miles north of Memory Rock with five million pesos on board; the *San Juan Evangelista,* vanished in 1714, near Grand Bahama Channel with 300,000 pesos.

Indeed, the Bahama Banks are paved with gold.

A quick tour of this part of the sea will tell you why so many ships have perished here. The Banks are gigantic sand-covered mountains that rise thousands of feet off the floor of the Atlantic and end only a few feet below the surface. They enclose the Bahamas from a point below the Tropic of Cancer northward beyond Bimini and the Berry Islands before plunging once again into the deep at the Northwest Providence Channel, just below Freeport, Grand Bahama. North and east of Grand Bahama, the Little Bahama Bank rises out of the sea and extends to Great Abaco and the deeps of the Northeast Providence Channel.

The peaks of this huge mountain range form the bottom of what may be seen as a great shallow sea covering thousands of square miles. This sea is a maze of shoals and sand bars bathed in emerald hues. It is punctuated by huge "blue holes" which plunge downward into a sunless abyss. With the constantly shifting shoals come uncharted cays, which rise up one day and are gone the next. There are low boulders and volcanic upthrustings as big as a modern office building, and only a few appear on the map. And there is the fickle weather—sunny blue skies at 9 A.M. can give way to howling gale by noon, which can dash any vessel to bits on that hypnotic bottom. Considering the elements, it is a wonder any galleons made the passage intact.

Even with our modern navigation aids the Banks are a challenge. After all, there is no way technology can fix the aspects of a sea that perversely changes its geography every day.

Touched by the "Triangle"

The "Bermuda Triangle" statistics are pretty alarming. I used to puzzle over it when I was younger, but until I nearly became one of those statistics I did not fully comprehend the forces at work in the Great Shallow Sea. The moment of truth came for me in 1979, while on assignment in the Caribbean. Our crew had chartered a single-engine aircraft out of Miami; our assignment: *Flying and Diving in the Bahamas.* We were to cover more than 2,000 miles of open water, and almost immediately we noticed peculiar magnetic anomalies that affected both cockpit compasses. For most of our journey this was of no real concern. We could see the islands we were flying toward, and the strange compass gyrations were shrugged off; shrugged off, that is, until we departed Cape Eleuthera bound for Great Exuma on a bright, cloudless morning.

This leg of the trip was the first time we were out of sight of land. As it turned out, the anomalies came back at us: the compasses were useless. We could not raise any ground control facilities on the radio or pick up the ordinary vectoring signals. Meanwhile, we were flying through rapidly thickening cumulus clouds above deep white capped seas. *This is not supposed to happen,* I told myself. *This is the stuff of Hollywood movies!* Forty-five minutes later, I was preparing to ditch, if necessary. I checked our survival gear: pitiful, worse than useless. The wave tops were creeping up, the water very deep, the color of coal. Finally, we found a deserted airstrip on a tiny cay, landed safely (and none too soon), raised someone on the radio, received bearings, and made it to Great Exuma, apparently on the vapors left in the gasoline tanks. Land never looked so good!

This story is not meant to alarm you; it's intended to remind you that the Bahama Banks are strange, unpredictable above or below, and must be treated with respect.

These days, a modern, well-equipped, and thoroughly seaworthy treasure hunter can explore the Banks at sea level and, at some point along the route, gold or silver will pass under the keel. But how does one stay out there long enough to get it on board? The unpredictable nature of the sea is always there, and to overstay your time is to beg the same fate as the New World sailors.

But I believe the Banks should and can be explored safely if you're willing to accept certain limitations. For instance, sailing the perimeters is fine if you know exactly where deep water is if you need it. A big wind over a shallow sea equals a wrecked boat—unless you can find depth quickly.

Literature about the site (which ought to be carried on board) is essential but not perfect. If you cruise the Banks, you'll need more information than any single source can provide, so do as much pre-checking as possible and use several local sources.

Check in with the harbor master or other authorities. Tell them your destination and estimated time of return. Do not venture out unless you have at least one marine radio on board. It's a good idea to head in to port several hours before sundown. I have known overnighters in these islands and I have no trouble confessing that they are braver souls than I.

One more point which I feel compelled to relate from my own experience and the experiences of others: As in centuries past, the Bahama Banks are an occasional haven for pirates. Today's breed are mostly drug runners, and even an inadvertent encounter could mean trouble. I realize that I am tossing cold water on the cheerful sunny face of charter boating, yet staying on the safe side keeps you cheerful longer. There was a time not so long ago when the suggestion of the existence of modern day pirates caused guffaws and even derision among those who should have known better. But this has changed lately, and the rules of sailing have changed, too. The age-old ethic of leaping immediately to the aid of any ship in distress has been officially rewritten by our Coast Guard, which now suggests standing clear and radioing for help unless the disabled vessel is clearly sinking or in flames.

Enough of this. A motivated explorer will not be able to resist the Bahama Banks. They are enticing ancient seaways, rich in treasure and natural wonders and haunted by a long history. If you set sail upon them, you may follow the admonition of my friend Eddy from Bimini: "Go good, mon."

Ancient iron cannons recovered by Marine Archaeological Research (MAR), a private salvage organization, are from the H.M.S. *Thunderer*, a British warship that disappeared during a hurricane in 1780, in the vicinity of the Caribbean island of Grand Cayman. Private salvors, treasure hunters, and archaeologists tend to be ticklish when it comes to making public the exact location of shipwrecks they are working, fearing that an outsider may jump the claim and loot the site. MAR President Captain Herbert Humphreys, shown here in checkered shirt, says the *Thunderer* is the largest historic shipwreck ever found and that it has remained "untouched" for more than two centuries. These cannons and their markings provided the first clue to the ship's true identity.
Photo courtesy Marine Archaeological Research.

CHAPTER NINE

Treasures in the Sand: Great Beachcombing

Stand at the high tide line of almost any beach in the civilized world and gaze out to sea; within a mile of your line of sight, hidden in relatively shallow water, lie most of the world's sunken riches. It would be misleading, of course, to imply that these treasures are as common as clam shells, but given the relative confines of most shorelines, there is more hidden loot in the sands than any other place I can think of. The odds favor the beachcomber. Sooner or later something will turn up—anything and everything from old coins and jewelry to ceramics, bottles, ship parts—even parts of spacecraft have been found. The only real limits are those imposed by time, persistence and the vagaries of weather.

There is, however, a rather explicit line of demarcation between the casual beach wanderer and the serious treasure seeker. Because there is so much lying about just awaiting a finder, the casual visitor will, with a bit of luck, eventually come upon some form of treasure. But the serious treasure hunter approaches the water's edge armed with two powerful attributes—motivation and purpose. This requires that one do a bit of homework, plan the route of the expedition, select the proper conditions of tide, wind and sea, prepare for an extended search and any surprises that may arise, and have a clear objective in mind.

Safety First: Planning

As in any undertaking in, on, or near the sea, safety should be the first priority. Avoid beaches that are off limits to the public, such as federal lands, private estates, and Indian reservations. Also, avoid barren clay banks, which are difficult to negotiate on foot. Narrow beaches near tall cliffs are especially dangerous. Unless you're familiar with daily tide patterns, it's all too easy to be caught in a rising tide, dangerous surf, and the backflow of water that can sweep you out to sea. As for driving on the beach, it's a tricky business without a specially-built dune buggy.

Good planning is the better part of luck. Get to know the area and its history. Read all you can about it and study local charts, especially older ones. No beach is ever the same twice; the water line changes in just a few short years. If you target a specific area of a beach, double check the maps and seek all the local knowledge you can get—from historical societies, librarians, folklorists, even oceanfront property developers. For each day you plan to comb a beach, spend the better part of a week doing your research. Read old newspaper articles, books, and pamphlets on local legends. Never discount the truth that invariably lies behind these so-called myths. Remember, you're a detective in search of clues perhaps long forgotten, so follow any lead to your objective, no matter how bizarre or "impossible" it seems.

Are you on your own or traveling in a group of like-minded treasure hunters? This is an important consideration, since the size of your party will determine divisions of labor and the amount of equipment needed. A large search party (from two to 12 participants) makes larger pooled resources and labor available and, of course, large parties tend to be rather social. The case for smaller parties (limit of six) is that they can be a lot more efficient. A small group tends to be more meticulous and to concentrate more on the common goal; the level of intensity is high, enthusiasm is better directed and focused. The small group can't carry as much gear, but it minimizes the diffusion of energies and skills.

On difficult terrain, such as the rocky coasts of Maine and Oregon, good communication is a must. Personally, I don't like it when someone in the party is out of sight for a long time. Your mind should be focused on the search, not on whether someone has gotten into trouble. It is not always possible to maintain eye contact or even keep each other in sight on the outings; in such situations, it makes good sense to keep non-togetherness to a minimum. If one explorer has a hunch about searching an area farther up the beach, go with the inspiration, but make sure your hunch-sniffer has a buddy. As with diving, do not go alone into dangerous or unknown territory.

Equipment And Techniques

What about special equipment, such as metal detectors? I believe a good metal detector, of which there are many varieties on the market, is an invaluable asset. A dry land metal detector and one that can be used in shallow water make a potent search combination. If you are after coins, silver, gold, firearms, and other metallic artifacts then, of course, the availability of one or more metal detectors turns pure chance into intelligent searching.

There are many brands on the market, ranging in price from $75 to $100 all the way up to nearly $1,000 for a hand-held portable model. There are basically two kinds to choose from: those that use horizontal coils and those that use radio double frequency coils. Horizontal coil detectors are suitable for most beachcombing, and are less expensive than the double frequency models, which are most often used by professional geologists, prospectors, and field engineers. A hand experienced with a simple detector gets better results than one with no experience using the most expensive machine on the market. So, the lesson is: practice, practice, practice. Practice at home over a set course where you've buried metal objects at different depths. If you're worried that the neighbors will think you've lost your mind, practice indoors by placing coins under your rugs. Remember, it is always possible to uncover objects using a random approach, but you are wholly in the hands of Lady Luck.

The Grid Search

One systematic method is called the "grid search." It works like this: Set up a baseline across the beach area to be searched. This baseline, or initial line, should be scribed from some large object on or near the beach, such as a tree, hill, or offshore island. Once this line is established, it can be reproduced later with good accuracy. On each side of the baseline, mark square sections in the sand from the edge of the beach all the way down to the waterline. The size of the squares should approximate the size of the items you hope to find. For example, if you're after a large sailing vessel that was driven onto the beach during a storm, the squares should be large enough to accommodate large ship fragments. If you're after coins or other small artifacts, the squares should be drawn much smaller. In the end, the baseline set up will produce something like a crude checkerboard pattern on the beach.

As an example, assume you are after a 100-foot sailing ship. Measuring 50-foot squares with a carpenters' tape is easy enough to do and will (hopefully) detect the various possible positions of the vessel along the beach. In this example, it will be practical to scribe ten or 20 squares on each side of the baseline. Each square should be marked with regard to its position on the compass. For example, the first southernmost square will be marked S-1; the first northernmost square should be marked N-1, and so on.

Generally, sample diagrams of search patterns come with the instructions of most metal detectors. In the sample used above, the explorer should walk slowly along one side of the baseline, sweeping the antenna plate of the detector as evenly as possible side-to-side at a rate of about one foot per second. Walk slowly ahead, sweeping a circle about three feet wide in one direction, and then back on another tack. Scan each square thoroughly, and avoid going back to re-scan squares. Your coverage on the first pass should be complete, otherwise you're heading for a lot of needless work and probably a bit of confusion.

Silver or Rust Iron?

Metal detectors work on a simple principle: When turned on and tuned properly, an electrical field is "excited" below the antenna plate. The field of detection can vary with the type of soil and even the amount of moisture in the soil. Also, the detector is affected by all sorts of metal items. Mel Fisher, while searching the Quicksands of the *Atocha* site off Key West, received thousands of meaningless "hits" on the magnetometers from bomb fragments and other junk laying in this Navy bombing practice area. It's virtually impossible, in most cases, to tell the sound of silver from that of a piece of rust iron. Newer detectors can discriminate between types of metals. Insist on a convincing demonstration before plunking your cash down on the sales counter.

The average metal detector is capable of picking up a two-inch square piece of metal at a depth of about two feet below the surface. The needle will swing toward the center of the object making the tone, thus indicating its approximate (if not exact) location in the sand. Mark this signal indication in a notebook copy of your grid pattern. Some searchers stop and dig at each "hit" they receive over the headphones. Some say it's better to keep going. It's usually more a matter of beach conditions. If the tide is coming in and your grid is about to be washed over, it may be best to dig at each hit.

Some metal detectors can pick up objects that are buried ten feet below the surface. Before you run out and buy such a detector, keep in mind that an object at that depth has to be about four feet square to register at all. The more typical ratio of size to detection depth is as follows: A piece of metal four square inches is detectable at 14 inches;

one-half square foot of metal can be detected at 42 inches, and a one-square-foot object can be read some six feet down.

It's important to remember that this device is first and last a *metal* detector; on a beach frequented by sunbathers, it will pick up the presence of beer cans, rings, cigarette lighters, silverware, keys, coins, watches, knives—the list goes on almost indefinitely. Very experienced operators say they can tell the difference between a beer can and a coin.

On beaches where shipwrecks have occurred, and where the sand has obliterated all visible evidence, the only practical way to search is by using a standard metal detector high up on the beach and, if possible, along the high and low tide lines. Of course, detectors can be used almost anywhere, on land or in seawater (if waterproof), and there are hundreds of sites from the tops of mountains to the deepest parts of the ocean. For purposes of this book, however, we are focusing on beaches and the practical necessity of what is called "methodical electronic search" as a means to an end—the discovery of historically important artifacts deposited along our thousands of miles of coastline. For the moment, I see no better instrument on the market. It's relatively inexpensive, works well and, like SCUBA, you can purchase it and begin to make important discoveries.

Metal detector technology is advancing rapidly. Visit a sporting goods or specialty shop that carries them for a quick education. Like any new piece of technology, they can be accompanied by a good deal of advertising and claims of success. It's far more prudent, though, to ask a lot of questions and read the specifications carefully.

It's remarkable that almost anyone can invest a few hundred dollars in such simple technology and make significant contributions to the discovery of historical artifacts—treasure whose value far exceeds the cost of the metal detector.

Dig We Must

Nothing good comes easy, as you will see in the second part of this chapter on beachcombing. It's fun. It's rewarding. It's personally invigorating. But it's also hard work.

Let's assume that you've accomplished the preliminaries and are now ready to examine the areas along your grid that show the presence of metal. Now begins the "dig we must" ethic. There are various tools and sifting screens that may make the job easier.

As to actual digging, be prepared to probe several feet below the surface. Very often, small objects are near the surface; items such as ship's fittings sink deeper. A long-handled shovel with a narrow blade is an excellent digging tool and though short-handled shovels can be fine, when the hole gets deep, the long-handled one is better.

Since holes in the sand have a way of caving in as quickly as they're dug, use a section of stovepipe—10 inches in diameter and three to four feet in length—to keep the hole from caving in. The pipe acts as a temporary caisson. Handles may be attached at one end to make placement easier. A trowel or a coal or flour scoop can be used to dig the sand out of the stovepipe.

Empty each shovelful of sand onto light, portable sifting trays. These can be wooden frames covered with ordinary window screens, or buckets, with screens secured over open bottoms trapping small items. Often, several trays are used. During the digging and sifting process, teamwork is helpful. While one person digs, another screens the sand. Do this for about an hour and then switch roles. It sounds simple—and it is. You may invent new types of digging and sifting tools to make the job go more efficiently. Imagination and invention are the two "I's" of successful beachcombing.

Best Bets: East Coast Beaches

To come upon a completely barren beach, one devoid of the remains of human dreams and commerce, is more difficult than finding one that harbors a wide variety of treasures. Virtually every known body of water, from the oceans bordering broad, sandy beaches that run for miles to tiny backwoods stone quarries contain vivid reminders of civilization. There are whole cities beneath the waters of major hydroelectric dams. The bottoms of wilderness lakes, such as Lake George in upper New York state, are paved (quite literally) with ancient American Indian watercraft and Revolutionary War relics. At the bottom of flooded rock quarries I have seen winding railroad tracks, wooden shacks, miners' lockers, and World War II "hedgehog" naval explosives. Forty feet below the surface of Willow Springs Quarry in Myerstown, Pennsylvania there is a large steam shovel, a miners' switch house, even an old wooden fishing boat. Florida's Suwannee River hides everything from the teeth of prehistoric sharks to flintlock weapons, and, in one spot, the ribs of a Civil War-era steamboat. The James River, at Yorktown, Virginia, is an incredible repository of colonial shipping. Our bays and harbors, such as the Chesapeake Bay, Biscayne Bay, Charleston Harbor, Baltimore and Boston harbors, and the ports of San Francisco, Galveston, and many others are storehouses of treasure and artifacts of every description.

In this section, however, we're focusing on beaches—public beaches in particular—places with easy access, known for turning up the stuff that glitters and that which captures the imagination. The list that follows is not all-inclusive; far from it! But each destination offers a real opportunity to the determined beachcomber. All come with excellent historical pedigrees and an impressive background of previous finds. They are fine starting points, areas rich in artifacts, and a realistic springboard from which to experience the thrill of discovery. Finally, they are *odds-on beaches*— locations that actually favor the treasure hunter.

The Florida Keys

This 100-mile-long strand of limestone and coral islands stretch across the sea like a jade necklace, strung from Biscayne Bay to Key West. The Keys are prime country for treasure, especially the New World variety. It's estimated that, between 1550 and 1800, more than 100 treasure-laden vessels were destroyed on the continuous shallow reef which borders the islands on the Atlantic side. The primary reef system is about six miles offshore, standing in ten to 40 feet of clear water. Most of the vessels that met their doom here wrecked on the eastern, or Atlantic, side of the islands; westerly winds pushed the sailing ships against the reefs where they shattered into little more than driftwood. However, there were times when the westerly storms lifted the vessels over the reefs, tearing out their bottoms in the process. These shoreward wrecks are the ones that have been depositing, bit by bit, a variety of artifacts—including silver coins— onto these beaches for four centuries.

The hook is that the Keys offer few beaches; most of the islands front the Atlantic with stoney "iron shore" virtually devoid of sand. These iron shores—the pitted, razor-sharp limestone remnants of ancient coral reefs —are difficult and dangerous, and they should not be searched without boots and heavy clothing, especially in winter when the sea surges straight onto the rocks. Far more amenable to the beachcomber are the beaches at Key Largo, Indian Key, Little Torch Key, and Grassy Key. These have given up a fair sampling of silver and gold coins. Another beach worth exploring is at Bahia Honda, north of Big Pine Key. Sea-blackened bottles, coins, coral-encrusted fittings, and a very substantial variety of artifacts have been found there, often on top of the sand.

The beachcomber may be surprised at the cramped beaches of the Keys, most of which are less than 100 yards in length, but by no means should they be underestimated; they contain large deposits, which are continually renewed by the action of wind and waves. Unfortunately for most sunbathers, the best time to search is December through March, a period of northerly winds and rough seas. It can be downright cold—but also downright rewarding. Each northerly blow churns the offshore deposits, pushing them landward; high seas and strong winds strip away top layers of sand, revealing objects hidden for centuries. On calm days, it can be fruitful to row off the beaches in a small boat and scan the bottom with a glass-bottom bucket or similar device that gives a clear view of the bottom. I have seen ceramics bouncing along in four feet of water and have snared them with a long-handled fishing net.

All along the Keys, on the western side facing the Gulf of Mexico, are inlets—some private, others totally uninhabited. A walk around the perimeters of these outcroppings can be rewarding, especially after a storm.

Sebastian Inlet, Vero Beach, Fort Pierce, Florida

This 24-mile stretch of Florida east coast beach is one of the most productive areas in the United States. It was a bonanza for Kip Wagner, whose Real 8 treasure hunting organization recovered more than $1 million in Spanish riches from the ill-fated 1715 and 1733 treasure fleets. The 1715 fleet was sent to the bottom directly offshore of this area by a hurricane. Although the fleet was salvaged by both the Spanish and by Wagner, it is by no means picked clean, and coins and bits of wreckage continue to wash ashore. Happily for the beachcomber, the remains of the Spanish ships are close to the beach—some only a few hundred yards out—and only a series of low sandbars stand between the meticulous treasure hunter and the Spanish loot.

There are eight known wrecks here, the richest being the "Wedge Wreck," just north of Fort Pierce Inlet, named for its stash of wedge-shaped silver ingots; the "Cabin Wreck," 2½ miles south of Sebastian Inlet, famous for its silver coins; the "Sandy Point Wreck," halfway between Vero Beach and Fort Pierce, known for its stores of silver *reales* and gold two *escudo* coins minted in Bogota; the "Gold Wreck," or "Colored Beach Wreck," down in shallow water about two miles south of Fort

Pierce Inlet. This last wreck produced, among other treasures, a series of gold disks, each $22^1/_2$ karats in purity and weighing nearly eight pounds apiece. These are the most visible artifacts, the ones that get all of the *oohs* and *aaahs,* and most of them have been salvaged from their watery graves—maybe! It seems that every storm brings in new surprises, and there are determined beachcombers in these parts who have recently turned up silver coins valued as high as $1,000 and gold coins with market values of $400 to $120,000.

Stories of bizarre and wonderful finds can be picked up all along this area, and one of the most vivid is the 1970 recovery of a golden brooch, fashioned in the shape of a bumblebee, which was sold to a New York socialite for $30,000. In the winter months, storms have uncovered what the local children call "lumps of coal"—actually oxidized silver coins. During the heyday of Real 8, a golden dragon hanging from a 12-foot gold chain was recovered by Captain Rex Stocker, and there have been numerous discoveries of single, double, and triple links of gold chains, apparently disconnected during the centuries-long journey from the wrecked galleons to the high- and low-tide zones of the modern shoreline. Many finds aren't reported, of course. And many long-time beachcombers would sooner die than reveal those special places that seem to be infinitely rich in artifacts. Certainly, one doesn't have to push away rare gold coins to find the sand on this span of oceanfront; one still has to work for the finds and spend long hours tracing leads. Still, this area is not hunted out by any means. Those who say it is are hoping to discourage new blood—and with good reason. They don't want to share the troves with any outsiders, or insiders either, for that matter.

In 1977, I was visiting the area on business, staying with friends, Norbert and Fran O'Hara, at Indiatlantic. While diving off the beach at Vero in choppy water, I ran smack into a mound of timber only eight feet below the surface. In almost zero visibility water, the heavy surge bashed me against this rather thorny pile of junk so often that I was forced to leave the immediate vicinity and find less harmful surroundings. A year later, I was informed that this "junk" was part of a galleon wreck that apparently had been swept into shallow water by a recent winter storm. The local divers, who had heard of my encounter from friends, later came away with a fair sampling of silver coins, several silver plates, a bag of shattered Ming ceramics, four pounds of small musket shot, and a gold serpent of Egyptian design. I have turned a deaf ear toward anyone who says the area is picked clean. I give it an AAA recommendation.

Boynton Inlet, Florida

About 15 miles south of West Palm Beach is Lantana and a relatively unsearched area called Boynton Beach. I have a feeling that more is being found here than gets reported. The Boynton Inlet area has recently been turning up silver and gold bar stock. The finding of coins is not an eyebrow-raiser in these parts, but bar stock is rare, indeed. To begin with, bar stock is a lot heavier than coins; it tends to sink deep into the offshore sands. In addition, there have been reports of very old jewelry being recovered near these bar stock finds. All of this leads to some speculation about a buried treasure trove—but it's nothing more than speculation at this time. Boynton Inlet and the beach area have consistently yielded bizarre and rare items. Gene Ballinger, a Boynton resident and author of a treasure hunting publication, *In The Steps Advisory Report,* says the general oceanfront area from Boynton as far north as Saint Augustine "will continue to produce where new fill has not already been placed to stop further loss of the dunes." Perhaps the fill activity in the area unearthed the bars of gold and silver from an inland trove. Ballinger, a very ardent and persistent searcher, may provide more information on this development. His address is P.O. Box 486, Boynton Beach, Florida 33425-0486.

Florida West Coast Beaches

Florida's west coast, referred to in advertising brochures as the "Sun Coast," lies directly along the New World sailing routes. The shallow, storm-ridden Gulf of Mexico claimed a number of 16th and 17th-century treasure ships. Few attempts have been made to locate and recover these cargos and, as a result, the area's reputation for treasure is several orders of magnitude below that of the east coast. Many of the locals would just as soon keep it that way, for obvious reasons. However, finds are being made along the sweep of coastline from Naples to Pensacola. Listed below are known treasure-producing areas.

Naples, Florida

At the western terminus of the Everglades Parkway ("Alligator Alley") is the town of Naples. Its wide, flat beaches, like many along the west coast, are rich in fossil deposits. An added lure, however, are the silver—and occasionally gold—coins that are found after the hurricane season (September through October) and through the winter months. The area has been producing these finds for nearly 30 years, sometimes in abundant quantities. Most of the recent finds have been at the high tide line, indicating that one or more vessels were driven onto the beach and pounded into matchsticks by raging surf. It's said that at least one Spanish ship sailing out of Veracruz was destroyed on the beach or very close to the shoreline. Treasure hunts and metal detector surveys are common in Naples. You'll have little trouble finding good local information.

Gasparilla-Boca Grande

About 50 miles north of Naples are Gasparilla Island and the town of Boca Grande, situated at the mouth of Charlotte Harbor. The island took its name from the activities of the pirate Jose Gaspar, who launched his attacks from the island. There are legends upon legends concerning Gaspar's bloody business. Every other coffee shop in the area has placemats dotted with "X's"—all purportedly pinpointing his various buried treasures. Coins and other artifacts turn up along the beaches here and along the quiet shores of Charlotte Harbor. These tend to be scattered finds; the more substantial ones are kept quiet. Gaspar believed in burying his loot, and the sketchy historical records indicate that he hid more than $2 million in different locations on the island, and that at least an equal amount was spread out to the neighboring islets. Gaspar's ship went down at the southwest tip, just off Boca Grande, carrying an estimated $9 million in treasure to the bottom. The ship's cargo appears to be finding its way shoreward along the harbor area.

Cedar Key

Spanish coinage has been found along Cedar Key, an exclusive island at the point of Waccasassa Bay, which forms a wide crescent between Yankeetown and Lukens. The western shore has produced most of these finds. No hard evidence exists to date on where these coins, mostly silver, came from; local history buffs believe they can be traced to one of many vessels that sailed in the New Spain armada.

Bradenton Beach

A few miles north of Sarasota is Bradenton Beach, situated on a long, sandy key which fronts directly on the Gulf of Mexico. I have been roaming this area for a decade and have found a variety of ship wreckage. At the middle of Longboat Key there was a wooden wreck in very shallow water that kept me busy for two consecutive years. However, Bradenton is the newest star in the Sun Coast treasure galaxy. Beginning in the spring of 1969, beachcombers working with metal detectors hit a cache of 300 rare ancient coins. One coin bears the inscription "Caesar Augustus." Still another was minted in Russia and dated 1765. One coin weighed nearly a half pound—and was solid gold. Other coins are of Italian, Spanish, French, Persian, Macedonian, Danish, British, and Irish origin. Many are dated between 1771 and 1797. Research on the Caesar Augustus coin seems to bear out the belief that the Roman ruler who first held this title reigned in 27 B.C., and that Julius Caesar succeeded him. Where this remarkable cache came from is still a mystery—and one certainly worth looking into. This area is now being developed by home builders, and the beaches are sometimes crowded with sunbathers. The best time to search is during the winter months, when cold weather keeps the beaches virtually unoccupied. I recommend an area-wide survey, over a period of time, beginning at Holmes Beach just north of Bradenton, and southward across Longboat and Siesta Keys. Wreckage of all kinds turn up in the sands— from coins and gold bars to ceramics and ship timbers. I rate it as one of the most promising new treasure grounds in a state famous for treasure.

The Gulf Coast

Padre Island, Texas

As the New Spain fleets sailed northward from Veracruz, they picked up the Gulf Gyre current, an offshoot of the Gulf Stream, and followed it up to the coast of Texas and then eastward across the Gulf of Mexico. At a spot near the twenty-fifth parallel the ships made a turn close to the Texas shoreline. Directly in the path was Padre Island, a 110-mile strip of sand which has gained the well-deserved reputation as the "Graveyard of the Gulf." The Gyre is erratic in this area, and a westward-flowing arm known as "The Devil's Elbow" flows into the center of the island. The amount of flotsam pushed ashore by the Elbow is truly phenomenal, and there is a constant stream of mahogany logs, cedar timbers, and coins of every variety deposited daily on the beach dunes. Two sand dunes in this locale are aptly named "Money Hill." One reason for the rich inflow has to do with the ocean bottom, which is hard clay rather than the soft sand found in other areas. It appears that sunken treasure tends not to sink in, but rather "roll" along until it finds its place on shore. Bronze cannons have been found buried in the dunes, as have bronze spikes from Jean Lafitte's vessels. There may be as many as 20 wrecks giving up their treasures to Padre Island, including $2.5 million in gold thought to have been smuggled out of Austria by the Emperor Maximilian. In 1940, when

Humble Oil Company was drilling in Laguna Madre between the mainland and Padre Island, 70 "Maximilian Dollars" were pumped from the ocean floor during dredging operations. The treasure, packed in flour sacks after his death, was headed for Mexico when it was sent to the bottom in a storm. Many details of this story remain to be confirmed, though it's certain that the treasure has found its way to Padre Island.

The remains of three well-documented Spanish wrecks, the *San Esteban,* the *Santa Maria de Usasi,* and the *Espiritu Santo,* are located near Port Mansfield. There have been confirmed reports that one of these wrecks sits 4,000 feet offshore, some two miles north of the Port Mansfield Channel. Three 16th-century Spanish ships have been positively identified; these are the *Santa Maria de Guadalupe,* the *Capitana,* and the *San Crucifijo de Burgos.* There is no way to estimate accurately the millions of dollars buried at Padre Island, since fresh finds and new evidence turn up continually. The troves of ship artifacts seem almost endless—and endlessly fascinating. Be on notice, however, that anything found in these offshore areas belongs to the state, which has tough antiquity laws. There have been many lawsuits between the state and salvors, but none that I know of involving beachcombers or beachcombed artifacts. It's a shame that such a historically rich area is at the same time so strictly off limits, since Texas is doing very little actual shipwreck excavation. For beachcombers who wish to contribute directly to the history of the area, it's recommended that any significant finds be logged with the Texas Antiquities Committee. Of course, no one goes in search of legal trouble, but in Texas, where penalties can be severe, it's better to be safe than exceedingly sorry.

Outer Banks, North Carolina

Welcome to the infamous "Graveyard of the Atlantic"—a 100-mile sweep of barrier islands off the North Carolina coast. Along these shores no fewer than 642 ships are known to have been destroyed over the past four centuries. Dozens have been strewn along the beaches and buried in the dunes. Still others are clearly visible just beyond the breakers. And less than a mile from shore, countless others are churned and rechurned by storms, hurricanes, and stiff Gulf Stream currents. The offshore geography tells why this area is such a notorious ship killer. There are the ever-shifting sandbars and shoals. And at Diamond Shoals, off Cape Hatteras, the fury of two oceans come together. I have stood at the top of Hatteras

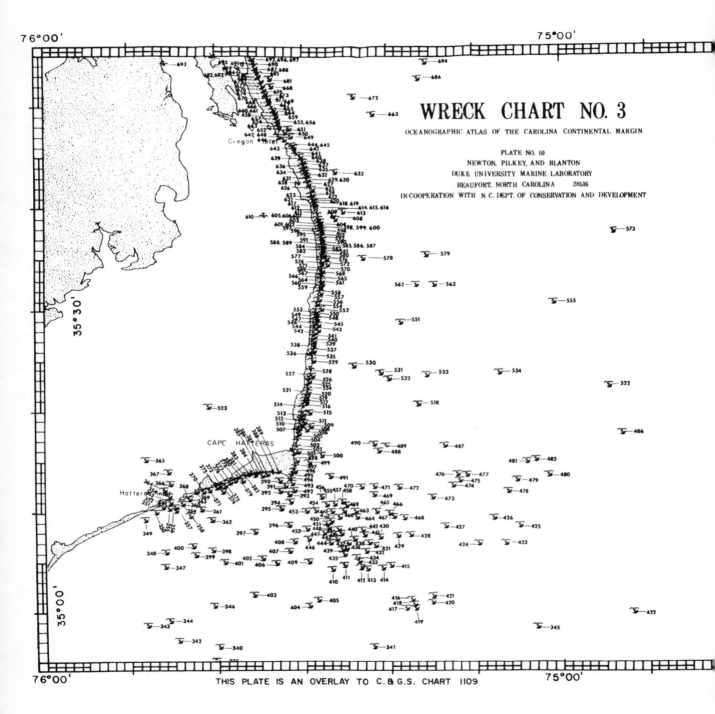

WRECK CHART NO. 3

OCEANOGRAPHIC ATLAS OF THE CAROLINA CONTINENTAL MARGIN

PLATE NO. 10
NEWTON, PILKEY, AND BLANTON
DUKE UNIVERSITY MARINE LABORATORY
BEAUFORT, NORTH CAROLINA   28516
IN COOPERATION WITH N. C. DEPT. OF CONSERVATION AND DEVELOPMENT

THIS PLATE IS AN OVERLAY TO C. & G.S. CHART 1109

74°00'

LEGEND

‌ Stranded

‌ Partially Submerged

‌ Totally Submerged

+ Position Doubtful

35°30'

483

485

484

Scale in Nautical Miles

0   5   10   15

35°00'

74°00'

The Graveyard of the Atlantic

More than 650 ships and 975 lives were lost along the treacherous shoals of the Outer Banks of North Carolina, a chilling fact that gives this 100-mile-long stretch of barrier island a well-deserved reputation as the "Graveyard of the Atlantic." So many wrecked vessels have been washed into the surfline that bathers must exercise caution to keep from being swept into the remains. The lost ships shown on this map span a period from 1526 to 1945. Yet for each documented wreck there are countless others, nameless and unknown, that have yet to be logged on any nautical chart. As seasonable storms sweep the Banks, mysterious relics are deposited on the beach, small clues that may lead the finder to discover one of these long-vanished victims resting beneath the waves.

Map courtesy North Carolina Department of Conservation and Development.

Light on stormy days and watched the northbound Gulf Stream collide head-on with the cold currents running southward from the Arctic. The result is an almost unimaginable confrontation, with the mountainous waves flinging spray 100 feet in the air. Here, the Continental Shelf drops into the abyss only 10 miles from shore. This means that the big westward-bound ocean waves suddenly encounter a shallow bottom. These waves become high enough and strong enough to overwhelm the unwary mariner. From Spanish galleons, which steered eastward from here in hopes of reaching Spain, to the steel-hulled merchantmen of World War II, ships and men have left a sad record along these banks. This record, however, has given the Outer Banks a reputation as a true beachcomber's paradise. Long ago, Edward Teach, better known as Blackbeard the Pirate, whose castle stood on nearby Ocracoke Island, made a bloody fine living luring ships to disaster on these sands. More peaceful residents did well by culling the pirate's leftovers. Today, the ribbing of lost vessels stands out clearly on the beaches, and it takes only modest poking around to find brass fittings, spikes, timbers, pottery shards—even fragments of cloth and leather. On calm days, it's not unusual to see the remains of old ships a few hundred yards offshore. These look inviting to an ordinary swimmer equipped with a mask, snorkel, and swim fins. But, the old hulks are a jumble of sharp timbers and one wrong move can end in trouble. Moreover, the currents are strong and unpredictable, so *stick to the beach.*

Occasionally you'll find coins in the sand, but the fare consists mostly of ship's parts, bits and pieces sufficient to draw the outlines of a long nautical history. The amateur beachcomber will find plenty of research material on the ships, and can solicit the local banks and stores. There are even markers pointing to various wrecks. This is an excellent place to try your beachcombing talents, to absorb a rich atmosphere of maritime lore and, if you're lucky, return home with something tangible for your own personal treasure chest.

Delaware Beaches

"Coin Beach," Indian River Inlet

Less than a mile north of Rehoboth is Indian River Inlet, a deep channel dredged in 1930 to provide inland safety for ships plying the Atlantic along the Delaware coast. And a few hundred yards north of the inlet is "Coin Beach," so-named after the wreck of an English vessel here in 1785. The ship, *The Faithful Steward,* had sailed from Londonderry, Ireland, bound for Philadelphia with 360 passengers. A little after midnight on September 2, 1785, the ship's captain and most of the crew were on deck celebrating the first wedding anniversary of one of the passengers, John McGreg. It must have been a very festive gathering, with plenty to drink and dancing under the stars. Only one crewman was on watch. A sounding was taken and it was immediately clear that *The Faithful Steward* was drifting far off course, hugging the shore in only 24 feet of water. Alarmed, one of the officers yelled, "Four fathoms, sir!" But Captain William McCasland failed to hear him above the noise on deck. By the time orders were given to alter course, disaster had seized the ship. She ran up on a shoal, broke in two, and began to sink rapidly. In the end, ten crewmen and 298 passengers drowned. For a reason no one can explain, *The Faithful Steward* also carried to the bottom an enormous cache of coins; these began to surface on the beach soon after the 1930 dredging operation. There were so many coins, in fact, that newspaper accounts tell of children gathering pails of British and Irish half-pennies. One reporter wrote that the coins were "numerous as clam shells." Some of these coins have found their way into a collection at the Zwaanandael Museum in Lewes, Delaware. But it seems the bank has not run out. The coins and other artifacts are still being found on the beach and in the shallows. A few years ago, Doug Keefe of Atlantic City, New Jersey, found 100 coins in five days; 15 of them were gold. The variety is fascinating: gold guineas dated between 1766 and 1782; Spanish *reales;* and numerous Irish and British coppers, some with holes drilled through King George's nose, perhaps an Irish slap at the colonizing English. The patient seeker may also find brass shoe buckles, whole and fragmented jewelry, and rings made of silver and gold. A metal detector is useful here, especially high on the beach near the dunes. On calm windless days, finds have been made in less than five feet of water. In summer, when the crystal clear waters of the Gulf Stream are drawn shoreward, it's possible to drift along with a mask and snorkel for a thorough bottom survey.

Rehoboth Beach

Another ship, *Three Brothers,* wrecked somewhere between Indian River and Rehoboth; its exact location is unknown. She was a British sailing vessel which broke up on a long sandbar close to shore in 1775. Her copper and gold coins have probably become indistinguishable from those thought to be from the nearby *Faithful Steward.* In the summer, Rehoboth is a popular refuge for visitors from the large cities of the mid-Atlantic region. The only times when the beach won't be crowded are just after sunrise and an hour or so before sunset. In the winter, however, the place is empty and the serious beachcomber can explore peacefully. *Three Brothers* coins can be found near the dunes, and a metal detector is virtually a must. Less valuable finds are common—especially ship wreckage of all descriptions.

New Jersey Beaches

Cape May

On March 9, 1877 the brig *Bethany* was wrecked within sight of Two Mile Beach. She was going in after a long, difficult voyage from Hong Kong with a cargo of china estimated to be worth more than $1 million on today's market. Gold was also aboard. Porcelain shards can be found along the beach here, but you have to look carefully. Gold coins, thought to be from the *Bethany,* have been found near the foot of Cape May Point Lighthouse.

The 34-gun Spanish frigate *Juno,* carrying a large but unestimated quantity of silver ingots and coins, went down within sight of land at the opening of Delaware Bay. She sank October 27, 1802, taking 425 people with her. Divers believe they have spotted portions of *Juno's* wreckage scattered in water 20 to 100 feet deep not far from the eastern rim of the bay. Gold and silver coins have been found here, but the finders did not record the dates, leaving us no conclusive evidence of their origin.

On the southwestern tip of the island, in line with Lily Lake, the pirate Captain Kidd came ashore for fresh water during his stay in the area. Interestingly, Spanish silver coins are occasionally found in this area, and clay pipes, silver matchboxes, and other artifacts have turned up at Lake Lily.

At Sunset Beach, facing Delaware Bay, beachcombers find the famous "Cape May Diamonds." The diamonds are not the real thing, but curious glassy crystals that range from the size of a pea and to as large as a golfball. They probably come from the *Atlantus,* a concrete ship of modern lineage that went down close to the beach. *Atlantus* is visible above the surface.

Silver ingots have been recovered along the Delaware Channel and around the small town of Milford. Their origin is unknown, but local history buffs believe they are part of a pirate treasure. In the early 1700s, the channel was used as a safe haven by pirates working this coast.

Though Cape May is a well-traveled resort, its beaches and shallows are only now beginning to give up their treasures. The beachcomber interested in extensive exploration is likely to uncover some rare finds. The area gets high ratings from this writer.

Long Beach Island

This 15-mile long Atlantic barrier island is steeped in history, rich in local lore, and inhabited by gritty treasure hunters, historians, divers, and seafarers of every description. Though it has plenty of modern accommodations, a walk along these beaches will instantly transport you into the past. Any summer weekend when the weather is fair, the dive boats cast off from Beach Haven, Ship Bottom, and Barnegat Light and head out to sea to explore the huge trove of shipwrecks located as far as 30 miles from land.

Off the beaches of Ship Bottom are the remains of the *Fortuna,* a 19th-century merchantman. She is only 300 yards off the beach, and on a windy day, relics bob in the low tide line. *Fortuna* was no gold carrier—but she has produced fragments and fittings that, to the true beachcomber, are endlessly thought provoking. *Fortuna's* anchor was recovered in 1983 and now decorates the lawn of Ship Bottom Borough Hall.

More glittery fare are the so-called "Long Island Beach Coins," including corroded silver pieces of eight and gold doubloons, which have been discovered in widely separated areas. Historians Walter and Richard Krotee speculate in their book, *Shipwrecks Off the New Jersey Coast,* that the coins issue from multiple inshore wrecks of 17th- and 18th-century origin—perhaps a combination of Spanish ships and pirate vessels. The meticulous beachcomber may find just the right clue to solve this long-standing mystery.

Another ship that scattered its remains on the beaches is the *Betsy,* a brig that broke up on the beach just north of Little Egg Inlet during a storm in 1778. Badly-corroded silver plates have been recovered in the area, and these finds appear to coincide with her primary cargo.

Across a narrow stretch of water, south of the town of Beach Haven, is Brigantine Shoals. Old records indicate that the schooner *Ellis,* a British vessel bound for New York, was destroyed on the Shoals in 1775. *Ellis* was primarily a tea carrier, but she also hauled silver plates, estimated to be worth nearly $1 million on today's market. The plates appear to have been swept by strong currents to Long Beach Island. Recently, plates have been found near Beach Haven, at the south tip of the island, and sources speculate that they came from the *Ellis.*

A storm also claimed the American privateer, *Fame,* as it capsized and sank quickly in February, 1781, off Great Egg Harbor. *Fame* was carrying prizes from a long voyage, probably rich in coins and other hard-core negotiables. This is pure speculation; more precise information is not available since privateers did not keep meticulous manifests. Their booty was constantly growing (they hoped) until the tour of sea duty ended. Finds of various artifacts including shot, ceramic shards, old glass, and pewter may be the last vestiges of *Fame.*

Before leaving Long Beach Island, or before you begin combing the beach, stop in at the Long Island Beach Museum (Engleside Avenue, in Beach Haven) and at the nautical museum at Barnegat Light. Both will provide eye-opening exhibits of just how many artifacts there are on area beaches and what they look like when you find them.

Long Island, New York

Around Greenport there are tales of a ship that burned within sight of land sometime around 1750. Nearly 150 years later, in 1894, dredging operations around the beach pulled up a cache of gold bars and an impressive number of gold and silver coins, nested in several tons of charred wood. The ship was never identified. However, pieces of charred wood are still found near Greenport, and with it the same gold coins. This will one day make a first-rate research project for some scholarly beachcomber. In the meantime, the casual visitor may profit from close inspection of the area. Who knows when the mystery of this "Greenport Wreck" will be solved.

Another mystery ship is dubbed the "Shinnecock Money Ship," named for the "beach dollars" it deposited at Shinnecock. The story goes as follows: On a brisk November morning in 1816, the residents of Southampton, Long Island, spied a ship with strange rigging apparently abandoned offshore. The next day it had drifted to Shinnecock and grounded on a long sandbar, where the masts toppled and the hull listed steeply. Twenty-four hours after the grounding an inspection party found the vessel devoid of life—but in perfect order. To many this sounds like the mystery of the Bermuda Triangle, but a ship is always put in order, if possible, prior to abandonment. Since we cannot determine if this is what happened, the point is made only to dispel notions of Little Green Men.

Once the hull settled, another group came aboard and found a silver dollar on the deck. They began to search for more. It was observed that the ceiling of the captain's cabin was sagging; when it was pried open, silver dollars rained down on them. Over a period of three or four days, more money was found, but the exact amount was never determined. Before the vessel could be cleaned out entirely, a storm destroyed it. Not long afterward, the money began appearing on the beaches. In a short time hundreds of silver dollars, dated around 1800, were recovered all the way to East Hampton. The mystery of the money ship was solved when it was subsequently learned that the crew had abandoned her during a storm. They attempted to gain the beach in longboats weighed down with the silver. Most of the boats capsized in the surf. The few crewmen who landed were murdered by Long Island's shore-bound pirates, called "wrackers." Today, the silver dollars still turn up. A close inspection at Shinnecock may prove fascinating—and profitable.

Scores of other vessels have met their doom on the shoals and sands of Long Island. Among those bearing treasure were: Spanish schooner *Ligera,* wrecked at Montauk Point, 1823; American privateer *Patience,* wrecked near Montauk Point, 1780; American coastal schooner *Marey,* wrecked at Montauk Point, 1763; and the Scottish merchantman *Elizabeth,* lost on the south side of Long Island in 1769.

This area deserves a high rating as a beachcomber's haven. It has sufficient reserves to occupy one's fantasies for a long, long time.

Massachusetts Beaches

Lynn Beach

After the first northeasterly storm of November, 1969, a local beachcombing carpenter, Howard Holbrook, recovered 250 coins in a single day. A few days after the second November blow, he found another 200 coins. Most of his finds predated 1925, and there were some rare items: "Barber Dimes" of 1886, quarters of 1902, Indian Head pennies, and a wide assortment of foreign money. At the time of his discoveries, Holbrook had been beachcombing for a year and his collection boasted more than 2,100 rare pieces of currency. Holbrook is only one of many who use metal detectors in this area, which is considered one of the richest off-the-beaten-track beaches in the state. Those who have worked it over the years agree that the cold winter months are best for coin and artifact hunting.

Wellfleet

This tiny community on Cape Cod is the site of the excavation of America's first known pirate ship, the *Whydah,* discovered off a public beach in 1985 by Barry Clifford, who estimates the value of the trove in excess of $400 million. The *Whydah* is below ten feet of sand, but it's possible that the wreck is giving up small samples. Silver and gold coins dated 1717 have been discovered along the beaches, as well as coppers dating back to King William. Silver cobb coins, roughly cut, are Spanish in origin, but it's unclear if they originated from wrecked galleons or from sunken pirate vessels, such as Black Sam Bellamy's *Whydah.* All sorts of ship wreckage floats ashore, perhaps dredged up by local lobstermen. The anonymity of much of this wreckage indicates that Wellfleet is amply stocked with sunken vessels of many nationalities. Every item found is another piece in a large offshore puzzle.

Orleans

Leif Eriksson landed here more than 900 years ago. Captain Bartholomew Gosnold visited in 1602 and gave Cape Cod its name after catching a "great store" of codfish. Orleans was also the scene of a great deal of piracy patterned after the style of the Outer Banks, where pirates attached lanterns to donkeys at night and lured unwary seamen onto the bars and shoals. The Orleans breed were called "Mooncussers." It was easier to lure in unsuspecting mariners when there was no moon. The only light the sailors could see was the glow from lanterns or fires built far inland. The Mooncussers were no less successful than Blackbeard on the Outer Banks, and the offshore sandbars continue to give up many relics. Oceanward, past the dunes, once lay a barrier island called Isle Nauset, which extended from Chatham on the south to Eastham. The island has been washed away, but the beaches nearby give the beachcomber a regular sampling of the havoc it caused mariners. At Nauset Beach, at low tide, one can find fragments of the lost island in the form of glassware, brass, fittings of various kinds, and occasional old coins dating back to 1602. In 1624, a small British ship named *Sparrow Hawk,* which carried settlers and supplies, was wrecked at Orleans. A number of artifacts are on display in the local museum.

Provincetown

This is the famous artist and writer's colony; it's also an historic fishing village. A couple of centuries ago, however, it was called "Hell-Town" because of the rogues and pirates holed up here. Where there is long history there are artifact-laden beaches, and Provincetown is one of the best in the state. Along the dunes and the Back Shore area the sea opens on limitless horizons and unlimited possibilities in the sand. There are many vessels lying offshore, and the expanse of unbroken sea is constantly pushing their bones shoreward. The off season is especially productive because of storms and high winds racing down out of the north. To comb these beaches is to piece together a diary of maritime history; whole conglomerates of materials wash up, often unrelated, as if the stormy sea were smashing the hulls of dozens of vessels together, entangling them in modern fish netting (of which much is lost among the wreckage) and hurling the bundles shoreward as salty potpourri to be deciphered by patient beachcombers. The wealth of Provincetown's waters is a consistent new delight to the beachcomber. One final note: It is believed that the American ship *Princess,* sailing from London to New York, was destroyed in a storm on April 27, 1813, near Provincetown. *Princess* was heavily laden with silver, all of it still awaiting new owners.

Hogg Island, Pleasant Bay (Cape Cod)

The ancient saying about Hogg Island, near a place called "Money Head," is that "it is Captain Kidd's money—so well hid, it is, no one shall ever find it." People have been digging at this cliff for more than a century, trying unsuccessfully to disprove the challenging commentary. Remember, the keen searcher is after clues here—and one clue is worth a thousand words. This is an off-beat adventure, one to test your skills as a master detective. No metal detectors allowed!

Martha's Vineyard and Nantucket Island

Two more perverse ship killers can hardly be found off the coast of Cape Cod than the Vineyard and Nantucket. Hundreds of vessels have run afoul of Nantucket Shoals, and if they were lucky enough to make it past the shoals safely, they were confronted by the cliffs of Martha's Vineyard.

The area has bedeviled mariners for centuries; therefore, it's almost impossible to pinpoint specific beaches that may be richer than others. Every beach has potential of yielding a good find. Generally, the eastern point of Nantucket offers slightly better pickings than the westward inlets, and the southern and eastern edges of Martha's Vineyard are likewise potentially more rewarding, depending on tides, winds, and the prevalence of storms.

Documented wrecks around the Vineyard include: two British merchantmen, *John & Mary* and the *Anne,* bound for Boston out of Barbados, 1731; seven unidentified vessels, caught in a hurricane on October 8, 1749; American merchant vessel *Clinton,* wrecked August 12, 1757, on No Man's Land, a small island off the tip of the Vineyard; American merchantman *Fanny,* out of Virginia in 1794; American merchantman *Charming Betsey,* out of Martinique in 1798; British merchantman *Delight,* arriving from Gibraltar in 1800; and the Irish ship *Alknomack,* transporting immigrants to New York in 1811.

There are many more—documented and undocumented—casting themselves up on the sands every day. They have given the Vineyard a first-class reputation for beachcombing.

Standing farther out to sea, Nantucket has taken an equally grim toll of shipping. Among the victims: British warship H.M.S. *Blonde,* 32 guns, 1778; ship of unknown registry, the *Fanciculetta,* arriving from Tobago, 1784; unidentified French brig sailing from the Caribbean to Europe, 1786; three merchantmen, *Clarissa* (British), *Margaret,* arriving from Amsterdam, and the American ship *Industry,* 1795; British ship *Julianna,* arriving from South Carolina, 1796; Swedish merchantman *Nordkoping,* routed to Boston out of Cuba, 1814; and the English merchantman *Robert Todd,* arriving from the Bahamas, 1817.

Whalers, pirate vessels, and modern shipping of all descriptions have left their remains here. You could spend years tracing them and never do more than strip away the top layers of history. Nantucket is endlessly fascinating, always challenging, and it's a destination sure to reward beachcombers today and those of generations to come.

Best Bets: West Coast Beaches

Baja Peninsula, Western Mexico

This rough, undeveloped region has more than 1,600 miles of shoreline—most of it virtually unexplored. For beachcombers, the good news is that Baja is inordinately rich in artifacts of almost every description. The competition for them is all but nil. The bad news is that getting to many of the coastal areas requires thorough planning, your own food and water, four-wheel drive vehicles, and plenty of time. Baja is definitely not for the casual weekend explorer. The inland road is far from the sea—in some spots as much as 100 miles—and except for the first 200 miles of highway, there are few communities to support the traveler.

But for the hearty souls who go in for the rough and ready, the beach at Malarrimo promises a good deal of excitement. Malarrimo is about 160 miles west of El Arco, just beyond Scammons Lagoon. Driving is the only sure way to get there, since there is no air strip and no safe offshore anchorage.

Finds at this beach add up to a lexicon of marine lore. Strewn along the high tide line are occasional silver coins, undoubtedly from the Manila galleons, and a remarkable collection of World War II articles, including airplane parts. Old bottles are also abundant, as are cedar logs from the Orient. The mix of items cannot be easily categorized, because at Malarrimo almost anything is possible, as winds and tides continually uncover new troves.

Malarrimo is prolific and you should plan to use a truck or some other vehicle to pack your gear, rations, and prizes. It's not uncommon to retrieve more than a dozen "keepers" (objects you will take home) in a single day. Many visitors camp out for days at a time and their prizes tend to be very substantial. Bring packing materials to hold delicate glass objects (green and blue Japanese glass floats are common). You will not need luck at Malarrimo. Sun screen, toughness, and good planning are the only requirements.

California Beaches

Santa Catalina Island

This island is well traveled and constantly explored. A short boat ride out of Los Angeles, Long Beach, or Newport Beach puts the beachcomber onto the shore of Catalina, where what is thought to be galleon wreckage has been uncovered. The richest galleons were those sailing out of the Spanish colonies in the Philippines bound for Acapulco. These Manila galleons, heavy with Oriental riches, used the eastward-flowing Kuroshio Current to carry them 9,000 miles across the Pacific. It is a long voyage, and the weather is vicious all the way. Typhoons and gales are common, and at least 36 galleons met death along this route. One of the earliest of these, the *Santa Marta,* wrecked at Santa Catalina in 1582 with more than 200 tons of cargo. Some of it was saved; most of it lies somewhere under the island beaches. Some beachcombers have found large disks made of beeswax which bear strange markings. The galleons carried a lot of this wax, used to caulk ship's timbers, out of the Orient. Its presence on Santa Catalina is a provocative sign.

The *Nuestra Señora de Ayuda,* a 230-ton galleon bound to Acapulco from Manila, went up on the rocks west of the island in 1641. So far as anyone knows, her Far East treasure was never recovered. Divers have recently spotted what they believe to be ballast stone in a shallow area on the west side of the island. On today's market the galleon's treasure would be worth at least $5 million.

Another galleon, the *San Sebastian,* was sailing through the outer Santa Barbara Channel in 1754 when a British pirate, George Compton, attacked her. *San Sebastian* went onto the rocks close to Santa Catalina and sank in 170 feet of water. Even though she is deep, the vessel's remains are close to shore near the west end of the island.

These treasure ships are known, documented Spanish wrecks; undoubtedly there are others, and clues end up on the beaches. A number of other ships have gone down in the area. Ancient wreckage, including ivory, occasionally turns up on San Nicolas and San Clemente islands, which stand to the west of Santa Catalina. The entire string of islands here make excellent searching grounds, and from a maritime historian perspective, they are among the most important on the West Coast.

Point La Jolla

Somewhere in this area near San Diego is the caravel *Trinidad,* destroyed in August, 1540, when a gale blew it off its moorings and dashed it against Point La Jolla. The *Trinidad* has been the subject of much research by the San Luis Rey Historical Society, which has concluded that the vessel was carrying a fortune that would bring some $4 million to $6 million at the time the research was done—but which today would amount to more than $60 million. Dr. J.J. Markey, who has been tracking the ship since 1951 through the Archive of the Indies in Seville, Spain, believes the *Trinidad* rests in 40 feet of water only 200 feet from shore. Roman coins have been found on the beaches—a fact which cheered Markey considerably. There are a lot of skeptics when it comes to the *Trinidad,* just as there were lettered men who doubted the existence of the *Atocha.* One day the *Trinidad* will be recovered, and the studious beachcomber who reads this book might be the one who finds it.

Point Reyes

This spot just north of San Francisco is an excellent hunting ground for all sorts of shipwreck material, old and new. One of the most sought-after treasures belongs to the *San Agustin,* returning from Manila in 1599, heading for Acapulco. A year earlier, the *Casa de Contratacion,* the Spanish New World shipping administration, ordered navigators to chart the inland areas—this to prepare for further conquest and colonization. The *San Agustin* anchored near Point Reyes and sent a party ashore, leaving a skeleton crew aboard. However, a southwesterly storm suddenly blew in and sent the galleon onto the rocks. In 1602, an expedition was sent to find the survivors and, hopefully, recover the ship's cargo—the usual priceless Manila haul of gold, silver, gems, ivory, porcelain, and wood. Portions of the hull were spotted, but very little was recovered. Storms had scattered the wreckage too widely for the divers of that time to thoroughly salvage the shipwreck. The vast majority is there today, washing ashore in tiny increments.

Point Reyes has captured more than galleons. It is a tricky—often deadly—area, and today modern vessels treat it with a great deal of respect. Those who have failed to heed the warnings litter the sands with their remains, curiosities for the beachcomber.

Cape Mendocino and Crescent City

The beaches that stretch northward from Cape Mendocino, past Humbolt Bay, to Crescent City are among the most promising in northern California. Like Baja, an unusually large amount of flotsam comes ashore here. Pieces of masts, brass fittings, dead eyes, rigging, teak, cedar, and the lovely glass floats from Japan are regularly deposited here. There are also relics from World War II. If these war remains are not in the same league with Spanish gold, they are still pieces of history which are now nearly a half-century old. We treat Civil War relics as treasures simply because of their age. One day, these modern military items will be considered historic, too. It is a function of time. And there is a certain magic in the battered sea ration cans that wash ashore. They remind us of days when the future hung in the balance, when brave men and women had to fight and give up their lives to crush tyranny. My diving mentor, Bob Landers, who now lives near Annapolis, is a true historian of World War II vintage ships; his home is decorated with the brass portholes and other memorabilia he retrieved from the deep, cold, and dark Atlantic waters off the coast of New Jersey. Each object reflects men and the age they lived in. "It's all passing into history," Bob once told me. "We spend time researching and bringing up the stuff because it means something important. Why else would anyone do it?" The same idea applies to the beach-combed materials. They are artifacts, part of the human experience, and therefore valuable to us. You will find a lot of wartime reminders along these wide beaches, a lot of memories that should not be allowed to fade. One note of caution: boxes of ammunition (American and Japanese) are found on the sand, and so are marine mines with their detonator horns; both ammunition and the mines may be dry inside, which means they are "live." Such explosives become unstable over time, so handle any of these finds with *extreme caution.* If you do not know anything about explosives, find someone who does. The war is over—so *no more casualties,* please!

Anacapa Island

The *Winfield Scott* sailed from San Francisco in 1852, bound for Panama with 200 passengers. On the night of December 2, the side-wheeler struck a rock near Anacapa, east of Santa Cruz, and sank quickly. The ship carried no gold consignment, but apparently many of the passengers did. This rumor was confirmed in 1965 by Glenn E. Miller, who explored the site with a party of divers. One of them, Ed Larralade, confirmed that the wreckage was that of *Winfield Scott.* Miller subsequently returned and used an underwater dredge to clear away overburden. In the riffle box he discovered gold nuggets. A lot of them, in fact. From time to time, they have been found at Anacapa—distinctive because, like the nuggets found by Miller, those picked up at the island have a vein of quartz running through them.

Oregon Beaches

Nehalem River Mouth

Oregon beachcombers came across a considerable trove of beeswax a few hundred yards from the mouth of the Nehalem River. The chunks weighed from ten to 200 pounds, and the larger pieces bore the inscription "JHS"—an abbreviation for *Jesus Hominum Salvador.* This indicated, it was said, that the wax was the property of the Catholic Church. The Pioneer Museum at Tillamook has a piece dated 1679 on display. Not long after the find, storms reshaped the beach and a beachcomber from Astoria came upon ship timbers in the sand. Other storms uncovered teak wood—quite a lot of it, in fact. The wax and the teak were both used to build ships, and speculation is that a galleon broke up in this area. Timbers of various kinds are still uncovered here after storms, but no more beeswax has been found. However, metal fasteners have turned up, along with fragments of ivory of unknown origin.

Clatsop Beach

Early explorers in this region found that the Clatsop Indians living near the mouth of the Columbia River, which empties into the Pacific, wore ornaments and various types of jewelry made from Chinese coins. These same explorers also noted that the Clatsop tribe had more than a few fair-headed members. The Indians told a tale of an ancient shipwreck, of five survivors who lived with the tribe. Then, in the 1950s, Chinese coins began showing up in the sands, dated from 1614 to 1796. Historian John S. Potter, Jr. believes that the combination of the coins and fair-headed Indians points to a Manila galleon. Other types of coins have been recovered, but none of Spanish lineage. This is a place looking for a studious beachcomber. The final story of what happened here would make an intriguing book.

Twin Rocks Beach

This magnificent seascape is named for the imposing rock formations standing like sentinels off the beach. Driftwood and a variety of ship artifacts are found here, mostly at high tide. It also has a reputation for the substantial amount of Oriental flotsam which washes ashore. Crates of dry silk have been found, but no galleon wear!

Coos Bay

Coos Bay owes much of its good reputation to a ship called the *Sunshine,* which capsized in a gale within sight of land. Unfortunately, we have no specific date on the event. We do know that she was an American schooner, and that after she was torn apart by the storm her hull drifted inshore and grounded at North Beach Peninsula. One other fact of interest: *Sunshine's* manifest listed a large keg of gold coins, probably Golden Eagles. Attempts to retrieve them from the hull have failed; in all likelihood I suspect that they fell into the ocean. Beachcombers keep a sharp eye out for glittery stuff in the sand, and they swear that sooner or later they will "find *Sunshine"* among the seashells.

Washington State

Cape Flattery

This bold outcropping at the very tip of Washington has long been a trove of ship relics. The Strait of Juan De Fuca, between the Cape and Vancouver Island, is a natural funnel for derelict materials waiting to be found. Shipping records reveal one known treasure wreck (though I am certain there are others)—the *Pacific,* an 875-ton three-masted paddle wheeler. On the night of November 4, 1875, the *Pacific* collided with a ship called *Orpheus* and went to the bottom almost in direct line with the tip of the Cape. Of the 277 aboard, there were only two survivors. The *Pacific* carried $79,220 in her safe, primarily paper money; there was also a store of gold currency and two large cases of opium. Somewhere among the nameless skeletons of ships and men hidden along these shores are the partial remains of the *Pacific*—a worthy prize waiting silently at the edge of the continent.

CHAPTER TEN

The Great Lakes and Canada

The ghostly television image coming from the bottom of Lake Ontario in March, 1983, caused the crew of the Canadian research ship to wonder if they were seeing things. In the green and gold twilight 290 feet below was a man in formal dress, hand over his heart, his eyes staring into the gloom.

It was not a real man, of course, but rather the bowsprit figure of Admiral Lord Nelson. The small boat the figure adorned carried Nelson's name until it was captured by the Americans during the War of 1812 and renamed the *Scourge*. Beamy and overburdened by cannons and 50 crewmen, the tubby little warship had been lost on August 8, 1813 in one of the nasty squalls that plague the lake. Yet after more than 170 years on the bottom, Lord Nelson and the *Scourge* looked as though they could be dusted off and sent back into battle.

The discovery of the *Scourge* and her sister ship, the *Hamilton*, by Ontario dentist and part-time marine historian Daniel A. Nelson, reminded the world once again of the remarkable preservative powers of cold water. Ships that go down in this part of the hemisphere remain in near-perfect condition, as do their human victims, up to a point. Human soft tissues have been observed at Isle Royale, Lake Superior, on vessels that were lost a half-century or more ago. There were no soft remains near the *Hamilton* or *Scourge*, but the video cameras did record a scattering of thigh and pelvic bones; there was a skull, mouth agape, teeth intact, empty eyes staring at the surface. Seaman Ned Myers, one of only eight survivors of the *Scourge*, later told novelist James Fenimore Cooper that the awkward little gunboats were "so tender that we could do little or nothing in a blow. . . . It was often prognosticated that she would prove our coffin." One day soon we will find out just how many men are still inside, and it would not be so shocking to find that Lake Ontario has preserved them, too.

The five Great Lakes have claimed more than 15,000 ships, but few were carrying treasure cargos. Like the Mediterranean, the Lakes haven't been natural shipping routes for gold or silver; these are commercial waters, and the ships that ply them are loaded with lead, steel, cooper, and iron ore. The lake bottoms are dotted with a fair collection of old automobiles and railroad rolling stock, farm machinery, steel rails, and a long, sad list of passenger vessels which may house jewelry and money or extensive stores of alcoholic beverages. When divers talk about treasure in these waters, they are usually referring to raw salvage value, such as the price of brass or copper on the scrap metal market. But commercial salvage is not the point of this book. If it were, I'd advise you to dredge your local harbors and marinas for outboard motors and other modern paraphernalia.

What is exciting about the Great Lakes is the history stored within them. There are many ships like the *Hamilton,* the *Scourge,* and the *Edmund Fitzgerald.* Be aware, however, that all salvage in Canadian territory is regulated by the Canadian Shipping Act, which requires that all recovered materials be delivered to the local Receiver of Wrecks. Another concern are local antiquities laws covering the removal of historic artifacts. Anyone planning to search in Canada should first contact the Canadian Department of Transport in Ottawa for a complete run down on the regulations.

The following is a small sample of ships lost on the Lakes:

The Great Lakes

Lake Superior

The largest of the five Great Lakes, Superior represents 31,800 square miles of open water. The U.S. National Park Service operates a fascinating underwater park preserve at Isle Royale. You can look and you can touch, but you can't remove anything from the ships in the park.

The man in charge here is Dan Lenihan, chief of the Submerged Cultural Resources Unit.

"We make history come to life," Lenihan says. Taken together, the submerged inventory, dating back to 1871, "represents a continuum of

The mournful wreckage of the passenger/ package freighter *Monarch* soon after she was smashed against Palisades Cliff, Isle Royale, Lake Superior during a fierce Great Lakes storm. Built in 1890 in Sarnia, Ontario, for the Beattly Line, she sank while "downbound" from Port Arthur with 12 passengers, 32 crew, and a cargo of grain and general merchandise. Only one crew member was lost. Remaining passengers and crew were rescued after four grueling days at Isle Royale.

Today the *Monarch* is part of a collection of ships mapped, plotted, and studied by National Park Service archaeologists, who maintain an underwater park for SCUBA divers visiting Isle Royale. Using waterproof maps and "trail guides," divers learn first-hand how lost ships adapt to their underwater graves. Since Isle Royale is a national park, visitors may look but not carry away any artifacts. *Photo courtesy National Park Service, Submerged Cultural Resources Unit.*

These National Park Service archaeologists may look like men from outer space, but in fact they are "innerspace" explorers preparing to search the frigid bottom of Lake Superior to chart the ghostly remains of the freighter *Monarch*. Their space suits are actually "dry suits" that trap warm air against the body and keep out the bone-chilling waters of the Great Lakes. Their air supply is provided by a set of twin tanks for extended bottom time and "octopus" air regulators—another dual array in which one air hose serves as a backup, standard operating procedure in deep, dark, cold waters. *Photo courtesy National Park Service, Submerged Cultural Resources Unit.*

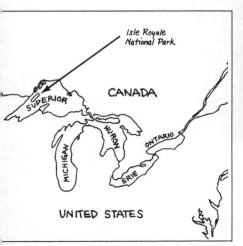

Using a special waterproof map, SCUBA divers visiting Isle Royale, Lake Superior, stop to inspect a large pipe on the port side of the freighter *Monarch*, the 1906 storm victim. The pipe was probably a sea cock or water intake for the ship's boilers. The unique maps and trail guides provided by the National Park Service give specific site information to divers who come to the underwater park. *Monarch* is only one of many ships to be seen at Isle Royale. *Photo courtesy National Park Service, Submerged Cultural Resources Unit.*

Tracking
Treasure
217

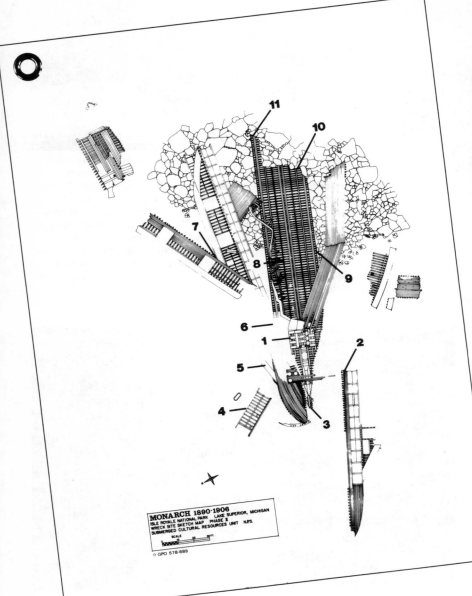

MONARCH 1890-1906
ISLE ROYALE NATIONAL PARK   LAKE SUPERIOR, MICHIGAN
WRECK SITE SKETCH MAP   PHASE II
SUBMERGED CULTURAL RESOURCES UNIT   N.P.S.

SCALE

☆ GPO 578-689

A Tour of the *Monarch*

**This waterproof plastic map,
carefully prepared by the
National Park Service, gives a
dive-by-the-numbers tour of the
sunken passenger/package
freighter *Monarch* at Isle
Royale, Lake Superior. The map
is two-sided. One side (*left*)
outlines the "lay" of the vessel
on the bottom and numbers the
major sights to be scrutinized by
SCUBA enthusiasts. By
following the numbers one gets a
feel for the ship as a whole
entity.**

　　**On the reverse side, (*right*)
numbered one through 11, is the
"trail number key." It explains
exactly what a diver is looking at
and tells him or her how to swim
efficiently to the next stop along
the way. Note the grommet that
allows the map to be attached by
a lanyard to a diver's wrist for
easy carrying.**

In the photo (*below, right*) a diver inspects a large mounting block aft of the engine bed plate. This served as the mount for the jacking gear which allowed the engine to be turned by hand during repairs.
Map and photo courtesy National Park Service, Submerged Cultural Resources Unit.

TRAIL NUMBER KEY

<u>Number 1:</u> Engine mount for the triple expansion, 900 horsepower, inverted vertical engine of the <u>Monarch</u>. Note the two shaft bearings.

<u>Number 2:</u> Forward portion of starboard stern section. The bilge attachment is on the right; the metal sheeting was toward the inside of the hull. This section may be followed out to the end, where the attachment to the stern deadwood may be viewed.

<u>Number 3:</u> Located on the stern deadwood near where the port stern section would have been attached. The shaft log, where the propeller shaft would have gone through the deadwood, was removed during the salvage operation in 1907.

<u>Number 4:</u> Swim to the port stern section near the bath tub. The number is located on a section of the aft crew quarters. This structure once contained port holes which have been removed by divers.

<u>Number 5:</u> From Number 4, proceed to the large upright pipe visible in the distance. This pipe was probably a sea cock (water intake for boilers). The number is on the main deck support shelf near the port stern termination of the arch support system. Note the decking nearby with the circular holes. This is from the part of the ship that held the coal bunkers. There are iron rings, gratings and covers, which fit these holes, on the site.

<u>Number 6:</u> Head towards the bow (shoreward). The number is on the metal sheeting on the inside of the port hull. There are metal rings for coal bunkers and a hardwood cargo winch in the area. Nearby is a hand-operated bilge pump, much like the one on the bow of the <u>America</u>. There are bottles and coal in this area.

<u>Number 7:</u> Proceed down and to the left over the cargo gangways on the top piece of hull construction. This piece is outboard side up, and is probably a portion of the starboard side of the ship. It is lying on the port hull which is inboard side up. The number is on a frame of the starboard portion. Two wood cargo winches may be seen in the gangway just ahead. Pass to the right (toward the stern) of the uprights into the bottom of the hull.

<u>Number 8:</u> Directly above the number is a scarf (bevelled joint) in the keelson cap. Near the number is a hatch in the ...ber boards for access to the bilge pump intake strainer

...mber 8. Number 9 is mounted
...tly out from the number is
...rd side up, the far edge

...arboard side you will reach
...resting on the wood and
...ock face.

...rt bilge keelson. Directly
...At this point the bow sec-
...r the dive terminated by

maritime history in the area. Some of the wrecks are fairly new, but we treat all of them as if they were historic."

Using students and volunteer sport divers, the Park Service has put together a fair slice of archaeological research. Research reports, along with the underwater trail and wreck maps, are made available to Isle Royale visitors. Lenihan thinks that increased public involvement will help support the Isle Royale concept.

"If we open up the field to the public, it will bring the interest we need to support our work," Lenihan says.

Two of the best shipwrecks at Isle Royale are the *Monarch* and the *Kamloops.*

The *Monarch* was built in 1890, and sank during a storm in 1906. It is a wooden vessel with a screw propeller, a crossover design between the eras of the wooden sailing ship and the steel freighter. Because the vessel is in shallow water, 20 to 70 feet, it's ideal for snorkelers and inexperienced divers. The water is cold but clear, and the visitor will get a good idea of what a sunken ship actually looks like.

The *Kamloops* is a bit more of a challenge. Built in 1924, it was wrecked in deep water three years later. She was a package freight vessel, and the packages are still on board. But *Kamloops* is for experienced Great Lakes divers, as the ship is deep, 170 to 240 feet below the surface. A visit to Isle Royale is bound to give you a feel for the kind of preservation that occurs in cold water. It's also a good place to survey large wrecks and ask questions about underwater archaeology and historic preservation. Here the treasure is knowledge, not goodies.

Other vessels of interest in Lake Superior, both inside and outside of Isle Royale park, are:

Smith More, a steamer that sank in 1889, five miles east of Grand Island. Reports indicate that 150 barrels of silver ore and 350 kegs of whiskey are on board. In 1960, the cargo was valued at $50,000.

Superior, another commercial steamer, wrecked off Grand Isle in 1856, with a cargo of various alcoholic spirits. Records also show a safe was on board and that some gold was in it, valued at about $40,000 in the early 1960s.

Algoma, a steamer that sank on the south shore of Isle Royale in 1885. Her cargo, consisting of 200 tons of steel rails, was partially salvaged in

1903. Many of the rails are still on board and cannot be removed without big league salvage gear, and, as part of the park, nothing can be taken from this wreck either.

Benjamin Noble is an intriguing wreck that went down in 1914. Her remains are at the base of Knife Island in shallow water. Her cargo was mundane, steel rails and such, but she's a big vessel with much to offer the casual explorer.

Gunilda, a fabulous luxury yacht, sank in 1911, off Rossport. She's one of those mystery wrecks everyone talks about but few have ever seen. *Gunilda* is 200 feet down, and reportedly loaded with cash and jewels. I've heard estimates of her worth ranging from $15,000 to $1 million or more. Finding her, of course, is no small feat; exploring her is only for the most experienced divers. As a history lesson, however, she may prove very rewarding. Budding marine archaeologists can practice their detective skills, tracing her whereabouts, her history, and her treasure.

Sunbeam, a commercial steamer, sank in 1863, about two miles east of Copper Harbor. There are rumors of money aboard this vessel. If so, it is stored in a steel safe. Estimates of actual cash range from $15,000 to $50,000 in silver and gold coinage. Given the preservative properties of the cold water, any paper money should be in fine condition as well.

Lake Michigan

This is the third largest of the Great Lakes, with 22,000 square miles of open water and depths to about 1,000 feet. Like its sister lakes, Michigan is a watery commercial highway. Among the cargos of pig iron and coal, however, are millions in cash and jewels lost aboard passenger ships and one intriguing (though unauthenticated) shipment of five chests of gold.

The Niagara, the *Prinz Willem V,* and the *Meeks:* A number of salvage operations have focused on these wrecks, and many artifacts have been found. Still missing, however, are five chests of gold thought to be from the *Niagara,* which went down near Poverty Island, north of Washington Island. Existence of this gold treasure has been variously linked to the *Prinz Willem V* and the *Meeks,* but more often the focus goes to the *Niagara.*

Lakeland and the *Wisconsin* are two prize automobile carriers. The *Lakeland* went down in 1924 in the area of Sturgeon Bay with various Detroit models on board. Salvage value is estimated at more than $1 million. The *Wisconsin* went to the bottom some six miles from Kenosha,

Wisconsin in 1929. The vessel was found in the early 1970s with its cargo of new Detroit cars and farm machinery. Salvage conducted at that time was reportedly partial, and a well-funded team may still turn the *Wisconsin* into a fortune.

Toledo was a passenger ship driven by steam. She sank in 1856, about a half-mile from Point Washington. There have been many estimates of her value, the lowest being $10,000 in money and jewelry, the highest about $250,000. The *Toledo* is deep in the bottom, and only a well-planned expedition could bring up her cargo.

Vernon: This was another lake luxury yacht, reportedly powered by sail and steam. She sank in 1887, approximately three miles off Two Rivers. Estimates place the value of personal items on this vessel at from $20,000 to $500,000.

Chicora: Many unknowns surround *Chicora*, not the least of which is her exact location. This steamer reportedly sank in 1895. The closest present fix on her final resting place is some seven miles to the west and south of St. Joseph. She carried cases of expensive liquors. Passengers' valuables and money in the purser's safe are valued at $25,000. With vintage bottles of wine selling at outrageous prices these days, a haul of *Chicora*'s liquor trove could escalate the values beyond $1 million.

Lake Huron

This is a clear water area and a favorite hunting ground for divers, explorers, and beachcombers. Including the Georgian Bay area, Lake Huron is the second largest lake, with 23,000 squares miles of open water and depths to about 700 feet. By far the most popular spot is Tobermory, near Ontario, at the end of the 50-mile stretch known as Bruce Peninsula.

Several factors combine to make this area popular: First, there are more wrecks than anyone can count; visibility in the water averages 40 to 50 feet year 'round; water temperatures in the summer get up to 50 degrees; and there are excellent accommodations and diving facilities.

There is one caveat: The entire area is now a provincial underwater park, and no artifacts may be removed. For some, this will be an immediate turn off. For others, Tobermory will be a challenge and a learning experience. After all, exploration and adventure are rewards in themselves, and what can be learned at Tobermory can be applied elsewhere.

Tobermory Harbor has two parts called Big Tub and Little Tub. At Big Tub there are two 80-foot-long sailing schooners off the innermost shore in about 20 feet of water. The schooners are so close to the surface, in fact, that you can stand on portions of them, head above water, and examine the hulls at your leisure.

At Little Tub there are four wrecks down in very shallow water. One finds wrecks like this at the Outer Banks of North Carolina, but at Tobermory the water is considerably less turbid, and there are no currents to speak of.

Forest City: This is the wreck of a converted schooner located at the northeast corner of Bear's Rump Island, about four miles north of Tobermory. The bow of the vessel is completely charred by the fire that sent her to the bottom. *Forest City* is a bit of a Hollywood set. She's on a steep incline, giving the appearance that she might slide all the way to the bottom at any moment. Her upper decks are 70 feet from the surface, with her stern rail at 150 feet. She's not to be taken lightly, even by experienced divers. However, with visibility at about 60 feet, she can be examined by snorkeling over her. Shallow dives, to 30 or 40 feet, will provide a good view of the ship. Experienced divers on deeper excursions should be wary of snagging themselves on monofilament line. Carry a knife.

Arabia is a schooner that sank in the 1800s, about three miles from Tobermory and approximately a half-mile north and east of Echo Island. *Arabia* is yet another Hollywood backdrop. Virtually in one piece, her anchors, rigging, and furniture are still intact. She's very tempting, but also very deep. The shallow portion is 90 feet down; the site dips to 110 feet. This is another vessel for experienced divers only, but it can be viewed and photographed on a relatively shallow excursion. Visibility in the water around the wreck can be 50 feet or more, so snorkelers can catch a glimpse of her eerie presence and SCUBA divers who don't mind hanging in mid-water at 30 to 40 feet will have a truly awesome vision before them. But unless you're sure you can handle the depth and the cold, don't go deep.

Mary L. Breck is a beat-up 396-foot schooner that went to the bottom in 1900, with a cargo of ordinary clay bricks. That's the so-so part. The upside is that she's in only ten feet of water at the south end of Bear's Rump Island. In my opinion, she's worth a look. *Mary L. Breck* reveals how battered a shallow-water wreck can get, and how important it is to save them before they deteriorate completely.

Lake Erie

One of the smaller Great Lakes, Erie covers 9,910 square miles. The area is extraordinarily rich in history. Long before her sister lakes became commercial shipping routes, Erie carried a substantial amount of water-borne traffic between the United States and Canada. As a result, the lake has a decided treasure aspect, and those who know her best say she hides more hard currency than all of the other lakes combined. Maybe. Certainly Erie has yielded many artifacts and, occasionally coins (big finds are seldom talked about openly). The shallow geography, less than 200 feet deep, makes it ideal for exploration.

Long Point: This peninsula stands out about 30 miles into the lake off the Canadian shore southwest of Hamilton, Ontario. The locals claim there are more shipwrecks on Long Point than any other place in the world. This may be debatable, but the claim cannot be dismissed easily. At the present time, there's no accurate count to rely on. Local nautical charts look like pincushions passed down from one generation to the next; indeed, it will take years to make an accurate survey. Thus it's open country. It combines plenty of variety with shallow depths (15 to 20 feet close to shore), long sandy beaches, and endless opportunities to search out a unique wreck. Among so many "no name wrecks," ships for which we have no records, you're bound to come across something.

Pascal B. Pratt is a wooden steamer that went up on the north side of Long Point about three miles from the Long Point Light. She wrecked November 16, 1908, and is down in 18 to 20 feet of water. She's fairly large, and still recognizable as a ship. Artifacts have been recovered in the area.

C.W. Elphinke is an old wooden vessel about which little is known. She's on the south side of the Long Point Light in about 25 feet of water. *Elphinke* is sometimes compared to the *Pratt* in size and vintage, but she's a little deeper and therefore more reclusive. She may prove to have a good store of scattered artifacts.

East Sister Island: A small outcropping located west of the north end of Pelee Island, the exact coordinates for the island can be found on Lake Erie Nautical Chart No. 36. Off the southeast side are a cluster of shipwrecks in depths of ten to 40 feet, and one can be found 200 yards straight off a very large dead, white tree in the middle of the shoreline. Among the other wrecks in the vicinity are the *Robert Burns,* wrecked in 1850; the schooner *Pearl,* sunk in 1855; and the schooner *Cornwall,* wrecked in 1865. All three ships are no more than 200 yards from the beach. Many artifacts have been recovered, including a ship's bell, numerous brass fittings, ceramics, and personal items such as watches and jewelry.

Counted among the classic glamour wrecks in Lake Erie are the following:

Gray Ghost was a rumrunner that sank under unknown circumstances in 1931 in the area known as Middle Ground, just north of Kelley's Island. Her cargo consisted of premium Canadian whiskey valued at approximately $100,000. An undetermined amount of money is said to be on board. The wreck has never been located.

Chesapeake: This classic steamer sank in a storm about three miles north and east of Conneaut. She went down about 1847, with a safe containing gold and silver worth about $300,000 on today's market. Passenger valuables are estimated to be worth $20,000 to $50,000.

Spanish Coin Wreck: There are no papers to determine the origin of this ship which sank in 1698, ten miles north and east of Erie, Pennsylvania. The vessel was discovered by accident when a dredging operation brought up a number of silver Spanish cobb coins minted in 1698. It was inferred that the probable date of sinking was the same as that stamped on the coin. There have been no investigations of the site in recent years. It's an unknown, and except for the coins and pieces of wood recovered during the dredging, the ship has left no other clues as to her origin.

Dean Richmond is a truly promising treasure wreck. The steamer sank in 1893, northeast of Dunkirk with a cargo of lead, zinc, and copper sheeting. There are indications that the *Dean Richmond* was also carrying $141,000 in silver and gold bullion, figured at 1893 prices.

Wheatley, Ontario: There are money beaches near Wheatley that produce Spanish pieces of eight, particularly after storms. There is speculation that a very old payroll ship, perhaps carrying specie for "Rogers Rangers," went down in the area.

Lake Ontario

This is the smallest and shallowest of the Great Lakes, encompassing 7,600 square miles, with many shipwrecks just below the surface. The lake is a trove of artifacts from the War of 1812. Among the vessels of interest:

Atlas is a schooner that sank two miles northwest of Oswego, date unknown. Her cargo was pig iron and valuable china, a very strange combination. She's never been found.

Lady Washington is another undated casualty. This sloop is believed to be on the bottom five miles west of Oswego with a cargo of china.

Black Duck is a sloop that sank in 1872, reportedly near the shoreline of Mexico Bay. She was carrying money and a large cargo of whiskey in kegs.

The Canadian Provinces

Quebec

Let me put it plainly: Quebec's waters are cold. Very cold. If you visit in mid-summer, water temperatures *may* be in the 50s or low 60s. But for hearty types, Quebec Province offers good treasure hunting—within the parameters of local laws. One of the most frequented areas is along the Richelieu River where it flows north from Lake Champlain. The Richelieu was the scene of a lot of action during the War of 1812, and a lot of reminders have been deposited on the bottom. Indian artifacts are also found regularly. The following areas are well-known for artifacts:

Ile Aux Noix: This is an island in the Richelieu at Saint Paul, Quebec. Its first claim to fame is its fabulous deposits of ancient Indian pottery, some dated back to 1500 B.C. Pieces of this pottery are found on the east bank of the river, just opposite the center of Ile Aux Noix. Keep in mind, however, that such finds are deemed important by archaeologists working the area, and the law is on their side. If you recover pottery, think of it as a contribution to their research, not as an ornament for your mantelpiece.

Some 30 to 50 feet off the east side of the island is an old sloop, quite beaten-up, in about 20 feet of generally clear water. The name of the wreck isn't known, but it's marked on nautical charts dating back 200 years.

At the southern tip of the island is Fort Lennox. Working out from the water's edge is a wide scattering of swords, muskets, cannonballs, and assorted war relics. Divers in the area have found a many as 50 different types of projectiles, from large cannonballs to the smallest pistol shot.

Lake Memphragog: An odd name, but a pretty fair hunting ground for relics. Located near Magog, about an hour's drive out of Montreal, the lake boasts somewhat warmer waters than those generally found in these parts. A lot of divers come here, and the facilities are excellent. Old bottles and 19th century war memorabilia are the main fare. Good intact ceramics are also found, along with odd bits and pieces of brass, pewter, and clay pipes.

Nova Scotia

Cape Breton (Eastern Shore): This area, which presents a rocky coastline flowing into sandy beaches, is about 200 miles east of Halifax. Water is clearest and warmest in the summer, with a visibility of about 30 feet. At the harbor near Louisburg, divers and snorkelers have been bringing up historic relics for years. The area just off Louisburg Fort is especially productive. The harbor entrance is well known for the wreck of the *Evelyn,* a 1924 vintage steel-hulled merchant vessel. She lies in 30 to 60 feet of water. Inside the harbor is a French warship which sank during the siege of Louisburg in 1758. Only 30 feet below the surface, this vessel has left 35 cannons on the bottom, along with a considerable amount of shipboard materials. For those who want a guided tour of shipwrecks, the Louisburg Historical Society can put you on track.

Saint Peters Bay: An easy, shallow area rich in artifacts, especially old bottles and coins. St. Peters trades on treasure and fresh scallops. There are probably more scallops than treasure, although some have argued the other way. It's definitely worth looking into, especially for beachcombers and non-divers.

Mahone Bay: A large, popular bay near Chester, Nova Scotia, Mahone has a wreck which the Canadians call "The Teaser." It's said to be an American privateer, but there's no substantial confirmation that I can find. More realistically, however, people are drawn to the area by the gold dredging operation at Gold River, which flows into Mahone. Just how much flows into the bay is a mystery, but evidently there's enough gold to keep divers coming back. Any of the glittery stuff found here does not have to be checked through the local Receiver of Wrecks.

Port Herbert: A good area for exploration, Port Herbert is on the Sable River in Shelburn County. Many ships went down in this area, so the supply of artifacts is plentiful. The local historical society has information on the maritime history, but much remains to be filled in. The difficulty is finding some context for the materials brought up by treasure hunters. The underwater wreckage has become so jumbled that it's difficult to trace individual finds to specific vessels. Contributions to this area's history will come through a labor of love fueled by hard-core scholarship.

Niagara River Area: For buffs interested in the War of 1812 this is a fine place to be. About a quarter-mile offshore on the Canadian side of the river is a heavy concentration of 19th-century arms—heavy and light cannon, muskets, and barrels of black powder. There is disagreement about how this weapons cache got there. The most popular theory holds that it is from a warship. Some wreckage has been found, but it hasn't been traced directly to the arms.

Fort Erie: The area five miles from the end of Peace Bridge on the Canadian side is famous for its 1812-era artifacts. The water is murky and shallow—a mixed blessing. Cannonballs are scattered from about 100 to 800 feet offshore. There are also old anchors and a large collection of muskets and shot. Swimming and snorkeling are easy here, the only problem being the poor visibility. It takes a lot of patience to grope around by feel. Canadian customs agents on the bridge can be helpful in showing visitors where to begin their search.

Sable Island: Melville Bell Grosvenor, whose grandparents were once residents of Sable Island, said the only real permanence on this tiny outcropping of the continental shelf is its loneliness. An examination of this northern graveyard of ships and men bears him out. Located 100 miles southeast of Nova Scotia, Sable is under constant assault by the Atlantic. As you might expect, the Atlantic is winning. In 1633, Dutch cartographer Johannes de Laet described the island as being "40 miles in circuit." Today, it's only 23 miles long and about a mile wide.

Sable's deadly sandbars and shoals have trapped and completely destroyed more than 500 ships and taken at least 5,000 lives. Anyone who has ever witnessed a winter storm in these regions will understand why the losses have been so great. A local historian has said these storms "strike the boldest with awe, if not with terror. The full force of the Atlantic . . . seems to cause the earth to quiver to its foundations." There's no saving a ship that goes aground; mountainous waves dash them to pieces and swallow them. Until the radio beacon was installed in 1947, grounded mariners were advised to stay with their vessels, despite the odds that they would not survive. Trying to make it to shore, even in relatively fair conditions, was considered an act of suicide.

Given its ominous reputation, it's not hard to understand why a visit to Sable is not a jaunt or a holiday; it's a major undertaking. Except in mid-summer when the sea provides brief surcease, the island is at war with the elements. The gale-force winds can sandblast skin from hands and face, and the surf rages in from the waterline up and over the dunes.

For these reasons, among others, the Canadian government doesn't promote tourism at Sable; if anything, it will discourage it. Those persistent souls who wish to visit anyway should have real business to handle and blue chip intentions. If you're a journalist on assignment, a researcher or historian, or a philanthropist involved in maritime affairs of direct interest to Canada, you'll have a strong bargaining chip.

The looting of artifacts and theft of the wild ponies that inhabit the island has given the Canadians a suspicion of would-be visitors. To obtain permission, it may be necessary to undergo a mild bit of personal scrutiny.

In recent years, the Mobil Oil Corporation has established drilling operations in the area, making access easier than it used to be. Still, transportation and housing are difficult and must be handled directly by the Ministry of Transport office in Nova Scotia.

Maps showing the location of wrecks in the area are available and Canadian maritime records are extensive. Getting at the wrecks, however, is a formidable challenge. SCUBA diving is out of the question. There are no facilities for it on Sable, and the currents are too dangerous even with the best equipment. A magnetometer survey would be risky and expensive, could only be performed during the few calm weeks in mid-summer, and would be of dubious value. Some of the wreckage located by such a survey would undoubtedly be scattered by storms before it could be examined.

Sable is most definitely a treasure island. Dozens of ships are buried deep in its sands, including the French vessel *L'Americaine*, lost in 1822. The ship sank with gold and silver specie worth more than $1 million. Getting at it would be extremely difficult. And anything found would have to be processed through the Receiver of Wrecks. Any visit to Sable on the profit motive will prove futile, if not illegal. Those in the best position to reap benefits are researchers with worthwhile and workable projects.

Despite this, Sable remains one of the few landfalls in the world that's still a challenge, begging exploration. In time, the island will disappear completely, and whatever can be done to document its maritime history will be valuable to future generations. If you believe you can contribute and aren't put off by red tape, you can apply for permission to visit Sable by writing to: William Parsons, District Manager/Administrator, Sable Island Coast Guard Base, Canadian Ministry of Transport, Box 1000, Darmouth, Nova Scotia, B-2Y328. Outline your project fully.

CHAPTER ELEVEN

Undersea Organizations You Can Join

The egomaniacal Captain Nemo learned the hard way: The world below the sea has no fences around it. Today we have many Captain Nemos who would like to claim it as their exclusive property, but fortunately it remains open to all persons lured by the deep and its countless mysteries.

The organizations listed in this chapter further the ongoing quest to explore the sea. Some are information-oriented and produce periodicals to keep you abreast of news and developments in the field. Others are action-oriented and devoted to hands-on fieldwork. Still others serve educational needs. No single organization can do it all and it generally takes a combination of forces to cover the field.

When considering which of these groups are best suited to your needs, it may be helpful to follow these guidelines:

- Go for action, if you are fit and able.
- Go for research, if you are patient.
- Go for philanthropy, if you have the resources.
- Go for all of the above, if the spirit so moves you.
- But *do not* go it alone. Getting the most out of undersea exploration requires being in touch with individuals and organizations that share your ambitions.

The groups listed here are divided into seven basic categories, with some unavoidable overlap. The categories are:

1. Exploration: These groups have developed a substantial amount of fieldwork involving surveys, searches, and recovery.
2. Museums: In addition to the typical museum functions of collection, conservation, and display of historic materials, the museums listed in this chapter maintain active at-sea projects which they operate directly or support through funding of other projects.
3. Colleges and universities: Unfortunately, academic study of nautical archaeology is rare. Only a tiny number of institutions award degrees or have full-time studies in the field. Those listed here offer degree programs at graduate and undergraduate levels; some offer only limited credits.
4. Government: Included are federal, state, and local government entities which promote

archaeology, and divisions which track legislative, legal, and conservation aspects of submerged cultural resources.

5. Historical societies: All states and many municipalities maintain active historical societies with well-defined goals. Those listed here focus on maritime activities.

6. Investment groups: These are organizations engaged in the business of searching for and recovering lost treasures. Some are funded by private capital; others receive grant monies. The groups are both for profit and non-profit, and all have reasonable records of success. No investment guarantees a return. After examining your own motives, *proceed with utmost prudence.*

7. Membership and professional associations: The organizations mentioned, with a few exceptions, boast a wide spectrum of members, from the most experienced explorers to the novice. The informational and public relations aspects of these groups are outstanding.

Please keep in mind that the listings are only a sampling. There are hundreds of maritime organizations in the United States and elsewhere. Those detailed here will get you started and help expand your personal horizons.

Exploration Organizations

CEDAM International, Department A, One Fox Road, Croton-on-Hudson, NY 10520.

This non-profit organization is named for its goals: conservation, education, diving, archaeology, and museums. Founded in 1967, CEDAM is open to all persons interested in marine biology, nautical archaeology, and terrestrial archaeology. Findings of its expeditions are reported in its quarterly newsletter, *Reef Report.* In October, 1984, CEDAM conducted major marine and on-land expeditions at Nueva Cadiz, on the island of Cubagua, Venezuela. Neuva Cadiz was a major pearl center for the conquistadors. CEDAM has also explored the Cayos Cochinos Islands in the Gulf of Honduras to determine what might be found in an underwater archaeological search. In 1982, the organization sponsored a shipwreck reconnaissance at the Chinchorro Bank, off the coast of Mexico.

Espey, Houston and Associates, Inc., P.O. Box 519, Austin, TX 78767.

EHA is an engineering and consulting firm that advertises worldwide oceanic capabilities. It maintains a cultural resource unit that provides a range of management services, with special emphasis on nautical archaeology and marine survey work.

Maritime Archaeological and Historical Research Institute, 224 Route 130, Bristol, ME 14539.

MAHRI is a first-rate non-profit organization under the direction of nautical archaeologist Warren Riess. Riess gained wide recognition during his recent excavation of an 18th century merchant vessel—on land! The ship was eight feet below street level at a preconstruction site in Manhattan. MAHRI engages in on-going excavations, including its work on the 1635 Bristol merchantman *Angel Gabriel,* and the *Snow Squall.* The group has a joint project with the National Oceanic and Atmospheric Administration's Northeast Undersea Research Program, which focuses on finding prehistoric and historic sites on the Continental Shelf. The organization publishes a newsletter, stays abreast of political developments, and encourages a wide membership. It's one of the best groups of its kind in the country.

Morning Watch Research, Inc., 2699 South Bayshore Drive, Miami, FL 33133.

Headed by former United States Ambassador to Jamaica Sumner Gerard, Morning Watch is a hands-on organization which operates archaeological expeditions in the Caribbean and elsewhere. Among its joint activities is a summer training school in Jamaica that focuses on shipwreck excavation and research on the sunken city of Port Royal, at Kingston.

National Institute of Archaeology, P.O. Box 690, Washington, DC 20004.

NIA is an exciting new organization headed by Daniel A. Koski-Karrell, president of Karrell Archaeological Services. The group's "Columbus Project" is especially timely. Koski-Karrell hopes to locate Christopher Columbus' flagship, *Santa Maria,* and the Great Navigator's first settlement in the New World, La Navidad, in Haiti. The federal government plans a 500 Year Anniversary gala to celebrate Columbus' voyage of discovery. President Ronald Reagan has established a Columbus Commission to handle the celebration in 1992. NIA is seeking input on this most ambitious project.

Sea Research Society, P.O. Drawer V, Sullivan's Island, SC 29482.

Sea Research focuses primarily on nautical archaeology and promotes research, exploration, and various educational programs. The contact at Sea Research is E. Lee Spence, a prolific writer and expert on the Charleston Harbor.

Sociedad Scientifica Interamericana, Avenue Del Cantaro, Andador 7, No. 1-1, Villa Coapa, Mexico, DF 14930

This is a productive research group based in Mexico that specializes in underwater digs and New World studies. It seeks input on the survey, excavation, and preservation of submerged cultural resources in the Americas.

Museums

Great Lakes Naval and Maritime Museum, P.O. Box A-3785, Chicago, IL 60690.

This museum acquires ships and maritime antiquities through donation and purchase and restores classic vessels. It offers excellent materials related to the maritime history of the region.

Kittery Naval and Historical Museum, P.O. Box 453, Rogers Road, Kittery, ME 03904.

KNHM collects, preserves, and exhibits items that record the history of the locality, with primary emphasis on the Portsmouth Naval Shipyard, established in 1880 as the first United States naval shipbuilding facility.

Mariner's Museum, Newport News, VA 23606.

Founded in 1930, the Mariner's Museum has the most extensive nautical collection in the country. Its main building occupies a 550-acre site and its exhibits are international in scope. The museum is involved in many aspects of marine history and archaeology, and maintains an outstanding collection of source materials. Marine archaeologist Warren Riess has joined the staff, which will certainly bring to the museum the kind of unique research he's noted for.

Peabody Museum, East India Square, Salem, MA 01970.

The Maritime History Department of the Peabody will trace shipwrecks with information you provide. You must know the name of the ship, date of sinking, and its approximate location. The museum boasts an excellent research facility and library.

Smithsonian Institution, Museum of American History, Washington, D.C. 20560.

The Smithsonian can provide information on all state and local historical societies in the maritime field. You can join as a Smithsonian Associate for a nominal fee, receive *Smithsonian* magazine and a steady flow of news, views, and announcements of Smithsonian-sponsored expeditions and projects.

Colleges and Universities

East Carolina University, Greenville, NC 27834-4353.

East Carolina's Department of History offers a program in maritime history and nautical archaeology which includes field study. Its major project is a cooperative arrangement with NOAA to excavate and possibly restore the Civil War ironclad, *Monitor,* which sank off the coast of North

Carolina. This is an exciting link; the *Monitor* work extends across many of the key disciplines required to master the art and science of bringing ships back to life. The school is also taking on other worthwhile marine archaeological projects.

Institute of Marine Studies, Haifa, Israel.

This operation has a world-class reputation. It offers a degree in nautical archaeology, and a student can go so far as to write a Ph.D. thesis here. The Institute is quite active in the field, with a good deal of hands-on work in the Red Sea—which just happens to offer some of the clearest water on Earth. Director of the Institute is Dr. Avner Aban, a scholar with impressive credentials.

NOVA University, Oceanographic Center, 8000 North Ocean Drive, Dania, FL 33004.

NOVA offers a course and a chance to get hands-on experience in nautical archaeology, but unfortunately does not offer a degree in the field. The course is run by Peter Throckmorton. In the late 1950s and early 1960s, Throckmorton, who was a journalist at the time, hitched boat rides with Turkish fishermen and sponge divers who knew where to find wrecks that were thousands of years old. It was Throckmorton's pioneering spirit that turned nautical archaeology into a workable art and science. He is currently working with NOVA to set up a research center in the Dominican Republic. A thesis on nautical archaeology may be written at the university.

Scottish Institute of Marine Studies, Saint Andrews College, Fife, Scotland, KY169AJ.

Dr. Colin Martin heads up a degree program at the Institute, which has an excellent reputation among American and European scholars. Martin oversees an extensive program of classroom and field study of a wide range of subjects.

Texas A&M University, Nautical Archaeology Department, College Station, Texas 77843-4352

Texas A&M is a pioneer in nautical archaeology and awards a degree in anthropology with a specialization in nautical archaeology. The program has an outstanding reputation and conducts digs all over the world. Students who have gone through the program swear by it. It is an excellent training ground for students and professionals.

University College of North Wales, Department of History, Bangor, Wales, LC5728G.

A complete program in nautical archaeology is offered here under the direction of Dr. John Illsley. Students may obtain a Masters Degree. The school has a fine reputation and conducts extensive fieldwork. Some academics say the program is the equal of Texas A&M's, though it places more emphasis on undersea technology. Students learn anthropological approaches to data interpretation. Learning how to operate complex oceanic equipment and do complex chemistry and preservation are two strengths of the program. Students are expected to complete detailed case studies of submerged cultural resources.

Government

National Archive and Records Service, National Archives, Washington, DC 20408.

The National Archives keeps records on shipwrecks between 1874 and 1939. It will make limited searches of its files based on information you provide. You must have the ship's name, the date of sinking, and the approximate location. Data on wrecks after 1939 may be provided by the Hydrographic Surveys Branch, National Ocean Service, 6001 Executive Boulevard, Rockville, MD 20852.

National Oceanic and Atmospheric Administration, Marine Sanctuaries Division, Office of Ocean and Coastal Resource Management, 3300 Whitehaven St., N.W., Washington, DC 20235.

NOAA heads an ambitious project to study and (hopefully) raise the famous Civil War ironclad, *Monitor.* Anyone seeking details about the *Monitor* Marine Sanctuary Program will receive published information, including a newsletter devoted to the warship, titled *Cheesebox.* NOAA also runs operations at Pennekamp Coral Reef Park, Key Largo, which shelters a population of historic ships within its 100-square-mile area. Information on Pennekamp and other areas of interest may be obtained. Do not underrate the role of NOAA in nautical research, even if you have never heard of the agency. It runs quietly but effectively, and should receive more public attention. Specific questions concerning the *Monitor* project may be addressed to Project Director Edward M. Miller. An extensive list of publications is available upon request.

National Park Service, Submerged Cultural Resources Unit, P.O. Box 25287, Denver, CO 80225.

The Park Service operates fascinating programs for divers and anyone else who wishes to volunteer for on-going underwater surveys, excavation, and preservation of submerged resources. It maintains and operates underwater parks from Florida and the Great Lakes to California and Guam. Like most federal agencies, it provides a steady flow of information, including the *Cultural Resources Management Bulletin* and a slick magazine, *National Parks.* Research reports and surveys are mailed regularly. NPS, though it is in a budget crunch, remains positioned to fund long-term projects. Those wishing to participate have an opportunity to work closely with professionals in various nautical disciplines. A general planning guide that outlines the legal framework of NPS activity is titled *Archaeology and Archaeological Resources.* It may be obtained from NPS in Colorado or by writing to the **Society for American Archaeology**, 1703 New Hampshire Avenue, N.W., Washington, D.C. 20009.

United States House of Representatives Merchant Marine Fisheries Library, 550 House Annex-II, Washington, DC 20515.

For the politically inclined, this library will keep you up to date on the latest "treasure wars" action. The library will send you transcripts of hearings and other documents related to shipwreck legislation and other issues. If you wish to make a political statement, a letter to your congressman and a listing with the library will place you in the thick of it.

Historical Societies

Champlain Maritime Society, P.O. Box 745, Burlington, VT 05402.

A non-profit unit founded in 1979, the CMS includes divers, historians, archaeologists, and others with an exploratory nature. In recent years, the Society has found a half dozen historic ships in Lake Champlain. In 1981, in cooperation with Vermont's Division of Historic Preservation, the CMS received a permit to study a vessel that produced more than 100 rare artifacts. Its work has received high scores as one of the most active and intensive underwater projects in the country.

Classic Yacht Restoration Guild, Inc., 683 Pond Neck Road, Earleville, MD 21919.

For anyone who has ever wanted to learn exactly how such ships are built, the Guild may provide good insight. The organization offers apprenticeship programs in ship restoration and maintenance, including carpentry, rigging, and other mechanicals. Restored seaworthy vessels are instructional platforms used in the Guild's piloting program.

Mary Rose Trust, Old Bond Store, 48 Warblington Street, Portsmouth, England, PO-12ET.

This prestigious society is headed by Prince Charles, who made a dive or two on the *Mary Rose,* King Henry VIII's flagship. It coordinates activities related to the vessel's restoration and display, and raises money to keep the work going.

National Maritime Historical Society, 132 Maple Street, Croton-on-Hudson, NY 10520.

This organization publishes a high-quality quarterly magazine called *Sea History.* It also supports restoration projects, maritime museums, and similar conservation efforts. The Society actively promotes hands-on involvement in the many projects covered in its publication.

National Trust for Historic Preservation, Department of Maritime Preservation, 1785 Massachusetts Avenue, N.W., Washington, DC 20036.

The Trust's Department of Maritime Preservation is getting into this field in a big way. It collaborates with The National Park Service on various ocean-related projects, including a survey of historic merchant vessels. The Trust also collaborates with NOAA on the *Monitor* project and plans to expand into the areas of marine survey and photography techniques. A documentation project is also in the works, along with an ambitious publications program. A newsletter is sent to Trust members. A special cooperative arrangement with *Yankee* magazine will give students an opportunity to participate in restoration projects. The Trust also takes an active role in legislation related to maritime cultural affairs, including the "treasure wars."

Nautical Archaeology Society, 1 Old Hall, South Grove, Highgate, London, England, N6.

NAS aims to advance education in nautical archaeology and publishes the results of its projects. It encourages public input. The Society publishes a newsletter and holds conferences, symposia, and lectures.

Nautical Archaeology Trust, 24-28 Oval Road, London, England, NW1 7DX.

The Trust was established as a charity in 1972 and focuses on education and training in the field. It publishes a quarterly, *The International Journal of Archaeology and Underwater Exploration.* In America, a subscription may be fulfilled through the Academic Press, Inc., 111 Fifth Avenue, New York, NY 10003. The publication provides excellent leads on European adventures and exploration.

Newfoundland Marine Archaeological Society, Box 583, Kelligreive, Newfoundland, Canada, AQA 2TO.

This group is organized to do research in the colder climes. It maintains an active calendar and is open to all interested persons. The organization has ties with groups in Canada and elsewhere, and keeps current records of activities in the area.

Society for the Archaeological Study of the Mary Rose, 3 Landmark Square, Stamford, CT 06901.

As the name implies, this is an extension of the *Mary Rose* Trust. Excavation and preservation of this ship reflect state-of-the-art technology and great historic importance. The Society can provide information on the dig, as well as information on the preservation and display of artifacts.

The Steamship Historical Society of America, 345 Blackstone Boulevard, H.C. Hall Building, Providence, RI 02906.

There is a large cadre of steamship fans here and in Europe and the SHSA gives them exactly what they want—news and information on the diverse line of steam-driven vessels. It offers a line of books and a quarterly journal, *Steamboat Bill.* It also sponsors national meetings. SHSA maintains a large library devoted to steamboat history and a collection of 30,000 prints and photo.

Wisconsin Marine Historical Society, 814 West Wisconsin Avenue, Milwaukee, WI 53233.

WMHS promotes the recovery, collection, and preservation of marine artifacts. It concentrates primarily on the commercial shipping of the Great Lakes and the Saint Lawrence Seaway.

Professional Associations

Advisory Council on Underwater Archaeology, 3610 Crowncrest Drive, Austin, TX 78759.

The ACUA provides professional advice on underwater digs and related research. It holds an annual conference and publishes its proceedings. These publications can very often provide excellent leads to on-going digs, persons to contact, and new directions in the maritime field. You do not have to be a lettered archaeologist to join.

Atlantic Alliance for Maritime Heritage Conservation, Inc., P.O. Box 27272, Central Station, Washington, DC 20038.

The non-profit Atlantic Alliance was founded in 1983 to bridge the gap between sport divers, archaeologists, history buffs, and others seeking to contribute their talents to the maritime field. It sponsors meetings and seminars and conducts field schools in underwater archaeology. The group has regional membership and concentrates on education. It also monitors shipwreck legislation. The Alliance has a wide range of publications, and is preparing an annual journal, *Seafarer.* A good starting place for those seeking hands-on experience in underwater exploration.

British SubAqua Club, 16 Upper Woburn Place, London, England, WC-1.

The BSC is one of the key diving organizations in the world. It is in touch with virtually every major expedition in Great Britain and Europe, and has played an important role in the excavation of the 1536 Tudor Carrack, *Mary Rose.* The club is open to all, and membership will put you in the mainstream of activity around the world.

Institute of Nautical Archaeology, P.O. Drawer AU, College Station, TX 77840.

INA was founded in 1973, at a time when its original organizers were working at five Mediterranean sites. Several INA staffers hold faculty positions at Texas A&M, though the Institute is not directly affiliated with the university. INA has ties with the Marine Maritime Academy and the Maine State Museum; it is excavating the American Revolutionary War vessel, *Defence,* in Penobscott Bay. Other activities include digs on the *Yorktown* in Virginia, the "Brown's ferry Project" in South Carolina, and investigation of the sidewheeler, *Black Cloud,* in the Trinity River in Texas. It maintains on-going projects in the Caribbean and Mexico. It is supported by public and private funds, publishes a good newsletter, and has reasonable membership fees for the public.

National Association of Underwater Instructors, 4650 Arrow Highway, Suite F-1, P.O. Box 14650, Montclair, CA 91763.

NAUI is a top-rated diver certification association which now offers an introduction to ship wreck research. A patch is awarded to those completing the program. The course is designed to make sport divers aware of the fragility of shipwrecks and covers basic technical points and the need for conservation. A good program for any certified diver.

Professional Association of Diving Instructors, 1243 East Warner Avenue, Santa Ana, CA 92705.

Like NAUI, the PADI is a diver certification association which currently offers a familiarization course in underwater archaeology for certified divers. It is a basic course, which includes classroom and water work. A certificate is awarded upon completion.

Underwater Society of America, Box 513, Christiansted, St. Croix, Virgin Islands, 00820.

USA has been around a long time, and in recent years it has become involved in many phases of marine archaeology, particularly the legal and legislative aspects. It is a diver-oriented group, though many non-divers belong. It publishes bulletins and news items. Its members are individually in touch with various exploratory projects.

Investment Groups

Historical Nautical Explorations, Ltd., 119 Segar Mountain Road, Kent, CT 06757.

HNE is mounting an expedition in the Turks and Caicos Islands. It is searching for ancient Spanish and French cargos, in cooperation with the British government. The expedition leader is Keith Jessop, the remarkable salvor who raised $80 million worth of "Stalin's Gold" from the *Edinburgh,* sunk in the Barents Sea in 1942. The Turks and Caicos operation is running on investment capital and is seeking treasure worth more than $300 million. The firm believes that investors may realize a 10 to 1 return on investment in three years.

Marine Archaeological Research, Ltd., P.O. Box 904, Grand Cayman, Cayman Islands, British West Indies.

Headed by Herbert Humphreys, Jr., MAR negotiates exploration rights with Caribbean and Latin American governments to search for and recover materials from vessels that went down along the old trade routes. MAR is based in Grand Cayman and also maintains corporate offices in Memphis, Tennessee. Artifacts recovered by the organization will be displayed at the Museum of Archaeological Research, Grand Cayman. In 1983, MAR discovered what it believes to be the 200-year-old British man o'war, H.M.S. *Thunderer,* which reputedly carried a rich Spanish and French cargo.

Treasure Salvors, Inc., 425 Caroline Street, Key West, FL 33040.

This is Mel Fisher's company. It operates in the Gulf of Mexico and along the Atlantic coast of Florida. New operations are beginning in Puerto Rico. It is a large, established organization funded by investors. TS sometimes takes on sport divers, historians, conservators, and others to help with its large workload. As a treasure hunting outfit, it is considered one of the most successful ever. Like Key West, however, it maintains an informal atmosphere. If you have never seen real New World treasures, the Mel Fisher Museum offers 47 tons of silver bars, plus a fascinating cross-section of the *Atocha, Santa Margarita,* and other New World artifacts. If you are persistent, you may even find a part-time job here.

Finding the illusive spot on the map marked "X" is anything but easy. But for the persistent searcher the rewards are worth the effort. Here a federal map reader, working with the National Park Service, tries to pinpoint the location of the Spanish treasure galleon, *San Jose,* lost centuries ago with a fortune in silver and gold off the Florida Keys. Using maps, historical records, newspaper accounts, folklore and legend, you, too, may make an important and rewarding discovery of your own.
Photo courtesy Florida Division of Archives, History and Records Management.

PART FOUR

The Treasure Hunt Contest

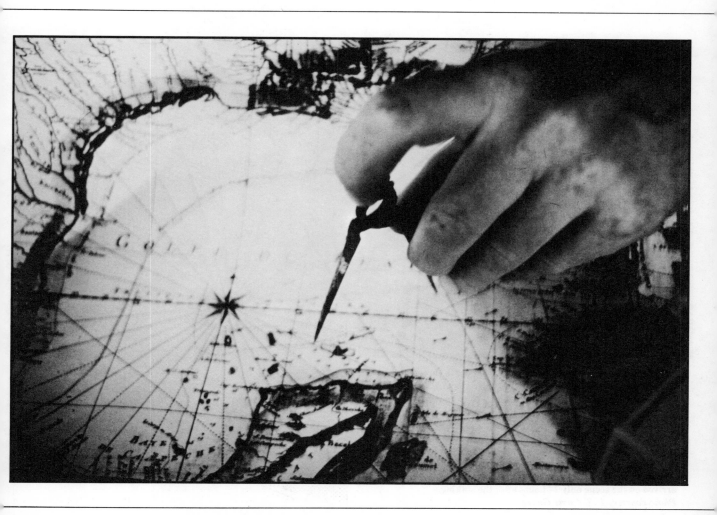

The Italian luxury liner *Andrea Doria* in her death throes on July 26, 1956, after a fateful collision with the cruise ship *Stockholm.* Some 40 miles south of Nantucket Island, this area is known as the "Times Square of the Atlantic" because of its heavy shipping traffic. The *Doria*, once considered the most beautiful passenger liner afloat, now lies forbiddingly more than 200 feet below the Atlantic. As the site where over 40 lives were originally lost, she has a reputation as one of the most dangerous wrecks waiting to be explored. The man who made the tragedy famous in his television epics, Peter Gimbel, arrived on the scene only 24 hours after the sinking.
Photo courtesy U.S. Coast Guard.

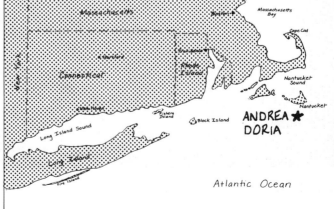

CHAPTER TWELVE

Five Mother Lode Destinations

Legend has it that pirates buried chests bulging with glittering booty along with maps and written clues leading the fortune hunter to that ever-illusive "X" on the map. Such tales make exciting fireside fantasy, but I have never heard of anyone actually finding such a bonanza. Real pirates were too clever even to leave their footprints on the sands of desert islands. But this treasure hunt breaks with tradition: It is real. *Tracking Treasure* does not trade in phony treasure maps! So if real hidden treasure piques your interest, and you love a good mystery, this updated 20th-century tale is for you.

Sorry we can't offer gold bars or jewels (such items properly belong in museums anyway), but we do offer to make your dreams of romantic tropic isles come true. Decipher the clues given below and polish up your best sleuthing skills and you can win a free dream vacation for two to one of five fascinating destinations—Aruba, Bonaire, Curacao, Cayman Brac, or Key West. You *must* be at one or more of these islands to win—not an unhappy situation considering the elegance and romance you'll find there.

The prize certificates are in containers clearly marked *Tracking Treasure.* Some are hidden on land. Others are beneath the sea. Finding them may not be a snap, but there will be no mistaking them when you do.

The prizes are as follows:

Aruba: Three treasure hunts to win three separate vacation packages.

- Eight days and seven nights for two at the Divi-Divi Beach hotel.

- Eight days and seven nights for two at the Divi Tamarijn Beach Hotel.
- Eight days and seven nights for two at the Divi Hotel's Dutch Village Luxury Apartments.

Bonaire: One treasure hunt.

- Eight days and seven nights for two at the Divi Flamingo Beach Hotel.

Cayman Brac: Two treasure hunts for two separate vacation packages.

- Eight days and seven nights for two at the Divi Tiara Beach Hotel.

Key West: One treasure hunt to win one vacation package.

- Four days and three nights for two at the Pier House Resort Hotel.

So much for the "goodies." I can personally vouch for each of these destinations. They are perfect "tens" among tropic resorts.

The Clues

Aruba: All of the prizes are above water and located at or near the following locations. The clues are:

- Tamarijn Beach Hotel: The action here is seldom slow, here they come, there they go. Above the fronds no sun to see, the ticket back unlocks the mystery.
- Divi Divi Beach Hotel: Recall place of the August moon; an oasis in an oasis will wing you back quite soon.
- Dutch Village Luxury Apartments and Casino: Progressive it is called, round and round they go; for some it is obsessive, best go slow. For you it is a chance, by the buck you will find romance.

Bonaire: This is a sunken treasure. The clues are: No beauty in the name, this reef's treasure is all below the surface. A pirate's refuse holds a diver's delight. Swimming east or west, 60 minutes will have to do.

Curacao: Seamen call her still, their ghosts be close by, dancing a jig in *Caracas Baai*. So drink your gin, and should you pass by, she's above the abyss in salty *Caracas Baai*. To hide her green, far from wave and tide, they buried her snug and deep in *Caracas Baai*.

Cayman Brac: The first prize is under water, the second on dry land. The clues are:

- Life's a "beach" and then you dive. Private it is not. For friend of glassy sweepers touch you *must*.
- Take it to the limit with the Louisville Slugger. It is a car wash of sorts with extra sponges.

Key West: The prize package is topside and located at or near the East Martello Museum. The clues are:

- T. Williams would have adored it, even when a mote. Return awaits 'neath the green side slab far from any boat.

I leave you now to track your own treasures. Good luck and good hunting!

A remote-controlled underwater vehicle is lowered beneath the waves to search out the remains of deep shipwrecks. A similar remote-controlled photographic robot was used by an American-French research team to find the world's most famous shipwreck, the R.M.S. *Titanic,* which rests in an underwater canyon $2\frac{1}{2}$ miles below the surface of the storm-tossed North Atlantic. As underwater explorers find more "pyramids of the deep," these unmanned search, photo, and recovery vehicles will be used to give us real-time tours of the ocean bottom, tracing our seafaring footprints back through the fog of time.
Photo by Joe Strykowski for the National Park Service.

APPENDIX

Treasure Values and Profit Potentials: An Analysis

by Burt D. Webber, Jr.

Within the last two decades a number of significant Spanish treasure galleon discoveries have been made on the ocean floor. Besides yielding considerable amounts of valuable artifacts, coins, and bullion to the salvors, these discoveries have provided material evidence substantiating the vast amounts of New World bullion production that was being shipped back to Spain during the Spanish Colonial period.

Unfortunately, these treasure recoveries have tended to lead to grossly exaggerated values placed upon the recovered treasure and upon the treasure galleons yet to be discovered.

As the dollar is the standard basis of our monetary exchange today, the peso (piece of eight) was its equivalent during the Spanish Colonial period in the Americas. Other methods of accounting sometimes encountered are in *maravedis* or *reales,* both subdivisions of the peso. Thirty-four *maravedis* equaled one *reale* of silver and eight *reales* equaled one peso of silver.

Research in the Spanish Archives rarely produces the complete itemized bullion registry of a shipwreck. The actual registry not only provides the total peso value of the treasure shipment, but also itemizes the quantities, weights, and values of gold and silver bullion and coins. To convert the Spanish peso into present day dollar values, you must:

1. Determine the total amount of troy ounces of gold and silver respectively. Multiply that figure times the current per-troy-ounce market value, thus deriving the "melt down"
   value of the treasure. This figure would represent the minimum value.
   Without an itemized bullion registry, the weight ratio of silver versus gold cannot be determined accurately.

2. Determine the approximate numismatical and antique "collectors value" of coins, silver and gold bars, jewels, artifacts, etc. And factor in the process of transforming much of the bulk gold and silver into commemorative type items, all of which would be sold under controlled marketing techniques.

The true intrinsic collector's value of coins, bullion, and artifacts is not easily determined, since any item is only worth what someone is willing to pay for it. For this reason, the only means by which an estimation of value can be derived is through the use of comparative examples of previous sales of treasure and artifacts recovered from other shipwrecks. The date of the shipwreck, the rarity of the coins and bullion, and the amount of publicity backing the sales are all contributing and generally varying factors that relate to the prices realized.

Table I
Treasure Values and Profit Potential Coin and Bullion Weight Table

Conversions

Troy Ounce System

1 grain = ...0.0648 grams
24 grains = ...1 pennyweight (dwt.)/1.55 grams
20 dwt. = ...1 ounce/31.1035 grams
12 ounces = ...1 pound/373.24 grams

Coin and Bullion Weights

1 silver *reale* = ...3.35 grams (34 *maravedis*)
1 *escudo de plata* (8 *reales*) = ...27.00 grams (272 *maravedis*)
1 *peso ensayado* = ...12.5 to 13 *reales*/43.55 grams
                                       (425-450 *maravedis*)
1 *escuda de oro* = ...3.40 grams (350-544 *maravedis*)
1 *peso de oro de minas* = ...4.6 grams (589 *maravedis*)
1 *castellano* = ...1/50th of a marc or 4.6 grams
6.76 *castellanos* = ...1 troy ounce

The gold *escudo* was equal weight and fineness with the silver *reale,* each being cut 68 to the marc. As gold and silver were fixed at a ratio of 16:1, the *escudo* (first struck in 1537) equaled two silver *pesos* of eight.

Using a ratio of 99 percent silver to 1 percent gold prevailing in the 17th century, a 1,000,000 peso treasure would consist of $6.9 million in silver and $430,000 in gold based on strictly "melt down" value. (A total of $7.35 million; an average of $7.35 dollars per peso.)

Silver registry average would be:

26 percent coins at 7.5 to 1   ⎫
74 percent bullion at 2.5 to 1 ⎬ "Collector" to "melt down" value
                                       ⎭

Table II
Gold and Silver "Melt Down" Peso Value   (9/85)

	PESO (WEIGHT)	CURRENT VALUE	AVERAGE
Gold Coin (*Escudo*).	3.4 grams	$36.00	
Gold Bullion (*Peso De Oro De Mina*).	4.6 grams	$49.00	$43.00
Silver Coin (8 *reales*).	27.0 grams	$ 5.35	
Silver Bullion (*Peso Ensayado*)	43.55 grams	$ 8.63	$ 6.99

The above figures are based on gold at $328.00 per ounce and silver at $6.00 per ounce. Applies to all tables where current values are used (9/85).

The following table provides *Concepción* treasure values relating to silver only.

Table III
Concepción Silver Coins Wholesale Prices**

Commercial Grades		"Wormy" Partials	
CHOICE	$300	CLASS "A"	$125
EXTRA-FINE	$250	CLASS "B"	$110
HIGH-FINE	$225	CLASS "C"	$ 90
FINE	$200	CLASS "D"	$ 70
HIGH-GOOD	$150		
GOOD	$125		

Dated/Partial Dated Coins		Rare Coins
CHOICE	$1,800/$450	RANGING FROM $2,000 to
EXTRA-FINE	$1,750/$400	$8,000
FINE	$1,700/$350	
GOOD	$1,650/$300	

** Market saturation of *Concepción* silver coins brought wholesale prices down to an average of $45 on commercially acceptable grades.

The smuggling of treasure, or contraband, was rampant practice throughout the Spanish Colonial period, particularly during the 17th century. It was not uncommon to find contraband percentages ranging between 50 to 75 percent of the registry. Contraband was usually carried in gold rather than silver for easier concealment due to the value to weight ratio. The motive for such excessive smuggling was not only to avoid paying the King's fifth, but also because of the Crown's common practice of expropriating entire treasure shipments on the basis of a "forced loan." In some cases the loans were never repaid, and those that were sometimes took as long as 20 years.

The following computations are based upon the treasure registry of the *Nuestra Señora de Atocha,* Almiranta of the 1622 fleet. This represents one of the rare few bullion listings found and now translated into English. (1985 Gold and Silver Standards)

Table IV
Treasure Registry: *Nuestra Señora de Atocha*

ITEM	SPANISH PESOS	WEIGHT	"MELT DOWN" VALUE	ESTIMATED COLLECTORS VALUE
792 bars of silver				
9 pieces of silver				
21 pieces of worked silver	589,731	825,720 oz.	$5,086,435	$12,716,088
2 pieces platinum		408 oz.	$ 129,744	$ 324,360
206,481 pieces of 8	206,481	179,249 oz.	$1,104,174	$ 9,291,645
79 gold bars 7				
38 gold cakes	20,484	3,029.44 oz.	$ 993,658	$ 2,484,145
582 disc of copper	2,071	30,000 lbs.	$ 19,800	$ 49,500
	818,767		$7,333,811	$24,865,738

Overall "Collector's Value" to "Melt Down" (3.4 to 1)
Overall per peso value = $30.00

Synopsis

Numismatics and artifacts are the most valuable items of treasure found in a wrecksite. The quantity, condition, and rarity of the gold and silver coins found cause a great fluctuation in the overall per peso value of the treasure. Based upon the analysis of *Concepción* and other treasure sales, it is reasonable to conclude that the average profit potential of treasure sold would be based on a 3.5 to 1 collectors value to melt down value ratio. A conservative estimate of the per peso value of treasure may be placed at an average of $30.00.

All of the figures used have been strictly based on the legal registry amounts. No allowance has been made for contraband treasure which commonly represented at least 25 percent of the registry. There are documented cases where, during Spanish salvage operations, nearly twice as much treasure was recovered as was listed in the registry.

Trying to determine the quantity and value of artifacts is difficult and can only be judged with limitations from results of previous sales.

Artifacts such as jewelry, glassware and ceramics, pewter and silverware, utensils, navigational instruments, tools and weaponry may well represent 15 to 30 percent of the treasure registry value.

Professional marketing outlets used for the realization of the highest profits may cost between 15 to 25 percent of the gross revenues realized.

BIBLIOGRAPHY

Ballard, Robert D., "How We Found the *Titanic,*" *National Geographic,* December 1985, p. 696.

Bass, George F., *Archaeology Under Water,* Penguin Books, Baltimore, 1970.

Branford, Ernie, *The Story of the Mary Rose,* W.W. Norton & Co., New York, 1982.

Burgess, Robert F., Carl J. Clausen, *Gold, Galleons and Archaeology,* Bobbs-Merrill, New York, 1976.

Clarke, Arthur C., *The Treasure of the Great Reef,* Ballantine Books, New York, 1970.

Cohen, Shlomo, *Bahama Diver's Guide,* Seapen Books, Tel Aviv, 1977.

Cousteau, Captain J.Y., and James Dugan (editors), *Captain Cousteau's Underwater Journal,* Harper & Row Publishers, New York, 1959.

Daley, Robert, *Treasure,* Random House, New York, 1977.

Digges, Jeremiah, *A Modern Pilgrim's Guide to Cape Cod,* The Modern Pilgrim Press, Provincetown, Massachusetts, 1947.

Directory of Maritime Heritage Resources, National Trust For Historic Preservation, Washington, 1984.

Fairbank, David, "How the Sea Gave Up a $400 Million Pirate Museum," *Parade,* January 27, 1985, p. 6.

Fleming, Robert M., *Primer of Shipwreck Research and Records,* Global Manufacturing Co., Milwaukee, 1971.

Franzen, Greta, *The Great Ship Vasa,* Hastings House, New York, 1971.

Grissim, John, *The Lost Treasure of the Concepción,* William Morrow & Co., Inc., New York, 1980.

Grosvenor, Melville Bell, "Safe Landing on Sable, Isle of 500 Ships," *National Geographic,* September 1965, p. 398.

Hampton, Capt. T.A., *The Master Diver and Underwater Sportsman,* Arco Publishing Co., New York, 1970.

Hartog, J., *A Short History of Bonaire,* DeWit NV, Aruba, N.A., 1975.

Heirtzler, J.R., "Project Famous: Man's First Voyages Down to the Mid-Atlantic Ridge," *National Geographic,* May 1975, p. 587.

Hickling, C.F., and Peter L. Brown, *The Seas and the Oceans,* Macmillan Publishing Co., Inc., New York, 1973.

Houot, Lt. Commander G.S., "Two and a Half Miles Down," *National Geographic,* July 1954, p. 80.

Hussain, Farooq, *Living Underwater,* Praeger Publishers, Inc., New York, 1970.

Laird, Marnie, "Raise the DeBraak!" *Country Magazine,* September 1985, p. 54.

Lyon, Eugene, *The Search for the Atocha,* Harper & Row, New York, 1979.

Maritime Folklife Resources, Library of Congress, Washington, D.C., 1980.

Marler, George, and Luana Marler, *The Royal Mail Streamer Rhone,* Marler Publications, Ltd., Tortola, BWI, 1979.

Marx, Robert F., *Shipwrecks in the Americas,* Bonanza Books, New York, 1983.

McKee, Alexander, *How We Found the Mary Rose,* St. Martin's Press, New York, 1982.

Nelson, Daniel A., "Ghost Ships of the War of 1812," *National Geographic,* March 1983, p. 289.

O'Keefe, Timothy M., *International Divers Guide,* Toss, Inc., Winter Park, Florida, 1975.

Peterson, Mendel, *History Under the Sea,* Smithsonian Institution, Washington, D.C., 1965.

Potter, John S., Jr., *The Treasure Diver's Guide,* Bonanza Books, New York, 1960.

Riesberg, Harry E., and A.A. Mikalow, *Fell's Guide to Sunken Treasure Ships of the World,* Signet Books, New American Library, New York, 1969.

Stick, David, *Graveyard of the Atlantic,* University of North Carolina Press, Chapel Hill, 1952.

Throckmorton, Peter, *Shipwrecks and Archaeology,* Atlantic, Little Brown, New York, 1969.

Underwater Archaeology, a Nascent Discipline, UNESCO, Paris, 1972.

Villiers, Alan, *Posted Missing,* Charles Scribner's Sons, New York, 1956.

Volker, Roy, and Dick Richmond, *Treasure Under Your Feet,* Henry Regnery Co., Chicago, 1974.

Wagner, Kip, "Drowned Galleons Yield Spanish Gold," *National Geographic,* January 1965, p. 1.

Weissman, Richard, "The Wreck of the *Andrea Doria,*" *Oceans,* Vol. 6, 1983, p. 42.

Wertenbaker, William, *The Floor of the Sea,* Little, Brown & Co., Boston, 1974.

Wilbur, Keith C., *Pirates and Patriots of the Revolution,* Globe Pequot Press, Connecticut, 1984.

Wilkes, Bill St. John, *Nautical Archaeology,* Stein and Day Publishers, New York, 1971.

Wood, Amos L., *Beachcombing the Pacific,* Henry Regnery Co., Chicago, 1975.

Woodman, Jim, *Key Biscayne, The Romance of Cape Florida,* Miami Post Publishing Co., Miami, 1961.

INDEX

Numbers in italics refer to photographs, illustrations or maps